Historians and Historiography During the Reign of Akbar

Harbans Mukhia

AAKAR

Historians and Historiography During the Reign of Akbar
Harbans Mukhia

First Published 1976
First Aakar Edition 2017
Reprinted 2019

ISBN 978-93-5002-520-8 (Hb)

Published by
AAKAR BOOKS
28 E Pocket IV, Mayur Vihar Phase I
Delhi 110 091, India
www.aakarbooks.com

Printed at
Sapra Brothers, Noida

To the memory of my Guru

Dr K.M. Ashraf

Contents

Prologue

This book happens to be substantively my doctoral dissertation with the same title written way back in the 1960s for Delhi University; the degree was awarded in 1970.[1] It was exciting to explore a somewhat different theme from the then prevalent "norm": composition of nobility, or the extent of exploitation of the peasanty, etc. etc. There was the feel of an adventure, almost. As an exploration, it did open up some new windows, though its shortcomings were to become evident soon enough.

One slim, though influential book that could—and often did—provide me with a reference point was Peter Hardy's *Historians of Medieval India*,[2] which analysed the works of five historians of the Delhi Sultanate. The thrust of its argument was that for medieval Indian historians, history was a branch of Islamic theology. As I proceeded with my research starting with the same historians that Hardy had studied and going on to those inhabiting the reign and indeed the court of Akbar, I found myself agreeing less and less with Hardy. I realised that his argument was more appropriate for medieval European historiography where ecclesiasts were virtually the only historians, imbued with the unquestioning faith that all history in reality manifested Divine will; in medieval India,on the contrary, courtier-historians established historical causation in human will or at best human nature, especially the ruler's disposition or nature. The events of a reign, with which they were primarily concerned, manifested the ruler's rather than God's will, notwithstanding the fact that the discipline of history for them owed its origins to Islam. This then became the thrust of this book's argument. I have not yet found a good reason to revisit it.

If there was one part of the book I would like redone, it is the latter segment of the book's central figure, Abu'l Fazl. In several ways

1. Published as a book by Vikas Publishing House, New Delhi, 1976.
2. Peter Hardy, *Historians of Medieval India: Studies in Indo-Muslim Historical Writing*, Luzac & Co., London, 1960.

Abu'l Fazl has stayed with me ever since my first acquaintance with the remarkably innovative historian. His presence in my book, *the Mughals of India*[3] is nearly pervasive. Since then every time I went back to his texts I made ever newer discoveries of meanings concealed in verbose prose. I have begun to refer to him as "my friend" indicative of my close "relationship" with him. The very different meanings he embeds in his famed "rationality", a theme barely touched upon in this book, fascinate me. It is much more than an inheritance from Islam's pantheistic traditions, as S.A.A. Rizvi had suggested long ago,[4] and much less than a half hearted emulation of European notion of rationality as Irfan Habib has argued more recently.[5] It is in fact rooted in the very authentic medieval *Indian* categories of thought at the ground level, especially of Kabir. I had missed some of these subtle nuances in the 1960s which I have tried to capture in several of my recent studies centred on him.[6]

But I leave the book in its original state. Revising it would have required returning to the many texts over again and would perhaps have resulted in a different work altogether, a rather tough call at my age. At any rate, it is good not to cover up one's earlier deficiencies.

I am very grateful to Mr. K.K. Saxena of Aakar Books for undertaking to reprint the book in its original format persuading me to bury my hesitation to let it go without even a retouch. Mr. Saxena has a wonderful way of overcoming an author's resistance. This is my fourth book to go into print under Aakar Books' very attractive logo. I am privileged to see my books in a large catalogue of some of the most prestigious books Aakar have published from around the world.

July 2017 Harbans Mukhia

3. Published by Blackwell Publishers, Oxford, 2004, as part of their Peoples of the World Series.
4. S.A.A Rizvi, *The Religious and Social History of the Muslims in Akbar's Reign*, Munshiram Manoharlal Publishers, New Delhi, 1974.
5. Irfan Habib, "Two Indian Theorists of the State: Barani and Abūl Fazl", D.N. Jha and Eugenia Vanina, eds, *Mind Over Matter. Essays on Mentalities in Medieval India*, Tulika Books, New Delhi, 2009, pp. 15-39; idem, "Reason and Science in Medieval India", D.N. Jha, ed, *Society and Ideology in India. Essays in Honour of Professor R.S. Sharma,* New Delhi, 1996, pp. 163-74, esp. 167-69.
6. Especially in "'No conflict between reason and faith': Reappraising Abu'l Fazl's rationality", forthcoming. A not yet final draft is accessible at academia.edu with the heading "Abu'l Fazl's Rationality Revisited."

Glossary

Aimah: Literally, plural of the term *imam* or religious leader. From the latter half of the 16th century, it came to denote the land granted in charity to such persons for the lifetime or in perpetuity

Ain-i-dahsala: Akbar's ten-year revenue settlement

Amil: Revenue collector

Amin: Revenue assessor

Amirs: The nobles

Amir-ul-umra: One of the highest titles granted by the Mughal Emperors. Literally, the chief noble

Ashrafi: A gold coin

Bakhshi: Head of the military department

Chahalghani: The group of forty nobles constituted by Sultan Iltutmish

Chaughan: The game of polo

Darvesh: A dervish, monk

Dar-ul-harb: An enemy's territory particularly in the content of holy war

Diwan-i-Buyutat: Official in charge of government stores and factories

Diwan-i-huzur: Probably the official in charge of general finance at the Centre

Diwans: Collections of poems, each *diwan* being the collection of one poet's verses. The word also means a minister of finance

Faujdar: Commandant of an area

Firman: Royal order

Ghazal: A short romantic poem comprising a number of couplets

Hadis: The "traditions" of the Prophet, source of Muslim law along with the Quran

Hakim: Physician

Ibadat Khana: Literally, House of Worship. Institution established by Akbar in 1575 to hold discussions on matters of religion

Ijtihad: Interpretation of Muslim law and theology

Imam: Religious leader, leader of prayers at the mosque

Imam-i-Adil: Literally, the Just Imam. Title assumed by Akbar in 1579

Iqta: Revenue assignment

Isnad: Arabic method of checking the authenticity of a piece of information by tracing the various stages of its transmission up to its origin

Jagir: Assignment of the revenue of a tract of land by the state to its officers by way of payment of their salaries

Jauhar: Rajput custom whereby women are burnt alive on the eve of battle and men go for an all-out war

Jehad: Holy war against infidels enjoined upon the Muslims

Karori system: Experiment made by Akbar in 1575 to make a long-term measurement of land and assessment of revenue to replace the earlier annual effort

Khalisa: Territory of the empire from which revenue was deposited with the central treasury

Khanqah: A monastery for Sufis (mystics) where Sufi ideals were propounded and practised

Khutba: Sermon preceding the Friday prayers in a mosque

Khums: One-fifth of the war booty which was in theory the share of the state

Khut: The village headman

Kos: A road measure of about two miles

Kotwal: Police official in charge of the law and order of a town

Kroh: Same as kos

Madad-i-ma'ash: Grants made in charity by the state

Maqamat: Stations by which the spiritual attainments of a mystic are measured

Mahdi: Reviver of Islam expected to appear towards the completion of the first millenium of the faith in order to restore its pristine purity

Mahzar: Document signed by the theologians in 1579 which made Akbar practically the arbiter in juridical and theological disputes

Maliks: The nobles

Mansab: Literally rank or office. Granted by the Mughal state to all its officials to determine their status and salary

Mansabdar: Holder of a mansab

Marsia: An elegy

Masnavi: Poetry composed of distichs corresponding in measure each consisting of a pair of rhymes

Mauza: A village

Mir-adl: Official in charge of administration of justice

Mujtahid: Interpreter of Islamic law and theology

Muqaddams: The village headmen responsible for the payment of revenue from their villages

Muqaddamas: Sections or chapters in a book

Nadim: The ruler's boon companion

Pargana: An administrative unit

Qarn: Vague period of time denoting a generation, an era, etc.

Qasidah: Long panegyric in verse

Qazis: Justices

Qisms: Parts of Afif's *Tarikh-i-Firuzshahi*

Qita: Distichs, whose first line does not rhyme with the second and the following even ones

Rajas: Literally Kings; mostly important chieftains who had accepted the Emperor's sovereignty; sometimes title given by the Emperors to individuals
Raos: Title by which many chieftains were known
Sadr: Official in charge of the ecclesiastical and judicial departments
Sadr-i-jahan: Chief sadr of the dominions
Sarkar: Administrative division; sometimes the administration of a prince or noble
Sayurghals: Grants made by state in charity
Shara: Islamic law
Shiqdar: Revenue official
Sijdah: Prostration
Subahs: Provinces
Tabqa: Section
Thanadar: Commander of a small fort
Ulema: Theologians
Umra: The nobles
Wahdat-ul-Wujud: Doctrine of the unity of human and divine existence
Wajah: Revenue assignment granted to soldiers being in theory equal to their salary
Wajahdar: Holder of wajah
Watan: Literally homeland
Zamindar: Holder of hereditary superior right in land

General Introduction

Historical writing has remained alive and creative because it is perennially assuming new forms, opening up new avenues of knowledge, and adapting itself to the changing needs of society. A desire to understand the past and make it relevant to the present, a commitment to shed, as far as is humanly possible, prejudices and preconceptions in the course of this quest—these are common to all the great practitioners of the discipline; but otherwise there is very little in common between them, and this is what gives the subject its zest and its drive.

Historians have, of course, been influenced by each other, but historical writing has not so much evolved as spread. Like a great river, it flows across the countryside, submerging new areas, picking up tributaries, drying up in old beds, but never petering out into the sands, and, unlike the great rivers, never reaching the sea.

So the history of historical writing is in itself an exciting pursuit; and nothing in it is more exciting than its latest chapter. In recent years the discipline has acquired vast, new dimensions. It is no longer a matter of finding out what really happened, particularly on the surface of politics, and stating this in elegant prose.

Beneath politics are the more basic, if less easily perceptible, changes in the economy and society, themselves resting on the seemingly impermeable facts of geography and nature.

To recognize these, to seek to grasp their influence, to note the gradual changes in the environment in which people live and to discern the interactions between the thoughts and actions of men and women and their social and economic context is to go some way towards comprehending the history of a people.

Writing this kind of history involves the study of more than the traditional kind of source material. Records and inscriptions are but a small part of the available material. There is archaeology, itself a manifold discipline and no longer limited to the elucidation of ancient history; we have the study of technology for the whole stretch of human development, and pre-industrial and industrial archaeology is today a subject in itself.

The analysis of myth, the unravelling of the language, the probing of the individual, and even more important, the collective unconscious, these are but some of the ways in which the past can be put together as a whole and therefore better understood. In fact, there is nothing that is alien to historical study.

In consequence, no historian can today afford to be a narrow specialist. He has, of course, to have a thorough grasp of his particular field; but the field has many layers. He has therefore to draw on many other disciplines—economics, law, politics, sociology, geography, psychology. The list is endless.

This it does by helping to lay bare the systems and structures that underlie the flux of the present. Here again the task has been made more difficult and therefore more vital and fascinating by the breaking down of the walls of dogma and the wing of rigid doctrine.

One does not have to renounce the truth in the writings of the great historical analysts in order to adapt and apply them to new knowledge and fresh problems. The only way, as Marx said, that history answers questions is by asking further questions.

The *Vikas History Series* seeks to combine the traditional virtues of deep knowledge of the sources and meticulous attention to detail with an awareness of the work being done elsewhere and an application to their own themes of the new methods of historical scholarship.

It is our hope that the series will give the public a chance to judge for themselves.

BIPAN CHANDRA
ROMILA THAPAR
S. GOPAL

Preface

The problem of analyzing the primary sources of medieval Indian history has, to some extent, always been at the back of the minds of modern historians of that period. This is obvious from the prefaces or the introductions, as also from the footnotes, to most of their works where the nature of the sources used by the author is sought to be analyzed and indicated in varying degrees.

The beginning in this direction was made by Elliot and Dowson in their *History of India as Told by Its Own Historians*. The shortcomings of this monumental work are no longer a matter of controversy. These shortcomings are not confined only to the technical flaws of translation pointed out so ably by Hodivala in his *Studies in Indo-Muslim History*. There are the more basic faults in the method of selecting excerpts from the sources. But these shortcomings apart, Elliot initiated the attempt at a critical study of the sources by prefacing the translation of excerpts from each source with his own evaluation of its worth, a practice continued by Dowson.

As translations of sources continued being published, the convention set by Elliot, of adding the translator's remarks on to the author and his work, was continued. Thus, for example, Major Raverty's chapter on Minhaj in his translation of the *Tabaqat-i-Nasiri*, Blochmann's biographical sketch of Abul Fazl in his translation of Volume I of the *Ain-i-Akbari*, Beveridge's remarks on Abul Fazl and the *Akbar Nama* in his translation of that work, Mrs Beveridge's on Gulbadan Begam in her English rendering of the *Humayun Nama*, and Beni Prasad's study of Nizam-ud-din Ahmad in the English translation of the *Tabaqat-i-Akbari*.

S.A.A. Rizvi has added similar remarks for each author in his series of Hindi translations of medieval sources. It is not suggested here that all these introductory remarks or short biographical sketches fall into the same pattern. Beveridge, for instance, deals mainly with the style of the *Akbar Nama*, while Blochmann mainly writes a biography of Abul Fazl. But the convention of introducing an author and his work was firmly set by Elliot and Dowson.

At the same time there have been independent studies of the sources. M.Habib and Wahid Mirza selected Amir Khusrau as the subject of their studies. Until very recently, however, such studies have generally been confined to articles published in various learned journals. In most cases these articles have dealt with individual sources. In some of these the attempt had been chiefly to draw attention to any additional information contained in a source that had not till then been brought to light or properly considered. Thus, for example, E.B. Cowell's article, "Kiran-us-Sadain of Mir Khusrau," *J.A.S.B.*, Vol. LXVII, 1898; Syed Hashimi's "The Tughlaq Nama," *Islamic Culture*, 1934; S. Nurul Hasan's "Sahifa-i-Nat-i-Mahammadi of Zia-ud-din Barani," *Medieval India Quarterly* (*MIQ*), Aligarh, Vol. I, 1950; and S.A.A. Rizvi's "The Munajat of Abul Fazl," *MIQ* Vol. I, 1950. Others have analyzed and interpreted the information contained in the known sources. Blochmann's paper "Badaoni and His Works," *J.A.S.B.*, Vol. 38, Part 1, 1869; Syed Sabah-ud-din Abdur Rahman's "The Futuh-us-Salatin," *Maarif* (Urdu), Vol. 44, No.2, 1939; and Dr Mahdi Husain's "Mahmud of Ghazna Idolized by Isami," *Indian History Congress Proceedings*, 1944, are instances of such an attempt.

A.B.M. Habibullah and Maulavi Hidayat Hussain probably made two of the earliest attempts at analyzing the nature of information contained in a *group* of sources. Habibullah analyzed sources bearing upon the political and cultural history of the Delhi Sultanate in his "A Re-evaluation of the Literary Sources of the Pre-Mughal History," *Islamic Culture*, 1941. In the same volume of that journal, Hidayat Hussain studied contemporary historians of the reign of Shah Jahan. A decade later M. Habib wrote his article, "The Chishti Mystic Records of the Sultanate Period," *MIQ*, Vol.I, 1950. In 1957 Mahdi Husain published a paper, "A Critical

Study of the Sources of Medieval India (1320-1526)," in *Islamic Culture*.

Habib later returned to a study of a single author and a single work, Zia-ud-din Barani and his *Fatawa-i-Jahandari*. It was first published in *MIQ*, Vol.III, 1957-58, and later incorporated into his and Mrs Afsar Khan's book, *Political Theory of the Delhi Sultanate*. This was the earliest detailed analysis and interpretation of the basic features of a work.

It was Peter Hardy who first devoted himself exclusively to a general study of the medieval sources in his book *Historians of Medieval India*, in which the works of five authors of the pre-Mughal period have been analyzed.

In 1966 the Jamia Millia Islamia, New Delhi, organized a seminar on medieval Indian historiography, the proceedings of which were edited by Muhibbul Hasan and published under the title *Historians of Medieval India*, Meerut, 1968. The volume contains some papers making a fresh analysis of well known works as well as others calling attention to hitherto unknown sources.

In the following pages an attempt has been made to analyze some of the explicit as well as tacit assumptions in the medieval sources of our information. It is these tacit assumptions which are the more significant for being largely involuntary on the part of the authors and for being the less perceptible. Inevitably, their influence on modern writing on medieval India appears to have been substantial.

To perceive this influence it may be necessary to make a general study of medieval Indian historiography. Such a study has been attempted in the pages that follow.

The life and work of three great historians of Akbar's reign—Abul Fazl, Abdul Qadir Badauni and Nizam-ud-din Ahmad—have been studied with an attempt at establishing a correlation, if any, between their life and their viewpoint as expressed in their works. An attempt has also been made to analyze the works of three other historians of the same period—Bayazid Biyat, Abbas Sarwani and Jauhar Aftabchi. The first chapter, however, is a study of the works of six representative historians of the Delhi Sultanate—Minhaj, Barani, Afif, Yahya Sirhindi, Amir Khusrau and Isami. This has been done in order to examine the background to history writing during the reign of Akbar and to see whether there was any further development in this field from the earlier period to the later.

I have tried to study the works of nine of these twelve historians under the heads Basic Form; Contents; Attitude Towards t Sources of Information; Treatment of History and Hist cal Causation; Style. (In the case of the historians of Sultanate period their viewpoint has been discussed instea their style.)

I have selected the heads under which to examine these works on the consideration that it might be as fruitful to study the basic framework and assumptions, attitudes and viewpoints of these historians as to investigate the authenticity of individual pieces of information in the passages of their works. In fact, even for the latter task one might first need to analyze the broad framework and assumptions, etc. of an historian. Thus, while many modern historians of medieval India have, through collation of plural evidence, worked out a generally accepted mass of information on individual events, or groups of them, they have done this largely within the medieval historians' framework of the treatment of history and historical causation.[1] It is by no means intended here to underrate the importance of their works, but only to submit that the information about a particular event is intrinsically linked with the broad framework of the historian and without an analysis of this framework an individual piece of information cannot be brought into proper focus and can, in some cases, be even misleading.

The three other historians—Bayazid, Sarwani and Jauhar—have been studied under a different category of heads for the reason that their works are not works of history, properly speaking: They are memoirs written to furnish information to Abul Fazl for his *Akbar Nama* and as such they do not lend themselves to investigation under the same heads as, for instance, the *Tarikh-i-Firuz Shahi* or the *Muntakhab-ut-Tawarikh* do.

I am aware of the fact that a meaningful study of any aspect of intellectual history should have for its perspective the broader social structure and the role of ideas in that structure. In a study of this nature one must also keep in view the levels of society to which

[1]This point will be discussed in the "Conclusion," *infra*, pp. 170-176.

the intellectuals and their ideas are related and the degree of their impact on the thinking of different social classes.

The medieval Indian historians were all courtiers and the focal point of their interest was the imperial court; such references as they made to matters falling outside the immediate precincts of the court were, at a remove, also related to imperial authority. The culture they represented and reinforced was the high culture of the upper echelons of the ruling class. Indeed, even within the ruling class, the lower echelons hardly ever found a sympathetic reflection in any of the important works of history. The books that were written and the small number of copies that were made of these were meant to influence only a select few.

Yet society as a whole, even its lowest orders, did not remain immune to the influence of their ideas, not because of any innate strength in those ideas, nor because they were widespread, but because they represented the thinking of the dominant social class in a structure where political power and economic resources increasingly tended to move towards a high degree of centralization. It has been suggested that there is a close correspondence between the dominant political thinking and popular religious ideas of the leaders of the Bhakti movement in medieval north India at least.[1]

It has not been possible for me to fully correlate the study of historiography to the social and political structure of the period. The absence of comprehensive studies of these aspects of medieval Indian history compels one either to make very broad generalizations or to wait for such studies to be made before a view could be stated confidently. Rightly or wrongly, I opted for the latter alternative, for the third alternative—of making the study oneself—poses too gigantic a task for any individual effort.

I must tender my apology here on two counts—absence of diacritical marks and occasional use of the word "ideology" or "ideo-

[1]Harbans Mukhia, "The Ideology of the Bhakti Movement—The Case of Dadu Dayal," *Nihar Ranjan Ray Felicitation Volume*, Debiprasad Chattopadhyaya (ed.); Savitri Chandra, "Tulsidas' Concept of Rulership," *Proceedings of the Indian History Congress*, 33rd session, Muzaffarpur, 1972, pp. 325-334; Madhu Tandon, *An Historical Analysis of Kabir's Poetry*, unpublished M. Phil dissertation approved by the Jawaharlal Nehru University, New Delhi, 1974.

logical." Diacritical marks, I thought, might appear to be mere pedantry in a book which uses hardly any technical terms except for names, most of which are quite familiar to the student of medieval Indian history. I am aware of the fact that the words "ideology" and "ideological," with all the present-day connotations and nuances, are not precisely applicable to medieval Indian intellectual positions. Yet I have used these words in the absence of any better expression that I know of, and in the hope that these would be understood in the sense which they are meant to convey, without invoking the modern intellectual feuds about their meaning.

This book is by no means a comprehensive study of the subject, but only a preliminary one. As such it is bound to suffer from shortcomings inherent in a preliminary study.

I have largely refrained from tracing influences from various sources—Arabic, Persian, Turko-Mongol—on medieval Indian historiography for two reasons—the magnitude of the effort is almost prohibitive, unless one talks in very general terms; and given all the influences, medieval Indian historiography had an identity of its own and could by itself be an interesting study.

In a subject so sensitive as historiography, it is possible that the area of agreement among scholars is limited, for one's approach to a source is willy-nilly affected by the object for which one uses it. A student working on a source for agrarian history will have a substantially different approach from one seeking information on the system of education. I hope, however, that I have been able to adopt rational principles of analysis, whatever the worth of my argument.

The debt of gratitude I owe a number of scholars who helped me in preparing this book is, indeed, large. I am very thankful to K.S. Lal who was my supervisor when I was writing the Ph.D. thesis for the University of Delhi on which this book is substantially based. Professor Lal bore with me very patiently and helped me through to the end. To my very esteemed friend and colleague Irfan Habib I owe more than language can express. He went through my typescript with great care and made many suggestions, but for which my dissatisfaction with the book would have been much greater. S. Nurul Hasan was also kind enough to read the typescript in his freer moments and make extremely valuable criticisms of many points. My thanks are due to my friend and colleague Iqtidar Alam

Khan for discussing with me Bayazid's work in great detail and for going through the chapter on the *Akbar Nama* and making many suggestions; to M. Athar Ali for letting me use the research library of the Department of History, Aligarh Muslim University, of which he was incharge, at my convenience. I also had the benefit of discussing with him many points during the course of preparing this book. To the staff of the Maulana Azad Library, Aligarh Muslim University, I am deeply obliged for allowing me the use of its manuscripts section; to the staff of the Delhi University library for their ungrudging help whenever I needed it; to the librarian of the Indian Institute of Islamic Studies, New Delhi, for his assistance rendered with a winning smile; to the staff of the National Archives, New Delhi, and the Jawaharlal Nehru University library for all their help in some of my most anxious moments.

My thanks are also due to my colleagues, Romila Thapar, S. Gopal and Bipan Chandra for editing the book for the series in which it is being published and for tying up the loose ends of the argument and suggesting new angles for viewing the problems afresh.

Needless to add that the responsibility for the views expressed in this book rests entirely with me.

HARBANS MUKHIA

CHAPTER 1

Historiography During the Sultanate Period

A study of the elements of historiography during the period of the Sultanate has necessarily to be tentative mainly because we have only a part of the historical literature of the period at our disposal. Our evaluation therefore has to be based on information thus crippled.

In the surviving literature, however, a sustained development, both in form and technique, can be discerned from Minhaj's colourless narrative of coronations and battles to Barani's vigorously interpretative arrangement of events to Afif's technique of studying the history of a reign in various phases. In Yahya, however, we come back to the narration of events in a listless, indifferent manner. What might have been a developing pattern of history writing is thus interrupted, though, as it turns out, only temporarily.

In this chapter an attempt is made to study some elements of the historiography of the Sultanate period on the basis of the works of six representative historians—Minhaj-us-Siraj, Zia-ud-din-Barani, Shams Siraj Afif, Yahya bin Ahmad Sirhindi, Amir Khusrau and Isami.

Basic Form

The basic form in Minhaj's *Tabaqat-i-Nasiri* is what Rosenthal has categorized as dynastic historiography.[1] That is, after a short

[1] F. Rosenthal, *A History of Muslim Historiography*, Lieden, 1952, pp. 77-82.

account of "the history of the world" from Adam to the pious Caliphs,[1] Minhaj deals with different dynasties each in a separate section (tabqa), which is equivalent to a chapter. The accounts of the reigns of individual rulers form the sub-chapters within the dynastic whole. A chapter begins with a brief sketch of the antecedents of the dynasty concerned and ends with the elimination of that dynasty from the political scene. A sub-chapter begins with the accession of a ruler of the dynasty and terminates with the end of his reign. At times, Minhaj gives the length of the rule of a dynasty or that of individual rulers; at others he does not. Thus, for example, while the period of the Samani dynasty is given,[2] that of the Ghaznavide or the Khwarazm Shahi is not. Similarly, while the duration of the reign of each Sultan of the Ghaznavide dynasty is mentioned, with regard to some of the Khwarazm Shahi rulers, Minhaj merely states, "he reigned for many years"[3] or "he reigned for a considerable time,"[4] etc. There are occasions when he makes no mention of the length of a reign at all, even in these vague terms. The reigns of Ali Shah of Khwarazm and Ghiyas-ud-din of the same dynasty may be cited as examples.[5]

Towards the end of his sub-chapters, dealing with the reigns of the Ghaznavide and the Ghoride rulers, Minhaj appends lists of the sons of each Sultan. In the case of Sultan Muhammad of

[1]This "history of the world" along with the account of eight dynasties not related to Indian history has been omitted from the Bib. Ind. text which opens with the 11th section dealing with the Ghaznavide dynasty. Major Raverty has, on his own admission, translated the first six sections but briefly; it is only from section VII onwards that he has translated the work fully. Raverty, *Tabaqat-i-Nasiri* (tr), Bib. Ind., Preface, p. xiv. I have used both the text and the translation but relied more on the latter for two reasons: The text has omitted, apart from the first ten sections, many details which one can find in the translation; as Raverty puts it, "not a page of it is correct."

The text of the *Tabaqat* edited by Abdul Hai Habib and published by Anjuman-i-Tarikh-i-Afghanistan, 2 Vols., 1963 and 1964, is unfortunately based only on one late MS for the portion omitted by the Bib.Ind.edition. For the rest it follows the Bib. Ind. edition and thus it is no improvement on the latter.

[2]Raverty, *Tabaqat-i-Nasiri* (tr.), p. 53.

[3]For Sultan Takish, *ibid.*, p. 244.

[4]For Sultan Yunus Khan, *ibid.*, p. 250.

[5]*Ibid*, pp. 253, 285 respectively.

Ghor a list of his qazis and maliks is also attached, along with a description of his titles and his standards, etc.[1] Similar is the treatment in the sub-chapter on Iltutmish[2] who was the father of the author's patron.

At the end of a sub-chapter Minhaj gives his own evaluation of the ruler. The remarks are generally perfunctory and relate to the personal qualities of the Sultan. There is hardly a ruler whom he has not extended the courtesy of a few good words.

When Minhaj reaches the reign of Nasir-ud-din Mahmud, to whom he had dedicated his work,[3] he turns the *Tabaqat* into an annual chronicle. The list of the Sultan's sons and maliks and the description of his titles is given at the beginning of the reign and not at the end of his account of the reign.[4] Since Minhaj wrote his book before the end of Nasir-ud-din Mahmud's reign, he could not have appended these lists at the end of that reign.

The dynastic periodization was handicapped by the overlapping of events and consequently involved much repetition. Many an event common to two or more rulers of different dynasties was repeated at as many places. In the process, events were at times likely to be misdated at some place or dated differently at different places. Thus, for example, two dates are given for the death of Khusrau Malik at the hands of Sultan Ghiyas-ud-din and his brother Muiz-ud-din Ghori: 598 H. and 587 H.[5] The former is given under the Ghaznavide dynasty and the latter under the Ghorides. In fact, still another date could be inferred from two cross-references to this event. At both the places referred to, he states that since the Ghoride Sultans (he calls both Ghiyas-ud-din and Muiz-ud-din Sultan simultaneously) became engaged in a conflict with Sultan Shah of Khwarazm, they considered it prudent to put an end to Khusrau Malik. This conflict is therefore dated 588 H.[6]

Barani did not have to face this problem of synchronization of events, for he was writing the history of a succession of rulers in

[1] *Ibid.*, pp. 489-491.
[2] *Ibid.*, pp. 625-627.
[3] *Ibid.*, author's Preface and Dedication, pp. xxxiii-xxxiv.
[4] *Ibid.*, pp. 671-674.
[5] *Ibid.*, pp. 115 and 456-457 respectively.
[6] *Ibid.*, pp. 378-379.

a succession of dynasties in one and the same land. He did not have to put down, for instance, the conflicts between two or more rulers or dynasties at as many places. The form of his *Tarikh-i-Firuz Shahi* is therefore different from that of the *Tabaqat* which he claims not only to have continued but followed in the manner of writing.[1] The basic arrangement of his book is based on successive accounts of reigns of individual rulers from Balban to Firuz Tughlaq. Of the reign of the last ruler, only the first six years have been covered.

Each chapter in Barani's *Tarikh* opens with a list of the maliks and khans of the concerned ruler. (In the *Tabaqat*, as noted earlier, such a list follows the account of the reign of the Sultan, and that not in all cases.[2]) After this list comes the date of the accession of a Sultan. The chapter does not close immediately with the end of a Sultan's reign, for Barani usually gives his own evaluation of the ruler and the events of the reign.

Each reign is formally treated as a whole in itself. Within each chapter, Barani has sub-headings for important events like, for example, "Ala-ud-din Khalji's Engagement with Qutlugh Khwaja"[3] or "Muhammad Tughlaq's Conquest of Various Territories."[4] Sometimes the headings of the sub-chapters are more general and are not related to any specific events. Thus, for example, "The Causes of Sultan Ala-ud-din's Hostility towards Sultan Jalal-ud-din who was his Uncle and Father-in-Law,"[5] or "The Qualities and Excellences as well as the Hard Headedness and Oppressiveness of Sultan Ala-ud-din."[6] It appears that Barani introduced sub-divisions of chapters from the reign of Jalal-ud-din Khalji onwards, for the reigns of Balban and Kaiqubad are treated without any such sub-divisions. What is significant however is that Barani never entitles his sub-chapters after any individual, which Minhaj always does—a feeble clue, perhaps, to Barani's wider

[1]Barani, *Tarikh-i-Firuz Shahi*, Syed Ahmad Khan (ed.), Bib.Ind., pp. 20-21.

[2]Again, as noted earlier, the only exception is Nasir-ud-din Mahmud, where the list precedes the account of the reign. There are numerous cases where no such list is attached.

[3]Barani, *Tarikh*, p. 259.

[4]*Ibid.*, p 468.

[5]*Ibid.*, p 221.

[6]*Ibid*, p. 338.

view of history.

When Barani comes to the reign of Firuz Tughlaq, his contemporary Sultan, the form of the *Tarikh* changes. The account of the six years of Firuz's reign that are covered by Barani is broken into eleven muqaddamas. The muqaddamas individually deal with various aspects of Firuz Shah's reign, such as the circumstances of the Sultan's accession to the throne,[1] the orthodox Sunni qualities of the Sultan which manifested themselves in his administration,[2] and the digging of canals.[3] The division of the six-year period is arbitrary; it does not follow either a time sequence or a phasing of the period according to changes in the Sultan's policies.

Barani confuses dates quite frequently. This he does partly because of his failing memory which was the chief, if not the only, source of his information[4] and partly because of his indifference to chronology. For history was no mere narrative of events for him; it had some general lessons and these lessons could be intelligible even in a complete chronological disorder of events.[5]

This form of history-writing undergoes further modifications in Afif's *Tarikh-i-Firuz Shahi*. The range of Afif's work is more limited[6] than that of Barani's, which in turn was smaller than that of Minhaj's. In the portion of his work that has survived, Afif deals only with the reign of Firuz Tughlaq.

Afif divides his *Tarikh* into five qisms, each consisting of eighteen muqaddamas. Of these, four qisms in full and fourteen

[1]*Ibid.*, pp. 531-538.

[2]*Ibid.*, pp. 548-558.

[3]*Ibid.*, pp. 567-571.

[4]Habib, "Life and Thought of Zia-ud-din Barani," in Habib and Mrs Afsar Khan, *Political Theory of Delhi Sultanate*, Allahabad, n.d., pp. 121,125.

[5]Barani, *op. cit.*, p. 468.

[6]Hodivala believed that Afif had written a history of the Tughlaq dynasty from Ghiyas-ud-din to Timur's invasion of India, *Studies in Indo-Muslim History*, Supplement, Bombay, 1957, pp. 117-118. Afif certainly wrote separate volumes for the reigns of at least four Tughlaq Sultans—Ghiyas-ud-din, Muhammad bin Tughlaq, Firuz-Tughlaq and Muhammad bin Firuz Tughlaq—but only the work dealing with the reign of Firuz has survived. He refers to the other three in his *Tarikh*, Bib.Ind., p. 36 (*Manaqib-i-Sultan Tughlaq*) pp. 42, 51 (*Manaqib-i-Sultan Muhammad*) and p. 428 (*Manaqib-i-Sultan Muhammad bin Firuz*) respectively.

muqaddamas and part of the fifteenth of the fifth have survived. The opening thirty pages (of the published text) are devoted to the praise of God and the Prophet, the spiritual achievements (maqamat) of Sufis and the virtues of Firuz Tughlaq. A summary of the qisms to follow is then added.[1]

The first qism deals with the period from Firuz Tughlaq's birth to his accession; the second with his two expeditions to Lakhnauti and Jajnagar, and Nagarkot; in the third Afif describes the Sultan's expedition to Thatta and his return from there along with the Jam of Sind and Bahambanah (the Jam's nephew), and the installation of the astronomical clock and gong; the fourth concerns the Sultan's abstention from major expeditions and his devotion to the "welfare" of the people; and in the fifth is an account of the Sultan's undergoing tonsure, and the death of Prince Fath Khan, going on to offer an account of some of the khans and maliks belonging to the later period of Firuz Shah's reign.

Afif's division of his *Tarikh* into qisms is in itself a kind of interpretation. The qisms appear to be the phases in which the historian studies Firuz Shah's reign, although the phases are not strictly chronological. The expeditions to Lakhnauti, Jajnagar, Nagarkot and Thatta were spread over a long span of time and it is not that only after these expeditions did Firuz take to "welfare" of the people.

Yet Afif's technique was indeed new. He claims merely to have added 90 muqaddamas to Barani's 11[2] to complete his predecessor's plan of writing 101 muqaddamas on the reign of Firuz.[3] But in effect he adopts a technique different from Barani's in that while Barani introduces the muqaddama as an arbitrarily determined form, Afif inserts into this form an element of studied interpretation.

With Yahya we come back to a bare narrative of mainly political events over a long period of time. Yahya opens his account with the reign of Muiz-ud-din of Ghor and brings it down to A.D. 1438, that is, up to the reign of the Syed monarch Muhammad Shah, the author's contemporary. The *Tarikh-i-Mubarak Shahi* is

[1]Afif, *Tarikh-i-Firuz Shahi*, pp. 31-36.

[2]*Ibid.*, pp 29-30

[3]Barani, *op. cit.*, p. 530.

at best a chronicle of the accession of rulers, appointment of nobles, battles fought by the Sultans, rebellions and their suppression, and, finally, the death (or deposition) of the rulers. Even in the details of these events, Yahya hurries through his narrative until he comes to the Tughlaqs. The later part of his work, that is from the Tughlaqs onwards, is more detailed and more consistent than the earlier.

The basis of his periodization is regnal. Each reign is complete in itself and stands in no relationship to the preceding or the following reign. Even within a chapter dealing with the reign of one monarch, there are no sub-divisions. No such formalities as inclusion of the lists of the khans and maliks, etc., are observed.

The entire narrative is written in an extremely impersonal vein. Few value judgments of an historical personage or event are made,[1] for, as he puts it, "pointing out the errors of the great is improper."[2]

A common stylistic feature in all these works is the frequent insertion of verses in the narrative. The verses do not materially affect the account; more often than not these are useless in terms of additional information. Generally, if not always, these are inserted either in celebration of some happening, or in mourning the death of a ruler, or, and this is particularly so in Barani's case, in expressing the author's helplessness against the tyranny of Fate.

A different form of history writing was versified history. Although both Amir Khusrau and Isami specialize in this form, each is essentially different from the other.

The theme of Amir Khusrau's historical works is generally a particular event or a group of events limited to a short span of time. The *Qiran-us-Sadain*, for example, has for its theme the meeting between Kaiqubad and Bughra Khan; the *Ashiqa* is woven round the tragic love of Dewal Rani and Khizr Khan; the victories of Mubarak Khalji in the Deccan are central to the *Nuh Sipihr*; the *Tughlaq Nama* is written to celebrate the enthronement and victories of Ghiyas-ud-din Tughlaq.

Around his theme Amir Khusrau builds an eminent edifice and

[1]One exception is the discussion on the causes of the failure of Sultan Muhammad Tughlaq, *Tarikh-i-Mubarak Shahi*, Bib. Ind., pp. 113-115.

[2]*Ibid.*, p. 117.

the details of almost everything that can even remotely be associated with the main theme are carved into it. In *Qiran-us-Sadain*, for example, he describes the march of Sultan Kaiqubad from Delhi to Awadh. By the end of the march we have a fair picture of the buildings of Delhi,[1] the changing seasons of northern India,[2] the convivial parties at the court and the flow of music and dance for the amusement of the Sultan[3] and so on. The *Nuh Sipihr*, similarly, while having the victories of Mubarak Khalji in the Deccan as the central historical events,[4] includes a description of the buildings of the Sultan,[5] praise of India,[6] and of its inhabitants,[7] a note on its languages,[8] and pieces of advice to the Sultans and the maliks,[9] etc. Such a wide range of subjects naturally required a wide range of poetical forms. Khusrau, therefore, tries his hand at a variety of these forms—the masnavi, the ghazal, the qita, the qasidah, etc.

Isami's *Futuh-us-Salatin*, on the other hand, is an account of the Ghaznavide and the Ghoride conquest of India and the history of the Delhi Sultanate down to Isami's own day—A.D. 1349.[10] Throughout the book Isami has followed the same metre. The arrangement of the *Futuh* is regnal. Within each reign separate headings are given to important events or to episodes which the author considers worthwhile including in history. Thus, there are headings like "The Martyrdom of Sultan Jalal-ud-din in the Midst of the Ganges and the Breaking out of Gurshasp Malik (Ala-ud-din) into Rebellion,"[11] as also "Mahmud Ghaznavi's Becoming

[1]Amir Khusrau, *Qiran-us-Sadain*, Maulavi Muhammad Ismail (ed.), Aligarh, 1918, pp. 30-37.

[2]*Ibid.*, pp. 37-39, 58-61, 68-72.

[3]*Ibid.*, pp. 36, 43-44, 52, 56-57, 66-67, etc.

[4]Amir Khusrau, *Nuh Sipihr*, M. Wahid Mirza (ed.), Calcutta, 1950, pp. 81-146.

[5]*Ibid.*, pp. 76-80.

[6]*Ibid.*, pp. 151-161.

[7]*Ibid.*, pp. 161-172.

[8]*Ibid.*, pp. 172-181.

[9]*Ibid.*, pp. 226-267.

[10]Isami, *Futuh-us-Salatin*, Agha Mahdi Husain (ed.), Agra, 1938, p. 582, where the date of the composition of the book is mentioned.

[11]*Ibid.*, p. 232.

Polluted at the Jama Mosque and the Springing out of Water Before Him."[1] Chronology is not one of the strong points of the *Futuh*. The only date given during the reign of Ala-ud-din Khalji, for example, is that of his death.[2] At times the dates given are wrong. The rebellion of Tughril during the reign of Balban is placed in the eighth regnal year of the Sultan.[3]

CONTENTS

All the works under review (with the possible exception of Amir Khusrau's *Qiran-us-Sadain* and *Dewal Rani Khizr Khan*) deal essentially with political problems facing the Sultanate or individual Sultans. They concern themselves with accession of the Sultans to the throne, expansion of the empire, threats, internal and external, to the Sultanate, problems of organization of the administration and of the ruling class, etc.

This fact places serious limitations on the kind of information contained in these works in that the subjects of information tend to remain confined to the four walls of the imperial court and its ramifications.

However, with differing techniques of history writing,[4] there appears to have been a vertical growth of the contents within the limits indicated. That is, with the succession of historians there is an increasing amount of information on the same subjects or differ ent aspects of them.

Thus the *Tabaqat-i-Nasiri*, in which Minhaj merely narrates political events, abounds with information on the enthronement of rulers, their wars, names of persons involved and such like events, and at times their genealogies.[5] At the beginning of each of his chapters dealing with the history of one dynasty or another, Minhaj attempts to trace the origins of the ruling house. Occa-

[1] *Ibid.*, p. 54.

[2] *Ibid.*, p. 336.

[3] *Ibid.*, pp. 159-160.

[4] *Infra*, pp. 16ff.

[5] For genealogies in *Tabaqat* see pp. 53, 57, 70, 312. No reference has been given here for the other points because every page of the *Tabaqat* bears testimony to them.

sionally he relates anecdotes.[1] But generally the information contained in his work is stereotyped and the language prosaic.

Barani's *Tarikh* also deals mainly with the political events of the Delhi Sultanate; but history, to him, was something more than mere narration of events; he sought to analyze the causes of the occurrence of these events, individually, as well as collectively, and tried to draw general lessons from the study of history. In his treatment of history the Sultan's nature becomes an independent entity, for it is the Sultan's nature which manifests itself in the formulation of policies and the occurrence of events during his reign. Administrative measures and institutions, which find scarce mention in Minhaj's work, are treated by Barani as an integral part of history.

Thus we have in Barani's *Tarikh*, apart from details of coronations, etc., notices on the personal nature of the rulers and on the policies that were pursued during their reigns.[2] There is also considerable information on experiments made with various administrative measures and institutions during the period of the Sultanate, including a very graphic account of the market system of Ala-ud-din Khalji.[3] It is indeed from Barani's repeated references to the zamindars, the khuts and muqaddams, etc. that we begin to understand the nature of this class and its relationship with the Turkish ruling class. In another one of Barani's works, the *Fatawa-i-Jahandari*, the author makes a distinct contribution to the political thinking of the period. Barani clearly observes and expressly formulates the contradiction between Islam and kingship and advocates the continuance of the latter.[4] The book is in the form of counsels to the Sultans on a number of subjects important for running the administration. The counsels are on subjects like the nature of state laws,[5] the need for moderation in state policies,[6]

[1] *Ibid.*, pp. 17-18, 500, 554-555, 734.

[2] There are notices on personal nature and policies of every Sultan dealt with in the *Tarikh*.

[3] *Ibid.*, pp. 303-319.

[4] *Fatawa-i-Jahandari*, (*FJ*) translated by M. Habib and Mrs Afsar Khan and published under the title *Political Theory of the Delhi Sultanate*, Allahabad, n.d., pp. 34, 39-40.

[5] *Ibid.*, pp. 64-71.

[6] *Ibid.*, pp. 55-57.

the organization of the army[1] and the unqualified necessity of keeping low born elements out of the official hierarchy,[2] etc.

Afif in his study of the reign of Firuz Tughlaq tries to analyze the causes which led to the liquidation of the Sultanate at the hands of Timur in 1398. He locates these causes in the weakness of Firuz Shah's policies in relation to the administration and the expansion of his empire. Consequently, Afif's *Tarikh* gives a vivid picture of the administration in actual operation during the reign of Firuz,[3] growth of the power of the nobility[4] and the Ulema,[5] the extent of corruption prevalent in the various departments of administration and the Sultan's indirect encouragement of it.[6] Towards the end of the book there are notices of some of the important nobles of Firuz Shah's court.[7] These notices are an advance over the mere enumeration of the nobles in Minhaj's *Tabaqat* and Barani's *Tarikh,* although in the case of Muizzi, Qutbi and Shamsi maliks, Minhaj has given very detailed sketches.

There are also, in Afif's book, details of the buildings erected,[8] cities founded and established,[9] gardens planted[10] and canals dug[11] at the instance of the Sultan as part of his pursuit of constructive activity. There is a long description of the astronomical clock and gong invented by Firuz[12] and of the way Asoka's pillar was brought and replanted in Delhi.[13] There are also references to low prices prevailing during Firuz's reign[14]; and there is the first reference in the works of the Sultanate period to the total annual revenue of the state.[15]

[1] *Ibid.*, pp. 21-27.
[2] *Ibid.*, pp. 91-96, 97-100.
[3] Afif, *op. cit.*, pp. 298-301, 302-304, 426, 474-475, etc.
[4] *Ibid.*, pp. 179-180, 288-289, etc.
[5] *Ibid.*, pp. 179-180, 287, 374-375, 380-381, etc.
[6] *Ibid.*, pp. 25, 226-229, 298-301, 341-342, etc.
[7] *Ibid.*, pp. 394-503.
[8] *Ibid.*, pp. 329-331.
[9] *Ibid.*, pp. 124-128, 134-136, 148.
[10] *Ibid.*, pp. 295-296.
[11] *Ibid.*, p. 127.
[12] *Ibid.*, pp. 255-260.
[13] *Ibid.*, pp. 305-315.
[14] *Ibid.*, pp. 293-294.
[15] *Ibid.*, p. 94.

The contents of Yahya's *Tarikh-i-Mubarak Shahi* closely follow those of Minhaj's *Tabaqat*, for Yahya sticks to a bare narrative of political events. There are once again the details merely of enthronement, rebellions, wars, etc. In this book, incidentally, there is the earliest mention of a famous remark attributed to Shaikh Nizam-ud-din Aulia, which has, in a modified form, for long become a proverb—"Delhi is (still) far away from you."[1]

In Amir Khusrau's works, however, we get information on a wide range of subjects. (The reasons for the great range have been discussed earlier.[2]) In the first place the beauty and simplicity of the Persian language as well as its ornate complexity have been amply demonstrated by the master craftsman in his different creations. The *Qiran-us-Sadain*, the *Miftah-ul-Futuh*, the *Nuh Sipihr*, and the *Tughlaq Nama* are works that can be read with comparative ease. The imagery, similes and metaphors in these works are exteremely charming and simple. The *Khazain-ul-Futuh*, on the other hand, or such non-historical works as the *Aijaz-i-Khusravi*, confront the reader with a very tedious language greatly taxing his patience.

The subjects covered in Amir Khusrau's works include the various seasons of north India,[3] the buildings constructed at the instance of the Sultans[4] and forms of their entertainment.[5] In the *Nuh Sipihr* there are two versified pieces of conversation between the bow and the arrow[6] and the club and the ball (used in chaughan or polo)[7] respectively. The conception of the conversation

[1](Dilli az tu dur ast) Yahya, *op. cit.*, p. 97. Sultan Ghiyas-ud-din Tughlaq was known to be hostile to the Shaikh, and on the eve of his march to Bengal he threatened to punish the Shaikh on his return. The Shaikh is said to have uttered these words forecasting the Sultan's death before he returned to the capital. What Yahya, however, fails to state is that the Shaikh actually predeceased the Sultan and thus could not live to witness the fulfilment of his prophecy. Yahya's account, in fact, implies that the Shaikh had survived the Sultan.

The modified version of the Shaikh's remark, which is used as a proverb in India, is "Delhi is still far away" (hunuz Dilli dur ast).

[2]*Supra*, pp. 7-8.

[3]*Qiran-us-Sadain*, pp. 37-39, 58-61, 68-72; *Nuh Sipihr*, pp. 158-161.

[4]*Ibid.* pp. 30-37; *ibid.*, pp. 74-80.

[5]*Ibid.*, pp. 36, 43-44, 52, 66-67; *ibid.*, pp. 372-400.

[6]*Nuh Sipihr*, pp. 284-318.

[7]*Ibid.*, Chapter VIII.

appears amateurish, particularly when the poet concerned is no less than Amir Khusrau, but incidental references to the types of bows and arrows then in use and to the details of the game of polo are of undoubted historical interest. In this work, again, there is a note on the Indian languages[1] and an appreciative description of the custom of sati and the religious beliefs of the Hindus.[2]

There are at the same time descriptions of wars of conquest waged by various Sultans—Jalal-ud-din Khalji's in the *Miftah-ul-Futuh*, Ala-ud-din Khalji's in the *Khazain-ul-Futuh*, Mubarak Khalji's in the *Nuh Sipihr* and Ghiyas-ud-din Tughlaq's in the *Tughlaq Nama*. The accounts of these wars and conquests are replete with excessive exaggeration for the greater glory of the Sultans, since this was primarily what the poet was commissioned to write.

Isami in a way stands in contrast to Amir Khusrau, for Isami's main objective in writing the *Futuh* appears to have been not to glorify but to demonstrate what he must have imagined was the ultimate in political degeneration of his contemporary Sultan, Muhammad Tughlaq. Incidentally, this would also serve to glorify, by contrast, Isami's patron, Sultan Ala-ud-din Hasan Bahmani,[3] the arch rebel against Muhammad Tughlaq. The *Futuh-us-Salatin* is therefore mostly concerned with the conventional political events —accession of Sultans to the throne, rebellions and wars, etc. The account of political events is at times interspersed with narration of miracles.[4] Isami however gives some details of political events that are not found in other contemporary accounts. Thus, for example, he alone among the historians of the Sultanate definitely tells us that Ram Dev Yadava of Deogiri had appealed to Sultan Ala-ud-din Khalji for sending someone to bring his, Ram Dev's, son to the path of obedience.[5] Ala-ud-din, therefore, despatched Malik Kafur to do the job. Again, it is Isami alone who informs us that Sultan Muhammad Tughlaq ordered the execution of all those soldiers who had survived the disastrous expedition to Qarachil.[6]

[1]*Ibid.*, pp. 172-181.
[2]*Ibid.*, pp. 161-172.
[3]*Futuh-us-Salatin*, pp. 574-575.
[4]*Infra*, p. 36.
[5]*Futuh*, p. 274.
[6]*Ibid.*, pp. 448-449.

(It is, of course, not to be understood that in all cases Isami's information is to be accepted as correct.)

ATTITUDE TOWARDS THE SOURCES OF INFORMATION

With regard to the attitude of our historians towards their sources of information, their works may be divided broadly into two categories for the sake of convenience—bare narratives of mainly political events such as are found in the *Tabaqat-i-Nasiri* and the *Tarikh-i-Mubarak Shahi*; and what may be called partly narrative and partly interpretative, or, at any rate, impressionistic works under which all others can be grouped. The books under the former head, in comparison to those under the latter, had necessarily to be based on some kind of investigated information. This for two reasons—they could not bear personal testimony to the events of the entire period they were covering; and they had no definite conclusion to prove by their study and narration of history for which they might even ignore the historicity of the events they had described so long as their objectives were not impaired.

It may be stated here that the two categories used here are not mutually exclusive; still they have been used only to indicate that whereas for the first group of works the writers had to depend more on investigation in comparison to the historians of the second group, the latter depended more on personal witness and hearsay due to the proximity of the period about which they were writing. It is also perhaps true that historians of the second group, more than those of the first, consciously tried to project certain "general lessons" (to use Barani's phrase) through their historical works; and as far as they were concerned, the historicity and the chronology of events were subsidiary to the projection of those lessons. Therefore, their impression of history, rather than a thorough investigation, relatively speaking, would serve their purpose. It is obvious that the narrative historians (of the first group) also carried in their works the stamp of "impression" not only of the period nearer their own lifetime but also of the books they had studied for narrating events of the distant past; it is equally obvious that the "impressionistic" historians also carried out some investigation of the past before they finished their works. The difference between them is in this sense one of degree than of kind.

Thus Minhaj often refers to the sources from which he had derived his information. He had derived it from "trustworthy chronicles,"[1] from sources unspecified,[2] from personal evidence[3] and from hearsay.[4] Yahya, unfortunately, does not refer to his sources except in a vague statement in which he says that he copied his account of the reigns of "past rulers" up to the accession of Firuz Tughlaq from "the different histories" and after that he had written on the basis of his own memory, observation and reliable information.[5] We are therefore left to conjecture as to what Yahya's written sources had been. But the fact that his information is fairly correct is testimony to his effort at collecting it from reliable sources.

Yet there is little evidence to prove that these authors adopted any definite method of ascertaining the authenticity of their information by questioning it, or vigorously using the isnad[6] form of investigation, or collating evidence from one source with that from another, something which, for example, Abul Fazl purports to do later on. In general they accept the evidence they obtain from books, hearsay, and personal testimony of others and their own. As a result, the historian of today, who has perforce to rely for his information on the works of these medieval authors, is doubly handicapped—not only do these authors not give all the information they have, but whatever they give is based upon dubious methods of historical investigation.

The other group of historians writes history with a view to proving certain given objectives. These objectives may be broad and theoretical as in the case of Barani and probably Afif, or they may

[1]Minhaj, *op. cit.* Vol. I, author's Preface, p. xxxiv. The books he refers to are numerous, pp. 56, 67, 69, 141, 231-233, 307, etc.

[2]*Ibid*, pp. 169, 387, 412, 446, 497, 892-893, 900, 935, 1160, etc.

[3]*Ibid.*, pp. 396, 864-865, where he states that he wrote the history of Iltutmish's dynasty on the basis of his personal testimony, pp. 892-893, 1197, 1204, etc.

[4]*Ibid.*, pp. 302, 465, 963, 1294, etc.

[5]Yahya, *op. cit.*, p. 4.

[6]The isnad method had for long been used in Arab historiography and hadis literature whereby the original source of each piece of information was traced through all the successive stages of its passage; in the process, variations were accounted for.

be limited as in the case of Isami and Amir Khusrau. For Barani the one irrefutable lesson of history was the sanctity of high birth, and for Afif history proved that only strong rulers were great rulers and Firuz Shah was not one of them.[1] Isami wrote his *Futuh* to show how oppressive Muhammad Tughlaq was; Amir Khusrau wrote no history; he wrote poetry and prose on limited historical episodes wherein certain events were glorified. These objectives the historians sought to achieve by basing their works mostly on personal testimony and memory. History, for them, was not exactly a matter of investigation; they studied and presented history in such a way as to advocate the efficacy of certain lessons, or certain points of view, particularly regarding state policy. It was Barani who was the most clear headed and the most vocal in presenting these lessons to his readers. And he is the one to state most clearly that "history is a science that requires no proofs so long as the historian is a trustworthy person,"[2] that is, a person of high birth. Others follow him in principle, if not in detail, in that they do not engage themselves in actively questioning their sources and establishing the authenticity of events and submitting proofs for it.

Treatment of History and Historical Causation

The treatment of history by each author is different from the others except in the case of Yahya who comes fairly close to Minhaj. Yet some gradual development in this component of history writing, as in the basic form, may be discerned.

The "universal" history of Minhaj does not reveal any broad universal historical perspective. The *Tabaqat* is, in fact, more a bare narrative of the rise and fall of a number of dynasties than a study in causes, or in the relationship of the history of an individual dynasty to the history of the world as such.

The tenor of Minhaj's work is politico-biographical. He describes events as part of the lives of so many individuals. As observed earlier, it is significant that he seldom entitles a chapter or subchapter after an event; it is always after an individual (except in

[1]These and the following points will be discussed in some detail later on.
[2]Barani, *op. cit.*, pp. 13-14.

the narrative of Nasir-ud-din Mahmud's reign where the sub-chapters are entitled after the concerned year, this part being an annual chronicle). The last part of the *Tabaqat* is, however, devoted to a history of the Mongol menace to Islam.[1] Yet even in this part the narrative is in the old form of a dynastic history of the Mongols.

The events are not described by Minhaj against a general political background but as happenings in the lives of individual rulers. The narration of events therefore does not follow any independent chronological order. These events comprise a monarch's political career rather than stages in historical development.

Consequently, history, for Minhaj, is not one whole, of which the rise and fall of dynasties, or even the occurrence of individual events, are parts. It is fragmented into dynastic units, each unit being independent of the others. The dynastic units are further fragmented into regnal units, each similarly independent of the others.

The causation in history, for Minhaj, lies in human volition. From the beginning to the end of the *Tabaqat*, events are described in such a manner as to reveal calculated designs of menat the helm of affairs. To take a few random examples:

"This monarch (Mahmud of Ghazni), by his manliness, his bravery and intrepidity, his wisdom and foresight, and his prudent counsels and wise measures, considerably extended the Muhammadan conquests in the east, and greatly increased the dominion of Islam in that quarter. The whole of Ajam, Khurasan and Khwarazm, Tabaristan, Irak, the territory of Nimroz, Fars, the mountain districts of Ghur, Tukharistan, all came under the control of his officers. The maliks or rulers, of Turkistan paid him obedience and acknowledged his superiority. He threw a bridge over the Jihun, and marched his forces into Turan and Kadr Khan had an interview with him, as had the Khans of the Turks likewise; and the Khakans of Turkistan came and presented themselves before him, and tendered him their allegiance."[2]

Or, "when Sultan Muiz-ud-din acquired the territory of Tigina-

[1]The heading of this chapter is "The Affairs of Islam and the Irruption of the Kafirs (Mongols)," Minhaj, *op. cit.*, p. 324 (text).

[2]Minhaj, *op. cit.*, p. 84.

bad, the Ghuzz tribe and the chieftains of that sept, who, retiring defeated from before the force of Khita, had moved towards Ghaznin, during a period of twelve years had taken the Ghaznin territory out of the hands of Khusrau Shah and of Khusrau Malik, and had brought it under their own sway. Muiz-ud-din was in the constant habit of making raids upon the Ghuzz from Tiginabad and assailing them and continued to harass that territory until the year 569 H., when Sultan Ghiyas-ud-din subdued Ghaznin, and placed Sultan Muiz-ud-din upon the throne (of that territory) and returned to Ghur again."[1]

Or, "when Malik Ikhtiyar-ud-din Aetkin became deputy, by virute of deputy-ship he took the affairs of the kingdom into his own hands, and, in conjunction with the wazir, the Nizam-ul-Mulk, the Khwajah Muhazzab-ud-Din, Muhammad-i-Iwaz the Mustaufi, assumed control over the disposal of state-affairs."[2]

However, Minhaj does not formally repudiate divine will or predestination ordained by divinity in matters of state. His account of events is occasionally interspersed with comments like:

"The Almightly gave them (the Saljuk rulers) strength and power, so that they possessed themselves of the territories of Khurasan, and the east and the west and whatever the dominions of Islam were, wholly and completely came under the sway of their descendants, in such wise that their fame will remain upon the records of time upto the judgement day."[3] Or, "since the Most High and Holy God, from all eternity had predestined that the states of Hindustan should come under the shadow of the guardianship of the great Sultan, the supreme monarch, Shams-ud-Dunya wa-ud-Din (Iltutmish) . . . was raised to the throne of empire and seat of dominion. . . ."[4]

Comments like these indicate Minhaj's personal preference for one or other dynasty or ruler rather than a basic causal relationship between divine will and historical events. Occasionally, Minhaj gives many material details which resulted in the happening of a particular event and then praises the Almighty for having brought

[1] *Ibid.*, pp. 448-449.
[2] *Ibid.*, p. 650.
[3] *Ibid.*, p. 122.
[4] *Ibid.*, pp. 597-598.

the event about. In the case of the second battle of Tarain, for example, Minhaj gives the details of the battle array of the belligerent forces, the divisions into which Muiz-ud-din's soldiers had been ordered and the tactics they had been instructed to follow. He then adds, "the Musalman troops acted according to these instructions and having exhausted and wearied the unbelievers, Almighty God gave the victory to Islam, and the infidel host was overthrown."[1] It is significant that the Almighty does not figure in the first battle of Tarain, when Muiz-ud-din had been defeated. Similarly, the predestination of Iltutmish's accession to the throne of Hindustan is simply one of the numerous praises which Minhaj showers upon the father of his patron, rather than an explanation of the cause of his accession. The actual circumstances of his enthronement have been given separately.[2]

For Barani, history is no mere narration of events in the biographical setting; it is a *study* of the past with a view to deriving lessons from it. "History," he says, "is a report *(naql)* of the laudable charity and malignity, justice and tyranny, worth and unworthiness, laudable qualities and offensiveness, obedience and defiance, virtues and vices (of the people) of the past so that those who study it now take lessons from it and are able to know the good and the bad aspects of government and good as well as evil behaviour of the people; from this knowledge they follow the path of virtue and avoid that of vice."[3] And the historians' purport is to bring to the fore these lessons and in this task he is not obliged to submit proof for his narrative provided that he "should command everbody's trust and should be known for his truthfulness and impartiality, so that everybody places his trust in whatever he writes even though there is no proof."[4]

Barani thus proceeds to write the *Tarikh* in a manner which would make the lessons of history intelligible to the reader. The *Tarikh*, though arranged as a sequence of reigns, is, strictly speaking, not a chronicle, for Barani had no particular regard for chro-

[1] *Ibid.*, pp. 465-468.
[2] *Ibid.*, pp. 605-606.
[3] Barani, *Tarikh*, p. 13.
[4] *Ibid.*

nology which he felt was unnecessary for his purpose.[1]

Events, for Barani, are not isolated happenings; together they form a pattern on which the attention of the historian is focused. Our author states that he had started his account from the point where Minhaj had left his[2]; that is, from (and including) the reign of Balban. But before he begins his account of Balban's reign, he prefers to examine the causes of the weakness of the Delhi Sultanate during the 30 years preceding the accession of that Sultan.[3] This is a kind of background against which the autocratic rule of Balban is studied. From then onwards, the reign of each ruler is some kind of backdrop against which the subsequent reign is assessed. In this respect, Barani's evaluation of a reign, which he makes at the end of each chapter, is of special significance. This evaluation is, unlike that of Minhaj, not in terms of personal qualities of the Sultan, but in terms of his policies. In fact, very often Barani evaluates not only the entire reign, but the individual acts and policies of Sultans. Thus, for example, he applauds Balban's determination to maintain the sanctity of aristocratic birth,[4] but regrets his despotic measures to suppress and, if necessary, annihilate, the remnants of the chahalghani.[5] Similarly, while he is extremely critical of Ala-ud-din Khalji's disregard of the *Shara* in matters of state,[6] he nevertheless considers the Sultan's market regulations a near miracle.[7]

What makes Barani an extremely valuable historian is his interest in the details of administration in actual operation. The administration is not dealt with as an independent entity but as an integral part of the state system. The details are presented in a logical sequence, as the outcome of certain historical events or situations. Thus, even though Barani does not fully approve of Balban's administrative measures designed to suppress recalcitrant nobles,

[1]*Ibid.*, p. 468.

[2]*Ibid.* pp. 20-21.

[3]*Ibid.*, pp. 24-29.

[4]*Ibid.*, pp. 33-39.

[5]*Ibid.*, pp. 47-48, 65-66. "Chahalghani" was the group of 40 nobles who exercised considerable influence in matters of state during and after the reign of Iltutmish through the early years of Balban's reign.

[6]*Ibid.*, pp. 289, 338.

[7]*Ibid.*, pp. 339-340.

these are set by him against the background of the weakness of the Sultanate during the reigns of the successors of Iltutmish. Similarly, Ala-ud-din's economic and administrative measures were related to the necessity of reducing the rebellious rural aristocracy to utter poverty so that it was left with no leisure to think of rebellion.[1] The market regulations were introduced, according to our author, for the purpose of maintaining a large army at reduced expense.[2] Why should a large army be maintained? So that the Mongol menace could be successfully encountered[3]; and the rebellions, both of the "Hindus" as well as of the Turkish nobles, could be suppressed.[4] Why did the rebellions occur? Barani gives in detail four causes[5]—the Sultan was not in the know of the affairs of his people; the nobles held convivial parties and struck friendship with one another and plotted rebellions; they had contracted close relationships with one another; if one of them in any way suffered, a hundred others rose in sympathy with him due to their affection for one another; and certain persons possessed an abundance of wealth, which induced them to mischief. Or, "Regarding the Hindus, he (Ghiyas-ud-din Tughlaq) passed an order that they should not be left wit hso much (of wealth) as to induce them to rebellion or intrigue; nor should they be deprived of so much that they give up agriculture altogether. . . .Observance of this regulation in regard to the Hindus can be called the best form of administrative arrangement."[6]

Thus, better equipped as Barani is in his technique, his treatment of history and historical causation clearly represents an advance over that of Minhaj. He studies events in their inter-relationship and in relation to the administrative system. He does not merely narrate them, but attempts to trace their causes. Above all, he studies history in a conscious theoretical framework.

Barani has expounded his theoretical framework in great detail in his *Fatawa-i-Jahandari*. In a limited sense he was cognisant of historical change. He clearly exposes the contradiction between the

[1] *Ibid.*, pp. 283-284, 287.
[2] *Ibid.* pp. 303-304.
[3] *Ibid.*, pp. 302-303.
[4] *Ibid.*, pp. 283-284, 287.
[5] *Ibid.*, pp. 282-283.
[6] *Ibid.*, p. 430.

institution of kingship and the principles of Islam[1] but recognizes and approves of the necessity of kingship, because "the world had returned to its old wickedness."[2] Similarly, he allows the Sultan to adapt old laws or frame new ones in accordance with changing circumstances.[3] During the period he has covered in his *Tarikh*, he had witnessed many changes, like the gradual absorption of the "lowly" elements into the ruling class. Barani abhors change of this nature, but abhorrence is implicit recognition.

This abhorrence stems from the basic tenets of Barani's thought. The central theme of his thinking is aristocratic birth. His contempt for the low born is unreserved. He carries this theory of the sanctity of high birth to absurd limits when he attributes to God Himself a preference for the high born. "God," he declares, "selects only possessors of merit and virtuous characters for nearness to His Court . . . . They do not permit any man who is wicked, unclean, or victim of vices or meannesses to occupy a place of distinction before the Divine Throne."[4] It may be noted here that merit and virtue, like uncleanliness, vice and meanness have been, in Barani's opinion, "apportioned at the beginning of Time and allotted to their souls,"[5] and these are hereditary attributes.[6] The recognition of this distinction between the high born and the low born is seen even in the Quran in plain contradiction of its original meaning.[7] Merit for him is high birth, and vice low birth and neither of them can be acquired through any amount of effort. These are qualities innate to different classes of people; and kings would be well advised to sacrifice even efficiency, if necessary, in order to maintain the supremacy of high birth in the official hierarchy.[8]

Barani's contempt for the low born transcends even his ortho-

[1]Barani, *FJ*, pp. 34, 39-40.
[2]*Ibid.*, p. 34.
[3]*Ibid.*, p. 66.
[4]*Ibid.*, p. 94.
[5]*Ibid.*, p. 97.
[6]*Ibid.*
[7]*Ibid.*, p. 98 and fn.
[8]*Ibid.*, pp. 92, 98-99. Also *Tarikh* where Barani complains of high offices being acquired through ability and efficiency rather than through the claims of heredity, p. 18.

dox religious affiliation. He detests the low born, Hindus and Muslims alike. In a false ascription to the *Ma'asir-ul-Khulafa* he fabricates an order ascribed to Caliph Mamun in which he prohibits education to the low born. In this order, in which Barani really doles out his own thought, the low born include Muslims by implication, since the order instructs teachers to teach people rules about prayer, fasting, and the Haj pilgrimage, etc., and Hindus as a corollary. "Teachers of every kind," he says, "are to be sternly ordered not to thrust precious stones down the throats of dogs or to put collars of gold round the necks of pigs and bears—that is, to the mean, the ignoble and the worthless, to shop-keepers and to the low born they are to teach nothing more than the rules about prayer, fasting, religious charity and the Haj pilgrimage along with some chapters of the Quran and some doctrines of the Faith."[1]

At another place, Barani warns the Sultans against appointing the low born to high posts, even if they were capable of setting the affairs of the world right.[2] At still another place he advises the Sultans to dismiss any sign of wisdom, learning, etc. in a low born for he, in his cleverness, tries to appear meritorious, while in reality it is not possible for a base born to attain any merit.[3]

Barani tries to rationalize this notion as a fundamental lesson of history about which "no disagreement is possible."[4]

Herein, indeed, lies the basic contradiction in Barani's approach to history—he would go with historical change to the extent of recognizing and approving the necessity of kingship even when it contravened the fundamental principles of Islam; but he would stop where history brought in changes inimical to his notions, like the one concerning birth.

Yet the fact that Barani studies the history of his period against a theoretical background is significant, irrespective of the validity of his theoretical understanding. And to the Sultans, who obviously did not hold the same view of the affairs of state, he offers positive alternatives—advice on the constitution of a permanent king's

[1] Barani, *FJ*, p. 49.
[2] *Ibid.*, p. 92.
[3] *Ibid.*, p. 98.
[4] *Ibid.*, p. 92.

advisory council where nobles, selected on account of their high birth, could offer their frank opinions[1]; advice on the nature of state laws[2]; advice on the advantage of protecting old families[3] and on a variety of other subjects which comprise the *Fatawa-i-Jahandari.*

At the same time, this approach involves a strong element of subjectivity, particularly with Barani, whose *Tarikh* was a kind of illustration of the truth of his theories.[4] He interpolates into the *Tarikh* many of his own views by attributing them to historical personages. The substance of Balban's opinions regarding the low born[5] is the same as that of Barani's own counsel on the subject in the *Fatawa.*[6] The alleged conversation between Qazi Mughis-ud-din and Ala-ud-din Khalji in the *Tarikh*[7] conveys the same sense which Barani's advocacy of all out operations against the Hindus does in the *Fatawa.*[8] More subtly, Barani praises Ghiyas-ud-din Tughlaq for his moderate policies in administration[9] because he pleads for moderation in state policies elsewhere.[10] He attributes the failure of Muhammad Tughlaq to an imbalance in the contradictory qualities in his nature[11] because he holds, on the theoretical plane, that while everyone's nature comprises contradictory qualities, it is a balanced mixture of these that results in success.[12]

At the same time, such a method probably indicates the thinking of at least one section of the ruling class, whose views the historian represents, one point of view from which contemporary

[1] *Ibid.*, pp. 8-13.

[2] *Ibid.*, pp. 64-71.

[3] *Ibid.*, pp. 101-109.

[4] This is so in spite of the fact that the *Tarikh* was written earlier than the *Fatawa*. M. Habib, "Life and Thought of Zia-ud-din Barani," p. 121 fn. While writing the *Tarikh* Barani must have had all those ideas in his mind which he soon afterwards expounded in detail in the *Fatawa.* Many of these ideas are common to both works, as will be pointed out and illustrated below.

[5] Barani, *Tarikh*, pp. 33-39.

[6] Barani, *FJ*, pp. 49, 91-96, 97-100.

[7] Barani, *Tarikh*, p. 290.

[8] Barani, *FJ*, pp. 46-47.

[9] Barani, *Tarikh*, pp. 427-429.

[10] Barani, *FJ*, pp. 55-57.

[11] Barani, *Tarikh*, pp. 459, 496-497, 505-507.

[12] Barani, *FJ*, p. 86.

history was studied.

Causation in history, for Barani, lies in the nature of the individual at the helm of affairs. He analyzes the individual's nature and finds in it the existence of contradictory qualities.[1] It is in terms of the Sultan's nature that he explains the existence of contradictory phenomena within the compass of a single reign, for instance, that of Balban and Muhammad Tughlaq. Ghiyas-ud-din Tughlaq's was an admirable reign owing to the moderation which he was able to observe, due to a balanced mixture of opposite qualities. What baffles Barani is the success of Ala-ud-din Khalji. Barani repeatedly censures him for his cruelty and his irreligious nature[2] and wonders "why does not the City (Delhi). . . collapse and be reduced to a heap of dust . . .?"[3] Still, whatever schemes he undertook, with or without a proper appraisal, were successful.[4]

To explain this, Barani, in accordance with his theoretical exposition in the *Fatawa-i-Jahandari*,[5] passes on the credit to the great nobles of the Sultan.[6] For Ala-ud-din's success in general he takes resort to a popular medieval notion which credited the presence of great saints with the success of their contemporary Sultans. Ala-ud-din's success was therefore due to the presence of Nizam-ud-din Aulia, who was a friend of God.[7] It may be noted that this is one of the very few instances in the *Tarikh* where Barani utilizes such extra-historical notions to explain historical phenomena. But his desperate resort to this kind of explanation of a phenomenon which defies his rational analysis proves the exception to the rule.

A departure which Barani makes from Minhaj in the treatment of historical causation is that, for him, the Sultan's nature does not manifest itself only in individual events but in the totality of his reign, or in substantial parts of it. He evaluates the entire reign of a Sultan, or different aspects of it, at different times in relation to

[1] *Ibid.*, pp. 85-89.

[2] Barani, *Tarikh*, pp. 261, 262, 289, 297, 338.

[3] *Ibid.*, p. 299. The words are attributed by Barani to Maulana Shams-ud-din Turk, but he quotes them with obvious approval.

[4] *Ibid.*, p. 324.

[5] Barani, *FJ*, pp. 8-13.

[6] Barani, *Tarikh*, pp. 336-337.

[7] *Ibid.*, p. 325.

the Sultan's nature and character, as has been illustrated above.

The use of the technique of phasing a reign was Afif's contribution to history writing during the Sultanate period. He probably observes contradictory phenomena during a single reign (that of Firuz Tughlaq), from fighting against fellow Muslims to renunciation of war; from extreme laxity in administrative control and tolerance of the offences of nobles to a strong suppression of Damghani's rebellion. Afif tries to reconcile these phenomena and divides them into phases, although, as observed earlier, these phases are not strictly chronological.

Why Afif wrote his *Tarikh* cannot be stated definitively. If he had ever stated the purpose of his work in any part of the *Tarikh*, that part has been lost to us. However, he certainly completed the book after Timur's invasion of India, for he refers to that event.[1] This could conceivably have given him a point of vantage from which to evaluate the immediate past.

Afif's general evaluation of Firuz Shah's reign is not free from doubt. It is possible to argue that in the midst of ruin and desolation left behind by Timur, the immediate past appeared golden to him and that Firuz Tughlaq, as the last great ruler of the Delhi Sultanate, was portrayed by him as an ideal monarch.[2] But the praise the author showers on the Sultan, coupled with his seeming approval of everything the Sultan does, seems to suggest that the excessive praise is not to be taken at its face value.

Afif calls Firuz the second Alexander (Sikandar-i-Sani)[3] but leaves no doubt that the Sultan shrank from an armed conflict, as far as possible, and struck a compromise with his few enemies at the first opportunity.[4] Firuz had a lingering desire for advancing his banners into the Deccan, for "kings are extremely eager, and make

[1]Afif, *op. cit.*, p. 314.

[2]For such a view, see Peter Hardy, *Historians of Medieval India*, London, 1960, p. 41.

[3]Afif, *op. cit.*, p. 101.

[4]In all his major expeditions—to Lakhnauti, Jajnagar, Nagarkot and Thatta (*ibid.*, pp. 109-120, 144-172, 186-189, and 230-247) Firuz seems to have been keen to establish mere formal suzerainty and leave the states to autonomous local rulers. Yahya corroborates Afif. When Firuz invaded Jajnagar and pursued its ruler, the latter sued for terms; and the Sultan, "*as was his habit*, returned from Jajnagar," *Tarikh-i-Mubarak Shahi*, p. 129.

great efforts to capture territories and bring them under their control."[1] and received petitions once each from Daulatabad and Ma'abar[2] inviting his intervention there, but failed to make up his mind because, "in these times things are different (from what they were earlier)."[3] Once the Sultan had fought his wars in Bengal, Jajnagar, Nagarkot and Thatta, and once he had realized the futility of an attempt to bring under his control the far-off Deccan, he gave up war because, in words attributed to his wazir, the disadvantages of war outweighed its advantages in the ratio of ten to one.[4]

Afif repeatedly emphasizes the Sultan's devotion to Sufi saints[5] and then takes note of how he was once caught drinking,[6] though earlier he had taken an oath of abstinence before Shaikh-ul-Islam Shaikh Qutb-ud-din Munawwar.[7]

It is from Afif that we learn of the gross inefficiency prevailing in Firuz Shah's army. On his way back from Jajnagar, the Sultan and his armies lost their way and for six months wandered among hills and marshes.[8] The same story is repeated on his withdrawal from Thatta, when a handful of men misled him into the Rann.[9] While at Thatta, the provisions for the army ran short and there was no arrangement for immediate supplies.[10] When Firuz proposed to undertake a second expedition to Thatta, a number of his soldiers chose to get away from the army and return home.[11] Such persons were captured and detained, but they suffered no material loss, much less corporal punishment. Says Afif, "This was due to the religious disposition of the Sultan; had such a thing happened during the regime of any other Sultan, it could not have been tolerated."[12]

[1]Afif, *op. cit.*, pp. 263-264.
[2]*Ibid.*, pp. 224, 261.
[3]*Ibid.*, p. 264.
[4]*Ibid.*, pp. 264-267.
[5]*Ibid.*, pp. 61-62, 194-196, 371.
[6]*Ibid.*, pp. 145-147.
[7]*Ibid.*, p. 79.
[8]*Ibid.*, pp. 172-173.
[9]*Ibid.*, pp. 207-208.
[10]*Ibid*,, pp. 208-209.
[11]*Ibid.*, pp. 226-228.
[12]*Ibid.*, p. 229.

Afif gives a graphic picture of the laxity of control and discipline in the administration in almost every department. Firuz acquiesced in gross irregularities in the muster of soldiers,[1] and refused to dismiss them even when invalidated by age[2]; he made most of the offices in the administration hereditary from that of the wazir to one of an ordinary clerk.[3] He would forgive any offence, big or small, including embezzlement and rebellion.[4] The accounts of the royal factories were annually audited by the Diwan-i-Wazarat, but the irregularities were not strictly examined, "not that the Sultan was ignorant of it; he was fully aware of it. But he would just close his eyes to it. The amils were indeed very happy and prosperous."[5] Referring to the promulgation of new rules regarding the salaries of the wajahdar soldiers, Afif remarks, "During the reign of the earlier Sultans and imams of the Faith in Delhi, this regulation was not prevalent. No village was given in wajah . . . . Sultan Ala-ud-din often expressed his doubt on (the desirability of) this measure (and said) that villages should not be granted in wajah, for in every wajah there are 200-300 persons and all these persons are under one wajahdar soldier. If a few of them, due to an excess of haughtiness and mischievousness, get together and rise in revolt, it would be no surprise. For this reason Ala-ud-din never granted any village in wajah to anyone. Every year the troops were given cash from the treasury. When Firuz Shah ascended the throne, he, "being one of the great saints who emulated them (the saints) for forty years, opened to the people the doors of kindness and completely brushed aside such suspicions."[6]

Afif, of course, does notice a state of general peace and prosperity during Firuz Shah's reign.[7] The Sultan's pursuit of peaceful activities like the construction of dams[8] and cities,[9] laying of

[1] *Ibid.*, pp. 298-301.
[2] *Ibid.*, pp. 302-304.
[3] *Ibid.*, pp. 302, 426, 474-475.
[4] *Ibid.*, p. 25.
[5] *Ibid.*, pp. 341-342.
[6] *Ibid.*, pp. 94-95.
[7] *Ibid.*, pp. 179-185, 288-292, 294-298.
[8] *Ibid.*, pp. 229-230.
[9] *Ibid.*, pp. 124-128, 134-136, 148.

gardens,[1] establishment of the department of charity,[2] and of a hospital[3] and the installation of the astronomical clock and gong,[4] etc. find a detailed description in the *Tarikh*. Afif repeatedly emphasizes the Sultan's patience in dealing with the affairs of state and his devotion to matters spiritual and qualities more of a Sufi than of a conventional medieval Indian ruler. For all this he duly eulogizes him.

Yet Afif does not fail to notice the gradual weakening of the state structure, thanks mainly to the mildness of Firuz's policies, to which he seems to trace the decline and disintegration of the Sultanate.

From the above analysis, it would appear that Afif studies and writes history in order to examine the causes of the decline of his contemporary state. If so, the causes he establishes lie within history and not outside it. He takes the period he covers in the *Tarikh* as one unit within which he studies change. This change, for him, is not an isolated phenomenon, nor the result of isolated events, nor that of any divine or supernatural intervention. It is the result of total change in the policies of the state during Firuz Shah's reign.

At the same time Afif locates the cause of this change in state policies entirely in the Sultan's nature or will, and not, even partially, in other historical conditions. That is, while he attributes the cause of the decline of the Sultanate to the mild policies of Firuz Shah, he fails to notice any causal relationship between the circumstances existing at the time of the Sultan's enthronement and the mildness of his policies.

Yahya's treatment of history is in the style of a narration of individual events. He rarely interprets history. The only interpretation which is implicit in his account is his choice of including or omitting some or the other events from his work. The most notable omission from the book, for example, is the economic reforms of Ala-ud-din Khalji. And yet, it cannot be definitively stated that he was completely indifferent to treating administrative measures as

[1] *Ibid.*, pp. 295-296.
[2] *Ibid.*, pp. 349-351.
[3] *Ibid.*, pp. 353-358.
[4] *Ibid.*, pp. 255-260.

an integral part of history, for he attributes the disintegration of Muhammad Tughlaq's empire to the enhancement of taxes and the transfer of capital among other, similar, causes.[1]

To capture the spirit of Yahya's discretion in the selection of events becomes all the more difficult in the part dealing with the post-Firuz Tughlaq period, the reason being that for the political history of this period, Yahya's book itself is one of our chief sources of information. This fact attests both to the importance of the work as well as to its limitations.

Yahya has no sense of an organic role of history. At his best, though rarely, he analyzes the causes of individual events or phenomena. But these causes he does not attribute to any unhistorical, supernatural force. The fact of his frequent attribution of the victories of the Sultans to God's favour[2] does not testify to a firm belief in a supernatural force directing history or causing the occurrence of historical events. Indeed, even the attribution of victories to God's favour conforms to a political principle. He intervenes on the side of the Sultan, whoever the Sultan may be, and not on the side of any particular person, least of all a rebel. Yahya relates the story of one Sarang Khan who was nominated by Sultan Mahmud Nasir-ud-din Shah to quell the rebellion of one Shaikha Khokhar. The two were engaged in a battle; ultimately, "God blessed Sarang Khan with victory."[3] Later on, the same Sarang Khan captured Multan from the royal nominee, Ghalib Khan. Sultan Nusrat Shah (at this time there were two Sultans ruling simultaneously—Nusrat Shah at Faizabad and Mahmud Shah at Delhi)[4] sent Tatar Khan to dispossess Sarang Khan of Multan and return it to Ghalib Khan. The matter was decided in the field of battle where "God blessed Tatar Khan with victory"[5] against His erstwhile favourite.

If and when Yahya tries to find the cause of an event, he finds it in human will or human action or both. Thus, "when Muiz-ud-din Bahram Shah was imprisoned, Malik Izz-ud-din Balban seated himself on the throne . . . . (But) the majority of amirs did

[1]Yahya, *op. cit.*, pp. 113-115.
[2]*Ibid.*, pp. 6, 11, 15, 73, 157, 162, etc.
[3]*Ibid.*, p. 157.
[4]K.S. Lal, *Twilight of the Sultanate*, Bombay, 1963, p. 12.
[5]Yahya, *op. cit.*, p. 162.

not agree (to this), (therefore) they removed him."[1] Or, "Sultan Ala-ud-din Masud fell under the influence of a group of Abyssinians and the low-born, therefore the killing of maliks and confiscating their property became a habit with him."[2] Or, "the affairs of state fell into neglect during the reign of Tughlaq Shah (grandson of Firuz) due to the Sultan's youth and inexperience."[3]

It is practically only at one place that Yahya has consciously tried to analyze the causes of the occurrence of a major historical event—the fall of Muhammad Tughlaq's empire. Among the seven causes he enumerates, there is not even a casual reference to any divine force, or God's displeasure with the Sultan having brought about that event. The Sultanate fell into disorder and disruption for the following reasons—Tarmashirin's invasion; famine and enhancement of the land revenue demand in the Doab; transfer of the capital from Delhi; annihilation of the 80,000-strong army sent to Qarachil; widespread rebellions; and the Sultan's large-scale massacre of people from all walks of life.[4]

The treatment of history in Amir Khusrau's works has to be viewed differently from that in the works of others because Khusrau does not make a systematic study of the past or of any particular aspect of it. He is ordered by his patron-Sultans to take up individual episodes[5] or a few main events of their reigns[6] and immortalize them in his craft. Khusrau therefore has little freedom of speech.[7] He has to praise his patron, whoever he may be, and this he does deftly. "Like a wandering minstrel he went from door to door, turned his lyre to a different pitch according to time and convenience, and sang with as much gusto the praises of a murderer as those of his victim."[8] This, despite the poet's

[1] *Ibid.*, p. 33.
[2] *Ibid.*, p. 34.
[3] *Ibid.*, pp. 142-143.
[4] *Ibid.*, pp. 113-114.
[5] Thus, for example, in *Qiran-us-Sadain* and *Dewal Rani Khizr Khan.*
[6] For example, in *Miftah-ul-Futuh*, *Khazain-ul-Futuh*, *Nuh Sipihr* and *Tughlaq Nama.*
[7] Habib, *Campaigns of Ala-ud-din Khalji* (being the *tr.* of the *Khazain-ul-Futuh*), Bombay, 1931, pp. xvii.
[8] Wahid M. Mirza, *Life and Works of Amir Khusrau*, Calcutta, 1935, pp. 234-235.

assurance that no one could purchase a verse from him just as no one could make a bargain over Paradise.[1]

Amir Khasrau does not purport to make a prosaic historical analysis in his works, for that was neither his genius nor his mission. If he had tried to analyze the causes of the achievements of the Sultans, he would be logically involved in analyzing the causes of their failures. This he could not always afford to do. His heroes, whatever their failures, had to be raised on to very high pedestals. At times he attains this objective by unceremoniously omitting unpalatable events like the invasion of India by the Mongols Qutlugh Khwaja and Targhi (from the *Khazain-ul-Futuh.*) But mostly he attains it by subjecting his literary flourish to effect rather than to analysis, "Like the rising of a pole (Qutb-ud-din Aibak) in the west, in the east a canopy of the sun of religion (Shams-ud-din Iltutmish) arose too."[2] Or, "in whichever direction his (Kaiqubad's) star turned its face, victory ran (up to him) and the doors of good fortune opened (themselves to him)."[3] Or, "if one could become a world-conqueror by one's own effort, nobody would be subject to Fortune."[4] This technique helps him to pass over unpleasant facts. He does not have to accuse Ala-ud-din Khalji, for instance, of the assassination of Jalal-ud-din. Ala-ud-din ascended the throne because "Providence had ordained that this Muslim Moses was to seize their powerful swords from all infidel Pharaohs . . . ."[5]

Amir Khusrau is further helped in this by his manner of treating events. A grand spectacle surrounds his treatment and he reaches the climax only after trespassing into numerous bylanes. The *Qiran-us-Sadain* and the *Nuh Sipihr* are the most obvious examples of it.

This however does not necessarily preclude his deriving lessons from history whenever it was safe for him to do so. The whole setting of the *Qiran-us-Sadain,* for example, is very suggestive. He leaves behind, in this book, the impression of an atmosphere of

[1]Amir Khusrau, *Ghurrat-ul-Kamal,* p. 52.

[2]Amir Khusrau, *Dewal Rani,* p. 48.

[3]Amir Khusrau, *Qiran-us-Sadain,* p. 23.

[4]Amir Khusrau, *Miftah-ul-Futuh,* Aligarh, 1954, p. 6. This remark is followed by a narration of Jalal-ud-din Khalji's first four victories.

[5]Amir Khusrau, *Khazain-ul-Futuh* (*tr.* Habib), p. 6.

revelry and pleasure seeking in Kaiqubad's camp at the cost of efficiency. The Sultan is unaware of Nasir-ud-din Bughra Khan's march towards Awadh with full military preparations; he is lost in convivial parties.[1] When he does become aware of it, he shows reluctance to advance personally and needs to be advised to that effect.[2] When the Mongols were beating their war drums as far inside the country as Lahore, Kaiqubad sent Barbak to check the menace and himself was unable to forsake the cup.[3] Amir Khusrau, indeed, feels sorry for the whole atmosphere in the court and particularly resents the attention the lowly elements and the flatterers receive at the Sultan's hands.[4]

Amir Khusrau's subsequent writings continue to project the same view. In *Dewal Rani*, for instance, he deems it proper to advise Ala-ud-din Khalji against an excess of indulgence.[5] He witnesses Mubarak Khalji's infatuation with Khusrau Khan and his complete absorption in pleasures, and censures him for it, though after his death. He says in the *Tughlaq Nama*, "Excessive indulgence soon overcomes the indulgent and destroys him. The Sultan in particular should exercise caution (in these matters), since he is responsible not only for his own security and well-being but also for that of his subjects. And infatuation of the kind such as Mubarak Shah's is particularly deplorable, for the Sultan ought to know that among his friends there would be many enemies."[6] Similarly, he advises the Sultans about the evil consequences of tyranny and injustice,[7] and holds that good administration is better than conquests.[8]

Yet these counsels—abstention from licence, efficiency of administration, prevalence of justice, etc.—are stereotyped and formal. These are not, as with Barani, theories arrived at from an analytical study of history. History, for Khusrau, is not a field for

[1]Amir Khusrau, *Qiran-us-Sadain*, pp. 35-36, 43-44.

[2]*Ibid.*, p. 88.

[3]*Ibid.*, pp. 86-87.

[4]*Ibid.*, pp. 243-244.

[5]Amir Khusrau, *Dewal Rani*, pp. 35-36.

[6]Amir Khusrau, *Tughlaq Nama*, p. 16.

[7]Amir Khusrau, *Dewal Rani*, pp. 23-36.

[8]Amir Khusrau, *Khazain-ul-Futuh* (*tr.* Habib), p. 7; *Nuh Sipihr*, pp. 226-243; *Dewal Rani*, p. 29.

inquiry; it is the raw material which he moulds into shape as the occasion demands.

To a small extent, and for different reasons, the decision to subordinate historical fact to literary effect relates to Isami also. Isami proposes to emulate Firdausi's literary masterpiece, *Shah Nama*, as the form of his work.[1]

Isami's personal frustration and his bitter hostility to Muhammad Tughlaq are ill-concealed. He claims blood relationship with some of the nobles of the Sultanate,[2] and throughout the *Futuh* he maintains a predilection for the nobility. Discussing the events of the post-Iltutmish period, Isami attributes to the nobles a much larger share of authority than they had actually possessed. And he refers to them as one undivided entity. They "granted" the kingdom to one ruler[3] and "dismissed" another from the throne.[4] He welcomes the enthronement of Razia, for she had come to the throne with the consent of the nobles.[5] But as soon as she begins to make her famous intrigues with Yaqut, Isami changes his tune and starts moralizing on the essential wickedness of womanhood.[6] He showers praise on Nasir-ud-din Mahmud and states, "His kingdom was stable, for he was a humble and compassionate king. (In everything) he sought the advice of his amirs. Everyone became his well-wisher. Without their knowledge he would not take a decision, nor undertake to implement a plan. Without their knowledge he would not even take water, nor sleep."[7] It is significant that to Isami there appear no dissensions within the nobility. All decisions are taken unanimously. When Altunia contravenes this principle and allows himself to be seduced by Razia and revolts against Bahram, whom the nobles had placed on the throne, he is derided by Isami as a wandering, stupid Turk with a small band

[1]*Futuh-us-Salatin*, p. 574.

[2]*Ibid.*, pp. 122, 142, 431. These claims are very convincingly challenged by Syed Sabau-ud-din in "Futuh-us-Salatin," *Ma'arif* (Urdu), Vol. 44, No. 2, 1939, pp. 110-113.

[3]They "granted" it to Rukn-ud-din Firuz, Isami, *op. cit.*, p. 124.

[4]They "dismissed" Muiz-ud-din Bahram Shah, *ibid.*, p. 137.

[5]*Ibid.*, pp. 127-128.

[6]*Ibid.*, pp. 129-130.

[7]*Ibid.*, pp. 140-141. It is interesting to note that Barani calls this Sultan ,'incompetent," *Tarikh*, p. 26.

of soldiers.[1] He is derided obviously because he revolted not so much against Sultan Bahram, for whom Isami had little regard anyway, but against the decision of the nobles who were responsible for Bahram's enthronement. Isami even treats Tughril, who had rebelled against Balban, sympathetically; nowhere does he condemn him for his rebellion. On the contrary, he calls him "brave"[1] very frequently,[2] and uses the term "martyrdom" for his death.[3]

When, however, Isami comes to the reign of Muhammad Tughlaq, his idiom begins to change. He views the Sultan almost as a sadist verging on madness, who completely throws overboard whatever our author had considered sensible. The burden of emphasis in his account of Muhammad Tughlaq's reign is on the interminable conflicts between the Sultan and his nobles, important as well as lesser ones. Even schemes like the transfer of capital, issuing of token currency and the expedition to Qarachil were undertaken by the Sultan, alleges Isami, in order to bring ruin to all that the earlier Sultans had nurtured so fondly.[4] What a contrast, indeed, he makes to Ala-ud-din Khalji.[5] Revolt against him was therefore justified; indeed, even the *Shara* permitted his extermination.[6]

Thus, Isami feels frustrated at the behaviour of his contemporary Sultan, whom he views as the destroyer of every established norm. Add to it the failure of the world to recognize his literary merit,[7] prior to his writing the *Futuh-us-Salatin* under the patronage of Ala-ud-din Hasan Bahman Shah,[8] the arch enemy of Muhammad Tughlaq.

Under the shadow of this frustration, Isami's frequent outbursts against the treacherous world[9] are quite understandable. So is his

[1]Isami, *op. cit.*, p. 132.
[2]*Ibid.*, pp. 160, 162, 163, 164.
[3]*Ibid.*, p. 165.
[4]*Ibid.*, pp. 430-441, 441-442 and 447-449 respectively.
[5]*Ibid.*, pp. 568-571. Significantly, Isami ignores Ala-ud-din Khalji's various administrative steps to crush the power of the nobles.
[6]*Ibid.*, pp. 491-492.
[7]*Ibid.*, pp. 12-13.
[8]*Ibid.*, pp. 22-23.
[9]*Ibid.*, pp. 12-13.

considerably frequent resort to the cup for solace,[1] as also his desire to leave his homeland for Mecca.[2] He tries to escape the world of his day sometimes by denouncing it, at others by expressing a desire for renouncing it. Nevertheless, Isami retains the urge for worldly fame[3] and regains hope when Bahman Shah extends his patronage to him.[4] Consequently he writes the *Futuh*.

Isami practically divides his work into two parts—the first covers the period from Mahmud of Ghazni to Ghiyas-ud-din Tughlaq; and the second deals exclusively with the reign of Muhammad Tughlaq. Each of these divisions is meant as if to contradistinguish the other.

In order to highlight the villainy of his contemporary Sultan, Muhammad Tughlaq, Isami tries to beautify the past. This he does not only by praising the material achievements of the earlier Sultans, but also by associating miracles with them or their reigns. Thus Mahmud of Ghazni is led out of the Rann on his march back from Somnath by a light projected from the Kaaba.[5] On the eve of the second battle of Tarain, Muiz-ud-din Ghori is given a key, in a dream, by an old man with which he could open the gates of Hindustan.[6] The abundance of foodgrains during Ala-ud-din Khalji's reign is the result of some magic seeds given to a doctor-peasant by the Devil of Ceylon in return for treating the Ceylonese ruler.[7]

In contrast to that, the reign of Muhammad Tughlaq is full of rebellions, destruction and madness which result in the "collapse of Islam"[8] (in India) which had been so sedulously nurtured by Sultan Mahmud[9] and Ala-ud-din Khalji.[10]

This contrast, indeed, appears to have been the sole objective for which he had written the *Futuh*. Isami therefore does not

[1]*Ibid.*, pp. 82, 98, 112, 115, 131, 152, 159, 292, 408, etc.
[2]*Ibid.*, p. 20.
[3]*Ibid.*, pp. 20-21.
[4]*Ibid.*, pp. 22-23.
[5]*Ibid.*, pp. 44-45.
[6]*Ibid.*, pp. 68-69.
[7]*Ibid.*, pp. 298-304.
[8]*Ibid.*, p. 569.
[9]*Ibid.*, p. 28.
[10]*Ibid.*, p. 569.

narrate events. He treats them as episodes designed to elicit commendation (for the earlier Sultans) or denunciation (for Muhammad Tughlaq). This, along with the poetic form, gives him room for inserting the supernatural element into his work.

Yet in Isami's treatment of history, the causation of historical events does not entirely belong to a force outside the domain of human volition. The court politics of the period between the death of Iltutmish and Balban's accession are planned and implemented by the nobles after due deliberation.[1] Ala-ud-din Khalji gets Jalal-ud-din assassinated[2] and Ulugh Khan poisoned[3] for the sake of kingship. The intrigues of Malik Naib, when Ala-ud-din Khalji was nearing his end and immediately after his death, have been given in detail by Isami.[4] These intrigues have been portrayed by him as the deliberate work of a cool calculating man. Indeed, Isami claims to have read even the thoughts of men who mattered in the affairs of state in their time.[5] His bitter hostility to Muhammad Tughlaq for all that happened during his reign is testimony enough that he attributes the cause of all those happenings to the Sultan's volition. And, finally, it is Sultan Mahmud of Ghazni and Ala-ud-din Khalji (in particular) who are responsible for the "manifestation of Islam" in India.[6]

The Viewpoint of the Historians

The works that have been reviewed in the preceding pages have the imperial court at Delhi as their point of focus. The authors of these works were themselves courtiers or aspired to such position. As historians, they on the one hand reflected, and on the other tried to influence, the ideology of the imperial ruling class or one section of it or the other.

Within this political framework, the relationship between the Sultan and his nobility became the main point of the historians'

[1] *Ibid.*, pp. 124-125, 127, 129-130, 132, 137, etc.
[2] *Ibid.*, pp, 231-235.
[3] *Ibid.*, pp. 272-273.
[4] *Ibid.*, pp. 329-341.
[5] *Ibid.*, pp. 179-180.
[6] *Ibid.*, pp. 28, 569 respectively.

interest. They generally advocated, explicitly or otherwise, the establishment and continuance of a particular type of state organization wherein a stable relationship would prevail between the Sultan and the nobility.

It would *prima facie* appear that a strong monarchy and a strong nobility were mutually antagonistic; and the historians therefore ought to have preferred the type of relationship that prevailed, say, during the reigns of the immediate successors of Iltutmish. That is, a nominal monarchy at the disposal of the nobility should have been their ideal. However, in fact there was little sympathy on the part of our historians for such an arrangement. They did not see any basic antagonism between the two institutions. They looked upon each of these as complementing the other. They did not fail to notice that a weak monarch might, in the short run, be an asset in the hands of his nobles, but in the long run, by the avenues this situation would create for dissensions within the nobility, as an institution it was detrimental to the healthy growth of the Sultanate and of the nobility with it. On the other hand, in a sound, expanding empire, under a virile ruler, there were great opportunities for the growth of wealth and power in the hands of the nobility through a healthy relationship between the Sultan and the nobility.

Therefore Barani's emphasis on the need for a strong monarch[1] and the simultaneous proposition regarding the establishment of an advisory council to aid and advise him[2] are an expression of his anxiety to establish such a relationship. The council should be a permanent institution; its members should be of high birth; they should be free of the fear of life and property; an established procedure should be followed in the meetings, etc.

None of the other historians has proposed, or explicitly seconded, Barani's idea. But their general attitude towards this problem suggests that what they had in mind was not very different from Barani's proposal. They did not, in general, support either a weak monarchy or royal despotism.[3]

[1]Barani, *FJ*, pp. 13-14, 71-72.

[2]*Ibid.*, pp. 9-10.

[3]Isami may be a queer exception, for the appears to support both (the post-Iltutmish rulers as well as Ala-ud-din Khalji, for example). Yet his hosti-

Now, if the historians were demanding a stable relationship between the Sultan and the nobility, they would appear to be placing a premium on the status quo in the character and composition of these institutions. That is, while the Sultan, according to Barani's proposal, should seek the aid and advice of his permanent advisory council, there should be no newer shades admitted into the nobility. Barani is the most outspoken on this point. The basic qualification, for him, of a noble is aristocratic birth, or heredity.[1]

The main threat to the exclusiveness of the nobility came naturally from the "Hindus," the rural aristocracy, the raos, rajas, khuts, muqaddams, etc. with whom the Sultans had been inevitably led to strike a compromise.[2] Another source of threat was the "base born" people with no hereditary claims, whether Hindu or Muslim. It is to these threats that our historians reacted violently, by showing great hostility to the Hindus in a language that would today be termed communal, and by fiercely denouncing the low born elements. The language used by them is no mere *form* of expression; it is a concrete, albeit crude, reaction to a concrete problem, that of preventing the entry of Hindus and the low born into the imperial nobility by appealing to religion and to aristocratic prejudice respectively.

The problem however was not basically that of religion, for even conversion to Islam failed to elicit the historians' charity. (Minhaj denounced Imad-ud-din Raihan in very abusive terms.[3] Barani carried this abuse to the point of obscenity with regard to Khusrau Khan.[4] Amir Khusrau pleaded for tolerance of the Hindus at the social level[5] but denounced them at the political level.[6] Isami accused Muhammad Tughlaq of falling from the path of the *Shara* when he found the Sultan indifferent to the claims of the

lity to Muhammad Tughlaq was precisely because, as he saw it, the Sultan had deliberately destroyed his established nobility, *supra*, p. 35.

[1]Barani, *FJ*, pp. 95, 97-98.

[2]*Ibid.*, pp. 46-48.

[3]Minhaj, *op. cit.*, pp. 827-828, 832, 835-836.

[4]Barani, *Tarikh*, pp. 409-410, 411, 412,

[5]*Nuh Sipihr*, pp. 161-172.

[6]*Khazain-ul-Futuh*, pp. 36, 50, 90, etc.; *Tughlaq Nama*, pp. 18-19, 21, 41-42, 48-49, etc.

Muslim nobility.[1]) The basic question was of maintaining the status quo in the structure of the ruling class and recruitment to it.

Barani, and presumably others, were conscious of the contradiction between the principles of Islam and the institution of kingship.[2] At the same time they recognized the necessity of kingship, presumably along with every other institution that had come into existence in spite of the Quran. They were not looking for an Islamic sanction for the institutions they approved but were trying to uphold and maintain them because those institutions were generally suited to the existing social structure. However, within this famework their thinking was conservative even in their own age. None of them dealing with Muhammad Tughlaq's reign, for example, could extend his support to the Sultan's policy of bringing into the official hierarchy the lowly, common men—a barber, a cook, a gardener, etc., as Barani contemptuously describes them[3]—and few of them were prepared to formalize any change outwards of the established norms. But the Sultanate kept on developing and changing in spite of the historians. It is for this reason perhaps that the general sequence of the histories of this period (except Minhaj's *Tabaqat*) is on the whole critical of the Sultans as well as full of denunciation of the world which did not remain stuck where the historians wanted it to. The development of the Sultanate did not follow the pattern our historians had outlined. A study of their mode of thinking is therefore useful not as a reflection of the policies and institutions of the Sultanate, but for noting and isolating the bias which colours their narrative.

[1]Isami, *op. cit.*, pp. 441, 491.

[2]Barani, *FJ*, pp. 39-40. Only Barani makes a definite statement to this effect. But it can be presumed that the others were not unaware of such a glaring contradiction.

[3]Barani, *Tarikh*, p. 505.

CHAPTER 2

I Shaikh Abul Fazl

Shaikh Abul Fazl's life can broadly be divided into two phases. The first comprises the period when Shaikh Mubarak and his sons, Faizi and Abul Fazl, were persecuted by the Ulema of the imperial court led by Abdullah Sultanpuri (the Makhdum-ul-Mulk) and Shaikh Abd-un-Nabi; and the second when Abul Fazl and his brother were on the ascendant in Akbar's court. The fact that after prolonged persecution of the family, which included destruction of their prayer house,[1] an attempt on their lives[2] (and the reluctance of some of the hitherto sympathetic friends to help them)[3], Abul Fazl was able to become one of the closest confidants of Akbar without the intercession of influential courtiers,[4] is testimony to the merit and perseverance of our author.

The story of this persecution has been told at length by Abul Fazl himself and has largely been corroborated by other authors. Shaikh Mubarak was, on all accounts, a very learned man.[5] Initially he was very orthodox in his personal conduct. Abdul Qadir

[1]Badauni, *Muntakhab-ut-Tawarikh*, Vol. II, p. 199. Abul Fazl hints at it vaguely, *Akbar Nama* (*AN*), Vol. II, Bib. Ind., pp. 303-304.

[2]Abul Fazl, *Ain-i-Akbari* (*Ain*), Vol. II, H. Blochmann (ed.), Bib. Ind., p. 269; Sujan Rai Bhandari, *Khulasat-ut-Tawarikh*, Zafar Hasan (ed.), Delhi, 1918, p. 434.

[3]*Ain*, Vol. II, pp. 268, 269-270, 271-272, 273.

[4]*AN*, Vol. II, pp. 303-304.

[5]*AN*, Vol. II, pp. 303, 387; Vol. III, pp. 642-643; *Ain*, Vol. II, p. 261; Badauni, *op. cit.*, Vol. II, p. 388, Vol. III, pp. 73-74; Nizam-ud-din Ahmad, *Tabaqat-i-Akbari*, Vol. II, Bib, Ind., p 472; Monserrate, *Commentary*, translated by J S. Hoyland, and annotated by S.N. Banerjee, Oxford, 1922, p. 55; Farid Bhakkari, *Zakhirat-ul-Khawanin*, Vol. I, Syed Moinul Haq, (ed.), Karachi, 1961, pp. 63-64; Shah Nawaz Khan, *Ma'asir-ul-Umra*, Vol. II, Bib. Ind., p. 584; Sujan Rai Bhandari, *op. cit.*, p. 434.

Badauni, who had known him intimately and had a certain amount of respect for him, tells us that if any one entered his assembly wearing a gold ring or silk or red gloves or socks (*moza*) or a red or yellow garment, the Shaikh would ask him to remove it immediately; and if he chanced to hear music even on the roadside, he would turn away.[1] In this Badauni is corroborated by Abul Fazl[2] and the author of the *Ma'asir-ul-Umra*.[3]

Later on, however, Shaikh Mubarak gave up orthodoxy and adopted a tolerant attitude towards other religions and sects. Badauni prefers this tolerance as a charge against him.[4] Father Aquaviva, who had led the first Jesuit mission to Akbar's court, considered him well disposed "to receive the light of our faith"[5]; and Father Monserrate, who had accompanied Aquaviva, says that the priests "were astonished at this old man's wisdom, authority and friendliness to Christianity."[6] Abul Fazl, indeed, never tires of harping on his father's eclecticism.[7] However, at what precise stage in his life and through what influences Shaikh Mubarak altered his mode of thinking we do not know.

It was Shaikh Mubarak's association with the Mahdawi movement sometime during the reign of Islam Shah that became the source of his and his sons' misfortune. Abul Fazl does not confirm this association fully; rather, he mentions it as an allegation which the Ulema had preferred against his father.[8] Badauni however specifically states that during the period of Afghan sovereignty, Mubarak had associated himself with Shaikh Alai.[9] The leaders of this movement in India, known for their erudition and oratory, challenged the Ulema at the court and refused to accept official patronage themselves.[10] It was when the movement threatened to

[1]Badauni, *op. cit.*, Vol. III, pp. 73-74.

[2]*Ain*, Vol. II, p. 275.

[3]*Op. cit.*, Vol. II, p. 584.

[4]Badauni, *op. cit.*, Vol. III, pp. 73-74, 74-75.

[5]E. Maclagan, *The Jesuits and the Great Mogul*, London, 1932, p. 38.

[6]Monserrate, *op. cit.*, pp. 55-56.

[7]*AN*, Vol. II, p. 388; Vol. III, p. 643; *Ain*, Vol. II, pp. 261-262.

[8]*Ain*, Vol. II, pp. 264-265.

[9]Badauni, *op. cit.*, Vol. I, p. 402; Vol III, p. 74. Also *Ma'asir-ul-Umra*, Vol. II, p. 585.

[10]S.A.A. Rizvi, *Muslim Revivalist Movements in Northern India*, Agra University, Agra, 1965, Chapters II and III.

envelop the imperial armies during the reign of Islam Shah[1] and disrupt the state, that the Ulema could, with the acquiescence of the ruler, launch their counter-offensive.

Apparently, the challenge of Shaikh Mubarak and his sons to the Ulema was essentially intellectual. But it was a challenge strong enough to elicit their retaliation. Abul Fazl gives instances when the confrontation took concrete form. During the reign of Islam Shah, when the Ulema accused Shaikh Alai of heresy and sedition and sought to destroy him, Shaikh Mubarak defended the Mahdawi leader. "From that day, girding up the loins of vengeance, they (the Ulema) accused him (Mubarak) of an attachment to that cause, and on so trifling a point as to whether the coming into being of the mahdi was based on a tradition of one man's authority (or otherwise), they, out of perversity, made such efforts that he was ruined."[2] On another occasion the Ulema tried to lay their hands on Miyan Abdullah Niyazi. The latter sought Shaikh Mubarak's opinion for his defence and the Shaikh obliged him ungrudgingly. At the court, the Miyan disclosed the source of his argument. "Those shameless, vainglorious men fell into the pit of bewilderment. When they discovered the source of their confusion they were inflamed with jealousy. Similar instances of assistance became known and they contributed to the turbulence of the ignorant."[3] On still another occasion the Makhdum-ul-Mulk presented himself at one of the lecture-assemblies of Shaikh Mubarak where he began his "crafty discourse."[4] Abul Fazl was so inflamed with the Makhdum's remarks that he confronted him publicly. The confrontation reached a stage where the Makhdum was "ashamed and the spectators were amazed. From that day he determined to

[1] *Ibid.*, pp. 127-128.

[2] *Ain*, Vol. II, p. 265. For the term "ahad" (one man's authority), see *Encyclopaedia of Ilsam*, Vol. II, M. Houtsma *et al.* (eds.), Leyden, 1927, p. 859 under "Khabar."

[3] *Ain*, Vol. II, p. 265, Abul Fazl refers to Miyan Niyazi merely as "one of the Syeds of Iraq" and subsequently as "Mir." J.N. Sarkar's guess is that the Syed in question was Miyan Abdullah Niyazi, *Ain* (*tr.*), Vol. III, p. 492, fn. It must be Abdullah Niyazi, for his persecution at the hands of the Ulema is attested to by various contemporary sources. See S.A.A. Rizvi, *Muslim Revivalist Movements*, etc., pp. 122-126.

[4] *Ibid.*, p. 266. The reference to the Makhdum-ul-Mulk is indirect but clear.

avenge his conviction of being an ignoramus."

As Shaikh Mubarak held his assemblies[1] where he lectured on problems of philosophy and theology,[2] the Ulema unrelentingly pursued designs for his (and his sons') physical annihilation. For this they had even been able to secure Akbar's sanction.[3]

In desperation, Shaikh Mubarak and his sons sought the intercession of Shaikh Salim Chishti with Akbar.[4] Shaikh Salim either did not wish to court the wrath of the Ulema by interceding on behalf of their adversaries or was not particularly agitated over the security of Mubarak. He merely advised him to flee to Gujarat and sent him some money to meet the expense of travel. It was then that Mubarak approached Mirza Koka, Akbar's foster-brother, for the favour of intercession on his behalf. The Mirza praised the learning and resignation of the Shaikh to Akbar and was able to secure a guarantee of safety for him.[5]

It was still, however, a long way from the lonely flights for personal safety to a position of influence at the imperial court. The Ulema had not yet abandoned their plans; and not even the Emperor could openly challenge them.[6] In fact, it was when Akbar had masterminded his scheme of gradual but sure erosion of the hold of the Ulema on the court, and ultimately imposing on them complete submission to his authority, that he needed the services of men like Shaikh Mubarak and Abul Fazl and, paradoxically, also of men like Badauni.[7] It was only then that Akbar could pro-

[1]Shaikh Mubarak set himself up as a teacher at Agra some time during the reign of Islam Shah, *Ain*, Vol. II, p. 263. For a long time he would admit only a select few into his assembly. From 1569-70, however, the Shaikh became a public teacher, *ibid.*, p. 266.

[2]*Ibid.*, p. 263; Muatamad Khan, *Iqbal Nama-i-Jahangiri*, Munshi Nawal Kishore Press, 1870, Vol. II, p. 277; Sujan Rai Bhandari, *op. cit.*, p. 434; Farid Bhakkari, *op. cit.*, p. 64.

[3]*Ain*, Vol. II, p. 269; Badauni, *op. cit.*, Vol. II, pp. 198-199.

[4]Badauni, *op. cit.*, Vol. II, p. 199.

[5]*Ibid.* Abul Fazl refers to "one of the chief nobles and greybeards of the imperial court" who pleaded their case with Akbar rather brusquely, *Ain*, Vol. II, p. 272. Later on he says, "well-wishers of Truth came to our rescue and men of awakened fortune girt themselves in our aid," p. 274.

[6]*AN*, Vol. III, pp. 203-234; Badauni, *op. cit.*, Vol. III, pp. 80-83; Farid Bhakkari, *op cit.*, p. 69.

[7]Akbar made use of both Abul Fazl and Badauni in the discussions at the

vide them with complete security and bestow upon them enormous favour.

Meanwhile, Faizi was emerging as a very talented poet. Word of his merit had reached the Emperor and he was summoned to the court.[1] The Ulema well understood the significance of his arrival at the court; therefore they tried to frighten him into flight. The men sent to fetch him, presumably with some ceremony, instead attempted to raze his house at the instigation of "a group of the wicked, ignoble ones, who were the scorched centres of the sands of envy."[2]

Faizi's introduction to the court however did not put an immediate end to the difficulties of Shaikh Mubarak and his family. It was not until a few more years had elapsed that peace descended on them.

*

Shaikh Mubarak's second son, Abul Fazl, was born on 14 January 1551 (6th of Muharram, 958 H.).[3] He expresses regret at having been born after Akbar, but consoles himself with the fact of having lived during his reign.[4]

During his early childhood, Abul Fazl showed signs of precocity. He had the advantage of the constant company of his father who was also his teacher. Abul Fazl claims that when just a child of a little over one year, he could speak fluently[5] and that by the time he was five he had acquired an unusual stock of information and could both read and write.[6]

Abul Fazl's early education at the hands of Shaikh Mubarak must have been, on the whole, traditional, for such was Mubarak's own learning.[7] Within the traditional framework, however, our author was able to establish acquaintance with diverse branches

---

Ibadat Khana to expose the hollowness of the Ulema, *infra*, pp. 47-49 and 96.

[1]*AN*, Vol. II, pp. 303-304. Faizi was summoned to the court in the 12th regnal year, 1567.

[2]*Ibid.*, p. 304; Badauni Vol. II *op. cit.*, 199.

[3]*Ain*, Vol. II, p. 276.

[4]*AN*, Vol. I, pp. 47-48.

[5]*Ain*, Vol. II, p. 276.

[6]*Ibid.*, pp. 276-277.

[7]*AN*, Vol. II, p. 387

of knowledge.[1] Yet he failed to put his heart into this kind of learning. Although he could defeat Makhdum-ul-Mulk in argument,[2] and on his own restore the motheaten half of every page of the gloss of Isfahani at an early age,[3] he "gained no deep impression from the school of learning."[4] Even later on, as he grew mature and wrote the *Akbar Nama*, he showed no particular predilection for any branch of traditional knowledge.

However, even without this predilection, Abul Fazl's mastery over the traditional branches of learning produced in him an arrogance of which he was not relieved till the end of his life. He confesses to this arrogance at many places.[5] At any rate, he seldom displays any disarming humility in any of his works except in relation to the Emperor (Akbar), Shaikh Mubarak and Faizi. On a number of occasions he contemplated withdrawal into solitary meditation.[6] But he kept postponing it until his engagements at the court made it impossible for him to do so.

The first 20 years of Abul Fazl's life, which he fervently devoted to studies, sometimes forsaking even his food for days together,[7] was also the period when he, along with his father and brother, lived constantly under the shadow of the Ulema's terror. It stands to their credit that none of them even *suggested* making a compromise with their ruthless adversaries.

Along with his studies, Abul Fazl took to the profession of teaching some time after he was fifteen.[8] All this while his restiveness at the limitations of the orthodox sciences grew in magnitude and he contemplated escapades, sometimes into discourses with the lamas of Tibet, at others with the padres of Portugal.[9]

[1] *Ain*, Vol. II, p. 277.
[2] *Ibid.*, p. 265.
[3] *Ibid.*, pp. 277-278.
[4] *Ibid.*, p. 277.
[5] *AN*, Vol. III, pp. 83, 84, 113-115, etc.
[6] *Ibid.*, Vol. II, pp. 387-388; Vol. III, pp. 84, 113-114; *Ain*, Vol. II, p. 278.
[7] *Ain*, Vol, II, p. 277.
[8] *AN*, Vol. III, p. 84.
[9] *Ibid.*, p. 84. S.A.A. Rizvi rightly interprets this to mean that "Abul Fazl was no longer satisfied with the religious and spiritual guidance which he could get from a man like Shaikh Mubarak," Introduction to "Munajat-i-Abul-Fazl," *Medieval India Quarterly*, Aligarh, Vol. I, Part III, 1950, p. 118.

Meanwhile, Akbar was founding his Ibadat Khana and was opening a series of discussions with the Ulema. The Emperor had planned to confront the Ulema and later on their detractors as well as other religionists. For this would divide the Ulema and weaken them into submission to imperial authority. In this, in destroying the Ulema, Akbar was able to unite men as opposed to each other as Abul Fazl and Badauni. Abul Fazl had mastered conventional knowledge without fully subscribing to its tenets. He claims always to have been critical of the traditionalists and formalists.[1] Therefore, when mention of him was made at one of Akbar's religious assemblies, he was summoned to the court early in the 19th regnal year.[2]

Abul Fazl arrived at the court and presented to the Emperor a commentary on the *Verse of the Throne*,[3] which, Badauni maliciously alleges, had been written by his father.[4] Akbar may have received the present graciously as our author claims, but in his urgency to march to the eastern part of India he could not pay any special attention to him. Abul Fazl was not able to enter the Emperor's service then, and it is only on his second introduction to Akbar, later in the year, that he was taken into service.[5]

However, during the expedition to the east and on his way back, at Ajmer, Akbar remembered Abul Fazl[6] the report of which was conveyed to him by Faizi. Abul Fazl wrote out the draft of a commentary on the beginning of the *Chapter of Victory* to present it to the learned assembly at the Ibadat Khana.[7] On Akbar's return to Agra, Abul Fazl made his obeisance to him first at the congregational mosque and later at the court. Akbar received him with kindness. "Once," says the author, "in that assemblage of realm and religion (the Ibadat Khana) where hundreds of thousands of sects and schools had gathered together he (Akbar) accosted this perplexed one of life's assembly (Abul Fazl) and described my condition beyond what I was myself conscious of to the special

[1]*AN*, Vol. III, p. 84; *Ain*, Vol. II, p. 277.
[2]*AN*, Vol. III, pp. 84-85.
[3]*Ibid*, p. 85.
[4]Badauni, *op. cit.*, Vol. II, p. 198.
[5]*AN*, Vol. III, pp. 113-114.
[6]*Ibid.*, p. 114.
[7]*Ibid.*

guests at the sacred society."[1]

At the Ibadat Khana Abul Fazl seems to have led very severe attacks on the Ulema. He is himself reticent in giving details of these discussions and particularly of his role in them. Having contributed his share to the destruction of his enemies he affects innocence on this score.[2] From other contemporary as well as later testimony, however, it is known that he had led sharp attacks on them.[3] For this he had the acquiescence of Akbar and his as well as his father's learning to back him.[4] His attacks on them became so sharp and devastating that the Ulema finally sought to conciliate him.[5] He was not however prepared to retrace his steps, having gone so far. Nor was it really in his hands to do so.

These discussions ultimately resulted in the banishment of the chief leaders of the Ulema, particularly Shaikh Abd-un-Nabi and the Makhdum-ul-Mulk, who were despatched to Mecca against their will. One could legitimately suspect Abul Fazl's hand in their exile.[6]

Thus when the chief Ulema and the Mashaikh had attested the Mahzar, the final draft of which had been prepared by Shaikh Mubarak,[7] and when the leaders of the Ulema had been exiled, to which Abul Fazl had, perhaps, made no small contribution, and when Akbar had read the khutba, in the composition of which Faizi had a significant hand,[8] the learned father and his sons had done their first job. After this Shaikh Mubarak probably withdrew himself from any association with the court for there is no more reference to him in this context in any one of our sources.[9] Faizi

[1]*Ibid.*, p. 115. Badauni interprets the welcome accorded to Abul Fazl in the Ibadat Khana to the effect that Akbar intended to use him against (literally box the ears of) the Ulema, *op. cit.*, Vol. II, p. 198.

[2]*AN*, Vol. III, pp. 386-387.

[3]Badauni, *op. cit.*, Vol. II, pp. 199, 203, 263; Monserrate, *op. cit.*, pp. 51, 56-57; Farid Bhakkari, *op. cit.*, pp. 69-70, 71. Abul Fazl also refers to these discussions without specifying the details, *AN*, Vol. II, pp. 388-390.

[4]Badauni, *op. cit*, Vol. II, pp. 199, 263.

[5]*Ibid.*, p. 263. Abul Fazl also makes an indirect reference to this, *AN*, Vol. II, p. 390.

[6]Badauni, *op. cit.*, Vol. II, p. 199; Farid Bhakkari, *op. cit.*, p. 71.

[7]Badauni, *op. cit.*, Vol. II, p. 272.

[8]*Ibid.*, p. 268.

[9]Shaikh Farid Bhakkari, however, states that towards the end of his life

and Abul Fazl, were however, destined to attain very high position in the imperial service.

After the fall of the Ulema the rise of Faizi and Abul Fazl was gradual but steady. Faizi accompanied Prince Daniyal to Ajmer on his visit there as Akbar's proxy in the 25th regnal year.[1]

The following year he was made the Sadr of Agra.[2] In the 28th year he was nominated to assist Prince Salim in the discharge of his functions as the superintendent of the royal marriage and birthday feasts.[3] Mirza Khan and Fathullah were the others appointed along with Faizi. In the 30th year Faizi, his brother Abul Barkat and a few others were sent to assist Mirza Aziz Koka in military operations at Bajaur.[4] Three hundred of Abul Fazl's horses were also despatched with them. In the 33rd year Faizi reached the summit of his glory when he was awarded the title of Malik-us-Shaura (the Poet-Laureate) by Akbar.[5]

Abul Fazl had been initially appointed to the mansab of 20.[6] Apart from his role in the discussions at the Ibadat Khana the services he rendered to Akbar were more or less of a personal nature rather than political or military. We find him, for example, collecting cow's milk for the children who had accompanied Akbar on one of his visits to Ajmer.[7] On another occasion, on the eve of the Emperor's march across the Indus to Kabul in the 26th

---

Shaikh Mubarak became a mansabdar, *op. cit.*, Vol. I, p. 64. The mansab, however, has not been specified. The very fact that Farid Bhakkari includes an account of Mubarak in his book is significant, for the book, as its title signifies deals only with the nobles of the Mughal empire. Yet the absence of any contemporary testimony to this effect and the not very reliable character of the *Zakhirat-ul-Khawanin* suggest that Shaikh Mubarak may really have gracefully withdrawn himself from the court in any case since his sons were still there.

[1] *AN*, Vol. III, pp. 316-317.

[2] *Ibid.*, p. 372.

[3] *Ibid.*, p. 404.

[4] *Ibid.*, pp. 476-477.

[5] *Ibid.*, p. 535.

[6] Badauni, *op. cit.*, Vol. II, p. 206. Abul Fazl does not mention his initial mansab; nor, in fact, does anyone else except Badauni. Badauni's evidence may still be correct, for both he and Abul Fazl joined service almost simultaneously and were given the mansab of 20 each, p. 206, to which, as beginners, they were entitled, p. 190.

[7] *AN*, Vol. III, p. 251.

regnal year, Abul Fazl was ordered to find out the state of opinion among the amirs regarding the expedition.[1]

The year after that Akbar appointed a number of overseers, one for superintendence of trade in each article. Our author was put in charge of the wool trade.[2]

In the 30th regnal year Abul Fazl was raised to the mansab of 1,000.[3] This mansab could not have been granted to him on account of any distinguished military service, for he had not performed any till then. In fact, at that time Akbar seems to have been sceptical of the author's merit as a soldier. Abul Fazl tells us that as the expedition to Swat, under the leadership of Zain Khan Koka (in the 30th regnal year), was not making any noticeable headway, the Emperor considered reinforcement. Abul Fazl promptly offered his services. One morning Akbar accepted the offer and promised to send "some tried soldiers" whose guidance the author was to follow during military operations.[4] Apparently not quite satisfied with this arrangement, Akbar changed his mind by the same evening. He suggested the casting of lots for a choice between the author and Raja Birbal. The lots favoured Birbal.[5]

In the 31st year Abul Fazl was made co-governor of Delhi, sharing the responsibility with Shah Quli Mahram.[6] Along with this, our author also kept discharging less formal duties. He was, for example, an investigator along with the Khan-i-Khanan, Azd-ud-daulah and Hakim Abul Fath appointed to enquire into the cause of a rift between Raja Todar Mal and Shahbaz Khan, then governor of Bengal.[7] In the 34th regnal year, when Akbar set out on his march to Kashmir, Abul Fazl accompanied him.[8] At Bhimbar, Akbar expressed a desire to visit the summit of the Kajiwar Pass and he ordered that no one should accompany or follow him except a few specified persons. Among the exceptions

[1] *Ibid.*, p. 355.

[2] *Ibid.*, p. 396.

[3] *Ibid.*, p. 457.

[4] *Ibid.*, p. 477.

[5] *Ibid.*, pp. 477-478. It must have been so managed, otherwise there was no point in casting lots.

[6] *Ibid.*, p. 511.

[7] *Ibid.*, p. 529.

[8] *Ibid.*, p. 538.

was our author; and he was in august company—that of the Khan-i-Khanan, Zain Khan Koka, Azd-ud-daulah, Hakim Abul Fath, Jagan Nath and Mir Sharif Amli among others.

Meanwhile, on 15 January 1590 (in the 34th regnal year) Abul Fazl's mother passed away at Lahore.[1] No details of this event are mentioned, but the author was understandably grieved.[2] However, he felt honoured at the Emperor's saying some words of consolation to him. Three years later, on 5 August 1593 (the 38th regnal year) Shaikh Mubarak died.[3] Abul Fazl had his parents buried at Agra in their old house.[4] In the 40th regnal year Faizi also died.[5]

Before the death of his father and brother, however, our author had his son, Abdur Rahman, married at the Emperor's behest to the daughter of Saadat Yar Koka.[6] The young couple later had a son to whom the Emperor gave the name Bishotan.[7]

Abul Fazl's rise to the mansab of 2,000 in the 37th regnal year[8] was on the one hand an evidence of the increased confidence Akbar placed in him, and on the other, for that very reason, a signal to many others to take notice of him. Our author states that he "was raised to this high dignity without having performed any (distinguished) service." This he says perhaps out of sheer modesty in relation to Akbar's favour. Yet he indeed had not performed any distinguished service till then except the more or less personal ones. Therefore, when Akbar granted him the mansab of 2,000, when there was no particular occasion for it, it signified only the Emperor's personal pleasure. However, as the Emperor's confidence in Abul Fazl increased, so did jealousy of him in the highest

[1] *Ibid.*, pp. 573-574.

[2] "Hundreds of thousands of eyes were needed for my heart's anguish that in solitude I might weep with each one of them," *ibid.*, p. 573.

[3] *Ibid.*, p. 642. Abul Fazl carries the story of his grief up to p. 644. Shaikh Mubarak was 88 or 89 years of age at the time of his death.

[4] *Ibid.*, pp. 654-655.

[5] *Ibid.*, pp. 672-673. Abul Fazl's grief was boundless, "I, who am of sewn lips, wept like a child and a tempest of lamentation arose," *ibid.*, p. 673.

[6] *Ibid.*, p. 579. When and to whom Abul Fazl himself was married we do not know.

[7] *Ibid.*, p. 596.

[8] *Ibid.*, p. 610.

quarters of the court. Ultimately, it was his unreserved loyalty to Akbar and Akbar's abounding confidence and generosity towards Abul Fazl that cost him his life.

It is not that Akbar's relations with Abul Fazl remained forever unblemished. There was at least one brief period when relations between them were strained. Abul Fazl tries to explain this away by making vague statements.[1] He says that he had not been attending upon Prince Salim because Akbar had kept him otherwise employed. This had resulted in Salim's annoyance with him which was fanned by his old enemies. This in turn hurt Abul Fazl most and he contemplated putting an end to his life, as he had contemplated on many previous occasions.[2] He tried to explain matters to the Emperor by saying that he had been misunderstood on account of the envious instigation of his enemies. Soon afterwards, the Emperor relaxed and once again Abul Fazl was rehabilitated in his favour.

Abul Fazl's account of the estrangement between him and Akbar has been considerably oversimplified by him. Fortunately, however, some of our other sources also refer to it in some detail. The *Iqbal Nama-i-Jahangiri* tells us that Akbar had been displeased with Shaikh Mubarak for his writing a commentary on the Quran in which there was no reference to him, and with Abul Fazl for sending its copies abroad without his permission after Shaikh Mubarak's death.[3] Badauni also refers to this commentary and states that in the Preface to it Shaikh Mubarak had claimed to be the Reformer of the age.[4] Further on, the *Iqbal Nama* says that Abul Fazl had committed many an act of presumption in regard to Prince Salim and was therefore excluded from attendance at the court for some days. Later on, however, Akbar rehabilitated him. This story is repeated by Sujan Rai Bhandari with the difference that in his opinion these facts were used by Abul Fazl's enemies to disillusion the Emperor with him.[5]

The version of the *Zakhirat-ul-Khawanin* (followed by the

[1]*Ibid.*, pp. 740-741.

[2]*Ibid.*, Vol. II, pp. 385-386; Vol. III, pp. 115-116, 643, 757; *Ain*, Vol. II, p. 251.

[3]*Iqbal Nama-i-Jahangiri*, Vol. II, pp. 457-458.

[4]Badauni, *op. cit.*, Vol, III, p. 74.

[5]Bhandari, *op. cit.*, 435.

Ma'asir-ul-Umra) is different from that of the *Iqbal Nama.* It tells us that Abul Fazl's rise to the mansab of 2,000 and Akbar's unreserved confidence in his loyalty and wisdom made even the Prince, not to mention the amirs, jealous of him. "He kept constant company with Akbar, like the setting to a pearl, and nothing was done without his approval. (Therefore, out of jealously,) some of the discontented ones persuaded Akbar to send him to the Deccan." Moreover, Prince Salim once went to the house of Abul Fazl and saw 40 scribes copying the Quran and a commentary on it. The Prince brought them all, along with the leaves of the books, before the Emperor and thus induced him to doubt the *bona fides* of Abul Fazl. The Emperor thought that Abul Fazl, while inciting him to traverse diverse paths in the field of religion, himself acted differently in the privacy of his house. From then on there was a strain in their intimacy and companionship.[1]

However, Abul Fazl's laments over the machinations of his enemies at the court appear genuine. His "enemies" might not have been the source of the Emperor's displeasure with him as he claims; but once they had spotted a breach between the two, they did everything to widen it. That Abul Fazl's separation from Akbar and his despatch to the Deccan were manoeuvred by the amirs is proved by much of the available evidence. Abul Fazl says this in so many words[2] and in this he is supported by the *Ma'asir-ul-Umra*[3] and the *Khulasat-ut-Tawarikh.*[4]

Abul Fazl never mentions his "enemies" by name, although he keeps wailing over their intrigues against him. The fact that he is unwilling or unable to name them, and the fact that they were influential enough to effect his separation from Akbar, suggest that our author had managed to contract hostility in the highest quarters of the court. His "enemies" most probably included Abd-ur-Rahim Khan-i-Khanan[5] and certainly Prince Salim himself, whose

[1]*Zakhirat-ul-Khawanin*, p. 72; *Ma'asir-ul-Umra*, Vol. II, p. 610. The former attributes this story to hearsay.

[2]*AN*, Vol. III, pp. 748-749.

[3]Vol. II, p. 610.

[4]P. 435. This separation took place in the 43rd-44th regnal years; by then Badauni and Nizam-ud-din had died. Hence there is no reference to it in their works.

[5]Abul Fazl's covert but strongly worded allusions to the Khan-i-Khanan

enmity proved, in the end, fatal to the author.

However, the despatch of Abul Fazl to the Deccan in the 43rd-44th regnal years, with the apparent objective of fetching Prince Murad to the court, proved a piece of good fortune for him. In the Deccan he performed excellent service and it is this, rather than his explanations to the Emperor, that must have brought him back into royal favour.

There are numerous positive indications in the *Akbar Nama* itself to the effect that in the later years of Akbar's reign his hold on the structure he had built had begun to loosen.

In the 43rd-44th years of Akbar's reign, the situation in the empire was not exactly promising. Weaknesses in the mansabdari system were coming to the surface and mansabdars were managing to maintain fewer soldiers than was required of them.[1] In the Deccan, Abul Fazl repeatedly speaks of confusion and dissensions within the imperialist camp.[2] The Khan-i-Khanan was able to exert his pressure in securing the nomination of one or another prince to the Deccan almost at his will.[3] Finally, the princes among themselves felt strong enough to defy the Emperor to a small or large extent.[4]

Against this background Abul Fazl served Akbar in the Deccan with unconditional loyalty and considerable military and diplomatic skill and this in the face of hesitation, even resistance to him, in his own camp.[5] He profusely used gold to break away part of the defending garrisons,[6] employed his troops to overcome their

suggest that there were no particularly cordial relations, binding one to the other. He accuses the Khan-i-Khanan of wickedness, selfishness and presumption, *AN*, Vol. III, p. 752. The allusion is indirect.

[1]*AN*, Vol. III, pp. 671-672; also Blochmann's note on the mansabdars, *Ain*, Vol. I (*tr.*), pp. 251-258.

[2]*AN*, Vol. III, pp. 754-755, 760-761, 765, 772-773, etc.

[3]*Ibid.*, pp. 698-699.

[4]"At this time (the 43rd regnal year) foolish and envious talkers represented that Prince Sultan Murad had no intention of coming to the court and they attributed unbecoming speeches to this or that person. They also pointed out improper behaviour on the part of Prince Daniyal who had already hastened off from Allahabad (on being called to the court)," *AN*, Vol. III, p. 745. Salim actually rebelled soon afterwards.

[5]*Ibid.*, pp. 760-761.

[6]*Ibid.*, pp. 777-778.

resistance,[1] and used persuasion to convince them of the futility of it all.[2] The fact that Abul Fazl was about to take the fort of Ahmadnagar when he was stopped by Prince Daniyal from doing so[3] is testimony enough to his capability. He pressed his son, Abd-ur-Rahman, into service at Daultabad.[4]

Meanwhile, in the 45th regnal year, Akbar himself marched to the Deccan.[5] His personal appearance in the Deccan was probably the result of his not being completely satisfied with the conduct of the war there in spite of Abul Fazl's excellent service. As he reached Malwa he recalled Abul Fazl to his presence, presumably for consultations. Abul Fazl was warmly received by the Emperor who on seeing him repeated this verse:

Serene be the night and pleasant the moonshine
That I may talk with thee on every subject.[6]

Along with this expression of trust in Abul Fazl's loyalty and capability Akbar raised his mansab to 5,000.[7] This was possibly not what our author's enemies had expected. And, therefore, when Abul Fazl remarked that "many sate down in the blackness of envy," he could not perhaps be far wrong.

[1] *Ibid.*, pp. 760-761, 764-765, 778.

[2] *Ibid.*, pp. 764-765.

[3] *Ibid.*, p. 766. Akbar had sent Daniyal to the Deccan after the death of Murad. Daniyal wanted to take the fort himself in order to claim the attendant glory.

[4] *Ibid.*, p. 758. It is nowhere mentioned as to when and in what capacity was Abul Fazl's son enrolled in Akbar's service. Nor is his rank at any time during Akbar's reign known. However, during Jahangir's reign Abd-ur-Rahman was granted the mansab of 2,000/1,500 and later on promoted to 2,000/2,500. *Tuzuk-i-Jahangiri* (*tr.*), Rogers & Beveridge, Vol. I, London, 1909, pp. 17 and 120-121 respectively. He was given the title of Afzal Khan, *ibid.*, p. 105 and made governor of Bihar, p. 143.

[5] *AN*, Vol. III, pp. 762-763.

[6] *Ibid.*, pp. 768-769.

[7] The continuator of the *Akbar Nama*, beyond the 46th regnal year of Akbar, states that in the 47th year Abul Fazl was made a mansabdar of 5,000, Supplement to *AN*, Vol. III, p. 805. Sujan Rai Bhandari and Bakhtawar Khan corroborate him; see *Khulasat-ut-Tawarikh*, pp. 427, 436; and *Mirat-ul-Alam*, Maulana Azad Library, Aligarh Muslim University, MS no. Farsi Tarikh 51, f. 113a.

Courtesies and consultations over, Akbar kept Abul Fazl employed in military operations. He was put in charge of guarding Khandesh.[1] His brother, Shaikh Abul Barkat, and his son, Shaikh Abd-ur-Rahman, were also commanded to the same duty. Soon afterwards we find Abul Fazl supervising the assault on, and capture of, Maligarh, on the outskirts of the fort of Asir, even as the imperial camp itself was divided regarding the advisability of the assault.[2]

The fall of Maligarh was a prelude to the taking of Asir. The attack on the latter was also led by Abul Fazl,[3] and when the fort fell, its keys were received by his son Shaikh Abd-ur-Rahman.[4] The surrender of the fort had in fact been negotiated through Abul Fazl.

As Asir was being reduced, there was some commotion in Ahmadnagar. Although its ruler had been defeated, strong local resistance had prevented the Mughals from occupying it. The Khan-i-Khanan was therefore ordered to proceed to Ahmadnagar and Abul Fazl to Nasik.[5] On the eve of his departure Abul Fazl was granted a robe of honour, a special horse, a banner and a drum.

Meanwhile, Akbar had returned to Agra.[6] Salim had established himself at Allahabad and was bent on defying Akbar's authority[7]; and this was apparently the primary reason of Akbar's return to the capital. On his return, Akbar recalled Abul Fazl to the court and ordered him to proceed unattended, handing over his soldiers and his charge to his son.[8]

Abul Fazl's journey to the court coincided with Salim's efforts at a reconciliation with Akbar.[9] Relations between Salim and Abul Fazl had never been very cordial; and the Prince must have been aware of the trust which Akbar placed in our author. Therefore Abul Fazl's return to the court could result in the frustration

[1] *AN*, Vol. III, p. 769.
[2] *Ibid.*, pp. 777-778.
[3] *Ibid.*, p. 780.
[4] *Ibid.*
[5] *Ibid.*, pp. 783-784.
[6] *Ibid.*, p. 789.
[7] *Ibid.*, p. 773; *Supplement to AN*, pp. 805-806.
[8] *Supplement to AN*, p. 810.
[9] *Ibid.*, p. 811; *Tuzuk-i-Jahangiri* (*tr.*), Vol. I, pp. 24-25.

of all Salim's hopes of regaining his father's favour. He therefore made the decision to do away with his adversary.

Abul Fazl was to pass through the territory close to the area controlled by Raja Bir Singh Bundela who was not impervious to Salim's overtures. The Raja was engaged to arrange the elimination of the lonely traveller.[1] At Ujjain, Abul Fazl was informed of the probability of an attempt on his life and was advised to change his route. Later on again, between Sarai Bir and Antri, one of his confidants, Gadai Khan Afghan, advised him to hasten to Antri where he would find supporters and to let him (Gadai Khan) engage the Raja's men. Abul Fazl, with somewhat misplaced bravery,[2] insisted on going ahead without bothering about precautions. Gadai Khan was still trying to persuade Abul Fazl when Bir Singh arrived and ambushed Abul Fazl and his men. They fought bravely and fell in the field. Abul Fazl's head was severed from the body[3] and sent to Salim as a souvenir. For this service Raja Bir Singh received the mansab of 3,000 when Salim became Emperor.[4]

*

[1]*Supplement to AN*, p. 811; *Tuzuk-i-Jahangiri* (*tr.*), Vol. I, pp. 24-25. The account of Abul Fazl's assassination in the *Supplement to the AN* is substantially based on that given by Muatamad Khan in the *Iqbal Nama-i-Jahangiri*, Vol. II, pp. 486-488. The contemporary account of the incident is, however, given in detail by Asad Beg in the *Risala-i-Tarikh-i-Asad Beg Qazvini*, Br. Mus. Or. 1996, Rotograph, Research Library, Deptt. of History, Aligarh Muslim University. Asad Beg had accompanied Abul Fazl on his way to Agra and had separated from him just before the assassination, pp. 2-3, 7 (the MS is marked in pp and not in ff). He claims to have been one of those who had seriously warned Abul Fazl of his impending doom, p. 3.

[2]Asad Beg quotes a couplet as his comment on Abul Fazl's stubbornness:

As Death flutters its wings downwards from the Heavens
It makes even the sagacious ones blind and deaf.

Op. cit., p. 4. Sujan Rai Bhandari also quotes this couplet in a modified form and adds another:

Do not conflict with soldiers greater in number
For one cannot strike a lance with one's fist.

Op. cit., p. 433.

[3]He died on 24 August 1602 (the 7th Rabi I, 1011 H), Asad Beg, *op. cit.*, p. 1. Almost all the authors give different dates for his death. Asad Beg, being a nearwitness to the event, can be accepted as the correct one.

[4]Jahangir, *op. cit.*, Vol. I (*tr.*), p. 24.

Abul Fazl had the distinction of being forever surrounded by controversy. His rise from practically being an upstart to the holder of the mansab of 5,000, and his becoming the keeper of Akbar's unreserved confidence understandably resulted in the animation of others' jealousy. His loyalty to Akbar was taken for hypocrisy.[1] He, with others, was charged with deflecting Akbar from the sane path of orthodoxy.[2] Conspiracies were hatched against him at the highest level. And he must have had the satisfaction of holding a place of which the future Emperor of Hindustan was envious.

Yet no one, except Badauni, challenges his learning.[3] It was diverse as well as deep according to the standards of his time. It extended from a study of orthodox Islamic literature to astronomy, to the system of revenue administration in Akbar's empire. Although in the writing of history he did not evolve any new concepts, his *Akbar Nama* is invaluable as a source book of extensive and fairly reliable information. Indeed, for a long time after Abul Fazl was gone, the *Akbar Nama*, which he had intended to leave behind as his memorial,[4] remained a model for subsequent historians.[5]

A charming trait of Abul Fazl was his enormous appetite. If the information given by the *Ma'asir-ul-Umra* is correct, his daily intake of food was 22 sers exclusive of water and broth.[6] His son, Shaikh Abd-ur-Rahman, served him as table attendant. The

[1]*Ibid.*, Badauni, *op. cit.*, Vol. II, pp. 199, 263 where he attributes a remark to Abul Fazl to the effect that Akbar's munificence was not ever lasting and therefore he was making the most of it as long as hecould.

[2]*Badauni, op. cit.*, Vol. II, p. 211; *Ma'asir-ul-Umra*, Vol. II, pp. 619-620; *Zakhirat-ul-Khawanin*, p. 72.

[3]Nizam-ud-din Ahmed, *op. cit.*, Vol. II, p. 1; Monserrate, *op. cit.*, p. 49; Jahangir, *op. cit.*, Vol. I (*tr.*), p. 24; Muatamad Khan, *op. cit.*, Vol. II, p. 277; Munshi Kazim, *Alamgir Nama*, Bib. Ind., p. 387; *Ma'asir-ul-Umra*, Vol. II, pp. 608-609, 620; Farid Bhakkari, *op. cit.*, p. 67; Sujan Rai Bhandari, *op. cit.*, pp. 337, 434, 436; Malik Zada Munshi, *Nigar Nama-i-Munshi*, Munshi Nawal Kishore Press, Lucknow, 1882, p. 4. For Badauni's view, see *op. cit.*, Vol, II, pp. 198-199, 204.

[4]*AN*, Vol. III, p. 3; *Ain*, Vol. II, p. 247.

[5]The *Badshah Nama* of Hamid Lahori, and of Waris and the *Alamgir Nama* of Munshi Kazim are all modelled after the *Akbar Nama*.

[6]Vol. II, p. 621. Also Farid Bhakkari, *op. cit.*, pp. 72-73.

superintendent of the kitchen stood by as Abul Fazl sat dining. If he helped himself twice from a dish it was cooked the next day also. If any dish were contrary to his liking he would give it to his son for tasting. The son, in turn, would admonish the cook, but Abul Fazl never said anything himself.

A complete list of Abul Fazl's brothers has been appended by the author himself to the *Ain-i-Akbari*[1] as well as the *Insha-i-Abul Fazl*.[2] Abul Fazl also refers to a son and a grandson as noted earlier. He probably had a sister, for Badauni mentions the death of his brother-in-law, Khudawand Dakkani.[3] Abul Fazl himself, however, does not refer to either a sister or a daughter.

1. The *Akbar Nama* is Abul Fazl's monumental work. The author had originally intended to write the *Akbar Nama* in five volumes.[4] Four of these were to constitute the narrative part, each covering a period of 30 years of Akbar's life. Our author's presumption was that Akbar would live 120 years and that he, Abul Fazl, would survive him in order to be able to complete his account of the Emperor's life. The fifth volume was to be the *Ain-i-Akbari*. Of these, Abul Fazl was able to write only three volumes, two of the narrative part and the *Ain*. The first volume covers "the history of mankind" from Adam to the first seventeen years of Akbar's reign; that is one cycle (qarn or thirty years) of Akbar's life for Akbar was around thirteen years of age at the time of his accession to the throne.The second volume brings the narrative to the close of the 46th regnal year of Akbar. In the first half of the 47th year, Abul Fazl was assassinated. The third volume, the *Ain-i-Akbari*, had practically been written by the end of the 42nd regnal year[5] with a small addition pertaining to the conquest of Berar which took place in the 43rd year.[6] After Abul Fazl's death the *Akbar Nama* was continued by one who is most probably known to be Muhibb

[1] *Ain*, Vol. II, pp. 280-281.

[2] *Insha-i-Abul Fazl*, Delhi University Library, MS no. MS 0164, 4J51x, ff. 288b-290a.

[3] Badauni, *op. cit.*, Vol. II, p. 372. Badauni specifically states that Khudawand was the husband of Abul Fazl's sister.

[4] *Ain*, Vol. II, p. 257.

[5] *Ibid.*, p. 256.

[6] *Ibid.*, Vol. I, pp. 476-485.

Ali Khan,[1] who brought the narrative to the end of Akbar's reign. Muhibb Ali's *Supplement* was written probably during the reign of Shahjahan. It is largely based on Muatamad Khan's *Iqbal Nama*, though the author attempts to imitate Abul Fazl's style.

Abul Fazl's plan of dividing the work he had finished into three volumes came to be modified some time after his death.[2] The first volume covering the history from Adam to the first seventeen years of Akbar's reign came to be split into two—one covering the history up to Humayun's death and the second from Akbar's enthronement to the first seventeen regnal years. The second volume in the original plan thus came to be regarded as the third. This modified form of the plan has been adopted by the editors of the published text. The text of the *Ain*, which had originally consisted of only one volume, was also divided by Blochman into two, and by Munshi Nawal Kishore and the Bib.Ind. translators into three volumes.

2. The *Maktubat-i-Allami* or the *Insha-i-Abul Fazl* consists of three parts—the first comprises letters and firmans written on behalf of Akbar by Abul Fazl to rulers and important nobles; the second is a collection of Abul Fazl's petitions and letters to Akbar and the nobles; and the third is a collection of Abul Fazl's comments on the Prefaces and Conclusions of books and other essays on certain subjects purporting to be models in prose style.[3]

3. The *Ayar-i-Danish* is a revised version of the *Kalilah Damnah*, commissioned by Akbar. It had earlier been translated into Persian by Nasrullah Mustawfi and Maulana Hussain Waiz, but the language of their translation was very difficult and tedious.[4]

4. Abul Fazl refers to a commentary on the *Verse of the Throne*[5] and another on the beginning of the *Chapter of Victory*[6] which he

[1]H., Beveridge, *AN* (*tr.*), Vol. III, pp. 1204-1205; also Rieu, *Catalogue of the Persian Manuscripts in the British Museum*, Vol. III, London, 1883, p. 929. For a different view, see C.A. Storey, *Persian Literature*, Vol. I, London, 1927-39, pp. 547-548.

[2]S.A.A., Rizvi, *Mughal Kalin Bharat—Humayun*, Part I (Hindi), Aligarh Muslim University, 1961, Preface, pp. 40-41.

[3]*Insha*, f. 3a.

[4]*Ain*, Vol. I, p. 116.

[5]*AN*, Vol. III, p. 85.

[6]*Ibid.*, p. 114.

had presented to Akbar on his two introductions to the court. The first of these has probably been lost but a copy of the second has been preserved in the *Insha-i-Abul Fazl*.[1]

5. The *Munajat-i-Abul Fazl*,[2] formally constituted Abul Fazl's invocation to God. But in the course of the invocation, he dwells on the nature of God's existence,[3] moralizes on self-control and on the necessity of suppressing one's selfish desire in search of nearness to the Supreme Being.[4] He also denounces mere formal worship of God and religious dogma and emphasizes the efficacy of personal devotion to God.[5] Thus Abul Fazl's views on questions of metaphysics as also of dogma have an indirect bearing on religious disputes in Akbar's assemblies.

The language of the *Munajat* is as ornate and tedious as that of the *Akbar Nama*, although the subjects of the two works are entirely different from each other.

6. Abul Fazl has also written the Preface to the *Tarikh-i-Alfi*, the history of the first mellenium of Islam written at Akbar's behest.[6] This Preface, however, is not found in the MSS of the *Tarikh*.[7]

7. Abul Fazl also wrote a Preface to the Persian translation of the *Mahabharata*.[8] The translation had been made by Abdul Qadir Badauni, Naqib Khan and Shaikh Sultan Thanesari.[9]

8. Blochmann reports having come across references to two more works by Abul Fazl, but he did not see any copy of either.[10]

[1]*Insha*, Vol. II, ff. 175b-177a.

[2]The text of this work has been edited and annotated by S.A.A. Rizvi and published in *Medieval India Quarterly*, Vol. I, Part III, Aligarh, 1950. Rizvi has also added an Introduction to it, pp. 116-123.

[3]*Munajat*, pp. 11-12.

[4]*Ibid.*, pp. 23-24.

[5]*Ibid.*, pp. 3, 6, 11-12.

[6]*Ain*, Vol. I, p. 116.

[7]C.A. Storey, *op. cit.*, Vol. II, p. 542, fn 2; Rieu, *op. cit.*, Vol. I, p. 117.

[8]Muhsin Fani, *Dabistan-i-Mazahib*, Munshi Nawal Kishore Press, Lucknow, n.d., p. 327. Fani says Abul Fazl wrote this Preface as a counterpart to his commentary on the *Verse of the Throne;* see also Rieu, *op. cit.*, Vol. I, pp. 57-58.

[9]Rieu, *op. cit.*, Vol. I, pp. 57-58; H. Ethe, *Catalogue of Persian Manuscripts in the Library of the India Office*, Vol. I, Oxford, p. 1081.

[10]H. Blochmann, "Biography of Abul Fazl," *Ain* (*tr.*), Vol. I, p. liv.

The works are entitled *Jami-ul-Lughat* (a lexicographical work) and *Kashkol* (a collection of anecdotes) respectively.

9. Rieu ascribes a Persian translation of the *Bhagwad Gita* independently of the *Mahabharata*, to Abul Fazl.[1]

10. Abul Fazl had also abridged the *Tuti Nama* of Zia-i-Nakhshabi, a collection of 52 tales, without, however, reducing the number. The abridgement was done on order from Akbar.[2]

II. TREATMENT OF HISTORY IN THE *AKBAR NAMA*

Basic Form

Abul Fazl begins the narrative part of the *Akbar Nama* from Adam[3] and brings it down to the 46th year of Akbar's reign.[4] To Abul Fazl, this beginning of his work from Adam was no mere medieval formality; on the contrary, by tracing back the descent of Akbar to the earliest human being[5] the author intended to show that his patron stood at the pinnacle of the progress of humanity.[6] This is also suggested by his treatment of the narrative in the *Akbar Nama* prior to the reign of Akbar—he hurries through this part, stating occasionally that his main object was to write of Akbar and his reign.[7] It is only when he comes to the immediate predecessors of Akbar that he is a little more detailed, but he still betrays a constant awareness of the secondary significance of this part to the reign of Akbar.

Abul Fazl takes up the relationship between Adam and Akbar as a mere notion, and elaborates it, as he does with many others. That is, he takes up the notion that Akbar stood at the climax of

[1]Rieu, *op. cit*, Vol. I, p. 59.

[2]*Ibid*, Vol. II, pp. 753-754. I have not included the *Ruqaat-i-Abul Fazl* in this list for it is considered by most modern scholars to be a forgery.

[3]*AN*, Vol. I, p. 52.

[4]*Ibid.*, Vol. III, p. 82.

[5]*Ibid.*, Vol. I, pp. 48-49. Significantly, Abul Fazl traces this descent not through the Prophet and the Caliphs but through the rulers of Central Asia.

[6]*Ibid.*, pp. 62-63, 324.

[7]*Ibid.*, pp. 120, 323-334, 368-369.

human history and from this he works backwards to Adam. It is significant that assuming a notion as true, and working backwards from it, is a method very commonly applied by Abul Fazl in the conviction that this method will by itself prove the particular assumption to be true.

The division of the *Akbar Nama* is regnal; that is, each reign is treated as a unit. Within the framework of a reign, however, each event forms an individual entity. The order of the succession of reigns as well as of events has been adhered to. As the author comes to the reign of Akbar, the book assumes the form of an annual chronicle. That is, one regnal year becomes the basic unit now, instead of the entire reign. Within the year events are described strictly in the sequence of their happening. Indeed, in order to maintain this sequence, Abul Fazl even breaks the continuity of an event. If the occurrence of an event is prolonged in time, and if meanwhile other events have also taken place, Abul Fazl would begin with describing the first event, snap the thread of its description where other events intervene in point of sequence, narrate those others and then resume his narrative of the first.[1] This

[1]Thus, for example, Abul Fazl opens the account of the siege of Mankot during the second year of Akbar's reign, *AN*, Vol. II, p. 50. He gives a brief description of the fort, etc. (p. 51). As siege is laid to the fort, Abul Fazl breaks the narrative of this event to inform us that Bahadur Khan, brother of the Khan-i-Zaman, "who had stirred up sedition and strife in Zamindawar," came and did homage and was pardoned (pp. 52-54). He then gives details of the arrival of Mariam Makani and other ladies of the harem from Kabul (pp. 54-56). Next he describes the Khan-i-Zaman's victory over Hasan Khan Bachkoti (pp. 56-57). Next in line is an account of the victory of Qiya Khan at Gwalior (p. 57). Finally, the author informs us of the marriage of Akbar to the daughter of Abdullah Khan Mughal (p. 57). All this had happened as the fort of Mankot lay under siege. From p. 58 onwards Abul Fazl resumes the narrative of the happenings at Mankot.

Similarly, Abul Fazl commences the description of Bairam Khan's estrangement from Akbar (p. 60). He interrupts it to relate the story of a wild horse who was not beyond Akbar's Divinity-aided control (pp. 60-61). The narrative of the affairs of Bairam Khan is then resumed (p. 62), to be interrupted again to inform us of Bahadur Khan's departure for Multan to put his jagir in order (p. 62). Once again the author comes back to Bairam Khan (p. 62) when he makes a pause, for it was too early for him to relate events which took place later.

From p. 90 to 99 Abul Fazl gives details of the events and of the thinking

however does not fundamentally alter the character of each event as an individual entity. The thread of continuity snapped at one place can easily be picked up at another. In preserving this continuity and the fundamental unity of an event, Abul Fazl's references back and forth[1] are of immense assistance.

The *Ain-i-Akbari* is divided into five books. The first of these deals with the imperial establishment. The account includes the descriptions of the various departments of the imperial household, the imperial mint, and prices of foodstuffs and manufactures. It also deals with the art of calligraphy and painting, the royal arsenal, guns, and the royal stables. Finally, it gives in some detail the prices of building materials and wages of labourers.

Book II deals with the institution of the army, its various divisions, the rules of payment, etc. There is one section on the sayurghals or grants of land and allowances in charity, another on the regulations regarding marriage and a third regarding education. Some of the royal amusements have been dealt with separately. Finally, there is a list of mansabdars holding the ranks from 10,000 to 200, and a list of the pious men, scholars, poets and musicians of the time.

Book III opens with an account of 20 different eras which were operative in different parts of the world at different times. It then proceeds to describe the qualities required of men appointed to some of the posts of the empire like the faujdar, the mir adl and qazi, the kotwal, etc. and the functions associated with these posts. There is the description of the four categories of land officially recognized for the purpose of the assessment of revenue,

---

of Akbar and Bairam Khan respectively which led to the latter's fall. Suddenly he breaks the narrative (p. 99) to describe the steps taken by Maham Anaga for the welfare of the kingdom. . .and goes on up to p. 100. He then resumes the earlier narrative (p. 100). From p. 101 to 103 he tells us of what had happened to Shah Abul Maali after his escape from Lahore, and returns again to the events concerning Bairam Khan.

Similarly, Abul Fazl informs us of the nomination and despatch of Raja Man Singh and others to fight the last battle with Rana Pratap (Vol. III, pp. 166-167), then breaks the narrative to describe a number of other events and picks up the broken thread again on p. 173.

[1] *Ibid.*, Vol. II, pp. 26, 34-35, 44-45, 48-49, 56-57, 84-85; Vol. III, pp. 173, 264, etc.

followed by the tables of revenue rates of crops of the spring and autumn harvests respectively in different provinces for nineteen years (from the 6th to the 24th regnal years of Akbar). The section of the *Ain-i-Dahsala* is followed by the revenue rates promulgated for different areas after the 24th year. Finally comes the account of "the twelve" (actually fifteen) subahs. Mahal-wise revenue tables for each province are prefaced, in each case, by a geographical and economic account of the province followed by a detailed historical note.

Book IV is mainly concerned with the various concepts of the Hindus—astronomical, medicinal, philosophical, etc.—and their customs and manners. Book IV is, perhaps, the weakest part of the entire work. This weakness arises on two acounts—the author has merely copied, at times from defective secondary sources, his information on the various schools of Hindu philosophy, science (particularly medical science), manners and customs, etc.[1] He has not tried to evaluate this information by discussing it with his contemporary scholars; and he does not describe the state of the Hindu society of his own day, which might have made his account more useful to the present-day historian. There is only one exception to this rule where he describes the various tribes amongst the Rajputs of his own day.[2]

Book V consists of a chapter comprising the wise sayings of Akbar, a Conclusion and a short autobiographical sketch of Abul Fazl.

CONTENTS

The *Akbar Nama*, apart from the *Ain*, contains extensive information on a variety of subjects within the limitations of the narrative of political events. The detailed information in it is related generally to the fields of battle, tactics employed therein, persons in command of forces, etc.[3] At times there are brief notices on

[1] *Infra*, p. 68.

[2] *Ain*, Vol. II, pp. 56-57.

[3] *AN*, Vol. II, pp. 111-113, 124-125, 134-135; Vol. III, pp. 165-166, 425-426, 430.

the history of other countries or territories.[1] Occasionally, too, there are genealogical data of persons concerned with events.[2]

Apart from battles and similar events, the author appends incidental notes on subjects such as the topography of an area[3] or elephants[4] or astrology.[5] This kind of information is given only on occasions when Abul Fazl is describing an event of which it forms an element. If he were telling us, for instance, of the Emperor's ride on a particularly difficult elephant, he would incidentally describe the kinds of elephants Akbar used to ride on.[6] Similarly, if he mentioned the birth of a prince, he would also refer to the horoscopes under different systems prepared on the occasion.[7]

The *Ain*, being altogether different in its character from the narrative part, is specifically meant to be some kind of gazetteer of information. It is in the *Ain* that Abul Fazl fully utilizes his potential as a compiler and editor.

The whole of the *Akbar Nama*, being circumscribed by its own character, generally lacks in incidental reference to men and manners outside the narration of political events centred round the person, and the court, of Akbar.

Attitude Towards the Sources of Information

Abul Fazl has the habit of rarely acknowledging the source from which he derives a specific piece of information. He has, however, given a general account of how he collected the information as a whole[8]:

1. The records of every circumstance and event connected with Akbar were collected.

2. The servants of the court and the old members of the royal

[1] *Ibid.*, Vol. III, pp. 224-227 and 587-592 (Persia), 553-556 (Central Asia), 662-665 (Turkey), 716-717 (Cooch-Bihar), etc.

[2] *Ibid.*, Vol. II, p. 21; Vol. III, p. 553, etc.

[3] *Ibid.*, Vol. II, p. 208; Vol. III, pp. 432, 512-513, etc.

[4] *Ibid.*, Vol. II, p. 222.

[5] *Ibid.*, pp. 2, 6, 7-9, 345-346.

[6] *Ibid.*, pp. 74-75.

[7] *Ibid.*, pp. 346-347, 354-355, 374-375; Vol. III, p. 524, etc.

[8] *Ibid.*, Vol. I, pp. 9-10.

family were subjected to long interrogations by the author and their accounts were reduced to writing.

3. Orders were issued to old servants in all directions of the empire to write out whatever they remembered of past events and send the notes and memoranda to the court.[1] The material thus collected was to be arranged and read out to Akbar and its use was first to be authorized by him. Other details, if Abul Fazl came across them later, could be included by him in the *Akbar Nama*.

4. In the 19th regnal year a record office (literally register of events) was established by Akbar's command where records of events from that year onwards were maintained.

5. Most of the royal orders issued to the various iqtas of the empire since Akbar's enthronement up to the time of Abul Fazl's writing were collected by the author in the original or in their transcripts.

6. Many of the "petitions" submitted by ministers and other high officials regarding events in various parts of the empire and in other countries were collected.

7. Abul Fazl personally exerted himself to collect notes and drafts (of memoranda) from well informed and prudent persons. Apart from these Abul Fazl uses his own testimony as evidence[2] as also that of his father.[3] Occasionally he quotes Akbar himself as his informant.[4] He is not immune from using even hearsay and dreams of certain individuals as his sources.[5]

Not an inconsiderable portion of the information, both for the narrative part of the *Akbar Nama* as well as for the *Ain*, has been derived from sources which have not been specifically acknowledged. Among these are not only the memoirs written exclusively for his

[1]As a result, at least four books were written which have continued to be independent sources of our information. These works are Bayazid Biyat's *Tazkira-i-Humayun-wa-Akbar*; Abbas Sarwani's *Tuhfa-i-Akbar Shahi* or the *Tarikh-i-Shershahi*; Jauhar Aftabchi's *Tazkirat-ul-Waqiat*; and Gulbadan Begam's *Humayun Nama*. A general study of the first three has been attempted in later pages, *infra*, Chapter 5.

[2]*Ain*, Vol. II, p. 255.

[3]*AN*, Vol. II, p. 153.

[4]*Ibid.*, pp. 145-146, 152, 164, 201-202, 233, etc.

[5]*Ibid.*, pp. 118, 126, 208, 215, 266, etc.

use but many others. This plagiaristic trait in him has been noticed by Jarrett who remarks, "The sources from which he drew his information are never acknowledged. This of itself would have been of no moment and their indication might perhaps have disturbed the unity of his design had he otherwise so incorporated the labours of others with his own as to stamp the whole with the impress of originality, but he not seldom extracts passages word for word from other authors undeterred by fear, or heedless of the charge of plagiarism."[1] It may, however, be noted that Jarrett's charge refers exclusively to Volume III of the *Ain* where Abul Fazl draws heavily on Alberuni as represented in Persian by Rashid-ud-din.[2] Taken as a general charge, it would appear to be somewhat exaggerated. Abul Fazl at least changes the words of his sources. Also, he is certainly not alone among contemporary, and even later, historians in making this a practice.

It would be impossible to analyze the entire *Akbar Nama* passage by passage and trace the source of information for each. A few examples, however, would show that the author made great efforts to secure information and has seldom acknowledged the source. In the *Ain*, for example, in the chapter on the literature of the Hindus, Abul Fazl copies the definitions of various forms of expression along with illustrations[3] from Viswanath Kaviraj's *Sahitya Darpana*.[4] The chapter on the Hindu system of the administration of justice[5] bears close resemblance to the relevant chapter in the *Manusmriti*.[6] Many of the details of the sarkar of Kabul[7] have been taken from Babur's *Tuzuk*.[8] In the narrative part of the *Akbar Nama*, Abul Fazl tells us of an oath of allegiance to Humayun taken by his nobles on condition that he takes a similar oath of allegiance to

[1]*Ain* (*tr.*), Vol. II, p. vii.

[2]Karl Jahn (ed.), *Rashid-ud-Din's History of India* (including text), the Hague, 1965.

[3]*Ain*, Vol. II, pp. 130-134.

[4]*Sahitya Darpana*, with *tr.* and commentary in Hindi by Vimla, Delhi, 1961, Chapter III.

[5]*Ain*, Vol. II, pp. 146-153.

[6]*Manusmriti*, Buhler's *tr.* Oxford, 1886, Book VIII, verses 1-420 and Book IX verses 1-250, 270.

[7]*Ain*, Vol. I, pp. 590-591.

[8]A.S. Beveridge, *Babur Nama* (*tr.*), Vol. I, pp. 310-311.

them.[1] The author's informant in this case is Jauhar Aftabchi.[2] The story told in the *Akbar Nama* of how Kamran was once publicly insulted in Humayun's court[3] is taken from Bayazid's *Tazkira-i-Humayun-wa-Akbar*.[4]

On the other hand, there are cases, although too few to be significant, where the author has acknowledged his source without giving any details. One such reference is to Khwaja Shams-ud-din Khawafi. Abul Fazl mentions his name and quotes his evidence but does not refer to his work, if any. Nor does he specify whether the evidence was oral.[5]

An interesting element in Abul Fazl's use of his sources is the alterations he makes in either the words or the nuances of the evidence. In this he does not spare even official documents. He copies in full, for example, Shah Tahmasp's firman to the governor of Khurasan on the eve of Humayun's arrival there[6] most probably from Bayazid's work.[7] In the process of copying, he makes some alterations and even omits some words. He adds, for example, three names to the list of those who were to entertain Humayun and omits the title "Jannat Ashiyani" given by the Persian Shah to his own father. Similarly, he omits the words "Sahib-i-dev-o-pari" from the list of Humayun's titles as described in the firman.[8]

[1]*AN*, Vol. I, p. 302.

[2]Jauhar, *Tazkirat-ul-Waqiat*, British Museum MS Add. 16711, Rotography, Research Library, Deptt. of History, Aligarh Muslim University, f. 113b.

[3]*AN*, Vol. I, p. 282.

[4]Bayazid, *Tazkira-i-Humayun-wa-Akbar*, Bib. Ind., p. 100.

[5]*AN*, Vol. III, p. 67. From the context it appears, however, that either Khawafi had been interrogated by the author and notes taken of his evidence or that he had written some kind of memorandum for Abul Fazl's use. Abul Fazl quotes him again in the first person, *ibid.*, pp. 301-302.

[6]*Ibid*, Vol. I, pp. 206-213.

[7]*Op. cit.*, pp. 12-31. No other author gives a copy of this firman. Abul Fazl must have copied it from the *Tazkira* unless he had another official copy of it. In any case, Bayazid's copy appears to be authentic, and therefore Abul Fazl's version can safely be compared with it.

[8]The omissions are understandable. "Jannat Ashiyani" was the title by which reference was officially made to Humayun in India after his death; and, "Sahib-i-dev-o-pari" was probably considered below the dignity of a Mughal Emperor, Beveridge, *AN*, Vol. I (*tr.*), p. 431, fn. 2.

At other places Abul Fazl gives in his own language the gist of Akbar's firmans to his amirs.[1] Significantly, he does not include a copy of the Mahzar, the final draft of which had been prepared by his own father in the *Akbar Nama* but merely gives a summary of it in his own language.[2] The making of the gist of a document and writing it in his own language provided our author with added avenues of altering words and nuances, if need arose. The absence of the text of the Mahzar and its substitution by a summary may illustrate this point. Whereas the actual document, which has been reproduced in Badauni's *Muntakhab-ut-Tawarikh*[3] and Nizam-ud-din's *Tabaqat-i-Akbari*[4] states, "If in matters of (Islamic) religion there is a difference of opinion among the interpreters (His Majesty) with his penetrating understanding and right thinking could, for the benefit of mankind and for the sake of administering the world, select one of these different opinions and issue an order to that effect which would be binding (on all the signatories),"[5] Abul Fazl makes Akbar the final arbiter in cases of disputation among all "sects and religions."[6] This was because when Abul Fazl was writing, Akbar was no longer content to be the "religious head" of the Muslims alone but of all the others as well.[7]

Secondly, the document empowers Akbar to issue any new orders provided that such orders did not contradict the Quran. Abul Fazl does not make even a reference to this clause probably because when he was writing he did not consider Akbar's authority of issuing orders limited by any qualification such as the one imposed by the Mahzar. Thus, to apply the attitudes, formed at the time of writing, uniformly over the entire reign, he tampers with an extremely important official document.

[1]*AN*, Vol. II, p. 31; Vol. III, pp. 351-352.
[2]*Ibid.*, Vol. III, pp. 268-270.
[3]Vol. II, pp. 271-272.
[4]Vol. II. pp. 345-346.
[5]Badauni, *op. cit.*, Vol. II, p. 271.
[6]*AN*, Vol. III, p. 270.
[7]Badauni, *op. cit.*, Vol. II, pp. 286-287. Abul Fazl understandably does not make such a statement but clearly implies it. I owe this point to Iqtidar Alam Khan, "The Nobility Under Akbar and the Development of His Religious Policy (1560-80)," *J.R.A.S.* 1968, Parts 1 and 2.

Another example of how Abul Fazl changes the shades of meaning from that of his evidence may be cited here. In the context of the rebellion of Ali Quli Khan, in the tenth year of Akbar's reign, Abul Fazl refers to a meeting between the rebel and Munim Khan. His source for this piece of information is Bayazid who was one of the very few persons present on the occasion. Whereas Bayazid remarks, "they wept to mourn the death of His Majesty Jannat Ashiyani (Humayun) as they had not met since then,"[1] Abul Fazl, referring to the same, writes, "Part of the time of the meeting passed in hypocritical weeping."[2]

Abul Fazl rewrites Todar Mal's memorandum concerning revenue administration and even Akbar's remarks thereon in the final version apparently because he considered the language of the original unsuitable to the dignity of his work.[3]

Limitations like these in Abul Fazl's attitude towards the sources of his information arise out of the framework of his undertaking. Within this framework, however, his attitude registers a great advance over that of the historians of the Sultanate. From his own account of his researches it appears that all the relevant information was first collected in the form of official documents as well as memoirs of persons involved in, or witness to, the events.[4] Each piece of evidence was then fully investigated and collated with others before being incorporated into the *Akbar Nama*.[5] For information on each event, Abul Fazl says he took the written testimony of more than 20 persons.[6] In these testimonies he found many a contradiction and discrepancy. He therefore proceeded by accepting the principal points common to all, and for ascertaining others he depended upon "prudence, truth-speaking and caution."

[1]Bayazid, *op. cit.*, p. 291.

[2]*AN*, Vol. II, p. 259.

[3]The original memorandum had been copied verbatim in the first draft of the *AN*, British Museum MS Add. 27, 247 (Rieu, *Catalogue of the Persian Manuscripts in the British Museum*, Vol.I, London, 1879, p.247b), f. 332b. See transcript of the variation between the first and the final drafts in Research Library, Deptt. of History, Aligarh Muslim University. The final version carries a paraphrase in a more literary language, *AN*, Vol. III, pp. 382-383.

[4]*AN*, Vol. I, pp. 9-10.

[5]*Ain*, Vol. II, p. 255.

[6]*Ibid*.

However, whenever Abul Fazl was uncertain of the authenticity of evidence for any piece of information, he submitted it all to Akbar and thus absolved himself of responsibility.

This use of official sources and the rigorous investigation of the authenticity of every piece of information makes *Akbar Nama* a genuine research work within its frame of reference and in the context of the time it was written. That is, it is not the author's purely impressionistic account of events; on the contrary, it is based on a certain authentic spadework and a systematic collection of data.

Yet, when Abul Fazl proceeds to write a "history of the world" with the *a priori* notion that this history had reached its fulfilment in the reign of Akbar, he places severe limitations on his work at the very outset. Add to this the restrictions imposed by what he thought was the ultimate proof of the authenticity of his information—prescription and approval of his sources beforehand by Akbar[1] who was also the final arbiter in cases of disputed plural evidence,[2] and the final outcome of the author's labours was subject to the Emperor's clearance.[3] This makes *Akbar Nama* a purely official history in which Abul Fazl played the role of a distinguished craftsman whose distinction lay in greatly improving upon the earlier achievements of his craft.

Treatment of History and Historical Causation in the *Akbar Nama*

History, for Abul Fazl, was "the events of the world recorded in a chronological order."[4] Unambiguous though the definition is, Abul Fazl adheres to it only in part. Except in a very formal sense, the *Akbar Nama* is not a record of the *events of the world.* Its commencement from the fall of Adam does not entitle it to being called a world history for two reasons—until Abul Fazl comes to the history of the Mughals he picks up some crude notions and

[1] *AN*, Vol. I, p. 10.
[2] *Ain*, Vol. II, p. 255.
[3] *AN*, Vol. II, p. 392.
[4] *Ain*, Vol. I, p. 280.

presents them as historical facts[1]; and the account prior to that of Akbar's reign has been written with the specific objective of setting Akbar's supremacy against a partly imagined and largely distorted historical background. That is, he does not write a history of the world—nor even a mere record of the events of the world—as such. On the contrary, writing under the patronage of Akbar and completely overwhelmed by his glory and that of his court, he feels that this glory is the most resplendent since the beginning of humanity and to prove this he looks back upon what he considers human history from Adam downwards.[2] To do this he is in great haste as he confesses at places.[3] In the process either due to his ignorance or for convenience, he does not mind picking up crude notions and treating them as historical facts.

Thus the vantage point from which he looks back is the reign of Akbar. Every word in the *Akbar Nama* is, directly or indirec-

[1]Thus, for example, the story of how Alanquwa, the 22nd ancestor of Akbar, became pregnant by a ray of holy light, *AN*, Vol. I, p. 65. Abul Fazl pleads that such a phenomenon was not beyond the comprehension of those "who had passed the stage of worship of the material causes but was inexplicable to those who had not advanced, their foot further than that stage." The author further remarks, "That day was the beginning of the manifestation of His Majesty the Emperor (Akbar). . . ." Arguments and opinions like these are characteristic of Abul Fazl whenever he has to explain inconvenient phenomena, *infra*, p. 78.

Similarly, the myths regarding Adam, Shis, Enoch, etc., have been accepted by Abul Fazl as true, *AN*, Vol. I, pp. 52-53, 53-54, 54 respectively, and he assigns the date of Adam's birth to 7,000 years ago. (This contradicts his own statement that the tradition that man originated 7,000 years ago is incorrect, *ibid.*, p. 49.)

Indeed, the basic presumption of Abul Fazl that Akbar was the direct descendant of Adam himself through the intervening 52 generations is a crude notion which, for him, is a self-evident historical fact. Similarly, as stated earlier, he had planned to write the history, in four volumes, of Akbar's 120 years, *Ain*, Vol. II, p. 257, presuming that Akbar would live as long and that he, Abul Fazl, would keep him company. He did not live long enough to see the presumption belied.

[2]At times this approach suggests a teleological view of history in that, to Abul Fazl, human history from its beginning appears to have drawn towards its end in Akbar's reign. Actually, however, his method is not teleological for he does not *reach* this conclusion after a study of human history but assumes this as a notion and elaborates it by looking back upon "human history" in the belief that this elaboration proves the assumption to be true.

[3]*AN*, Vol. I, pp. 120, 323-324, 369-370.

tly, related either to the Emperor personally or his empire or his reign. Even the notices on the history of other countries, which are interspersed in the book, have been inserted only on the basis of this relationship.[1]

Essentially, therefore, the main contribution of Abul Fazl in writing the *Akbar Nama* is the history of the reign of Akbar, including the information contained in the *Ain*, and at best a history of the Mughal dynasty from Babur to Akbar up to the year of writing.

The chronological sequence of events of which Abul Fazl speaks is adhered to only in the last two (printed) volumes of the book. This again is in keeping with the fact that the author has allowed himself to overlook certain forms in the first volume in a hurry to deal with Akbar's reign.

The most significant deviation of Abul Fazl from his own definition of history, however, lies in his explanation of the causation, rather than the mere recording, of events.

Abul Fazl does not formulate any general principles to explain causation in history. He does generalize. But his generalizations are mostly derived from individual events and hence are not comprehensive enough to explain total causation or causal relationship between two or more events or between the structure of state or

[1]There are some intimate details of the intrigues in the Persian court from the time of the death of Shah Tahmasp, in 1576, onwards, *Akbar Nama*, Vol. III, pp. 224-227.

The occasion for the insertion of this notice is a reference to the appearance of a comet in that year which could cast no evil influence on India owing to the presence of the divinity-aided Akbar, but which caused immense devastation in Persia where also it had been seen.

The arrival of Shah Abbas, Persia's ambassador at Akbar's court in the 36th year of Akbar's reign, again touches off a short account of the Safavide dynasty, *ibid.*, pp. 588-592.

Similarly, the mention of the arrival of Sultan Quresh of Kashgarh at Akbar's court in the 34th regnal year is followed by an account of the events in Central Asia from the days of Changez Khan downwards, *ibid.*, pp. 553-556.

The death of Sultan Murad of Turkey and the accession to the throne of his son, Muhammad, who had eliminated his 19 brothers starts off Abul Fazl on a short account of Turkey's events, *ibid.*, pp. 662-665. The incident of the Sultan's death is not essentially related to Akbar or his reign except that the news makes him unhappy. Abul Fazl, however, considers this account of Turkey a "digression" from his narrative, *ibid* , p. 665.

society and the nature of events in relation to that structure.

This may be clearer if we examine one of the chief features of Abul Fazl's style of writing. Abul Fazl treats history as a collection of individual events, and, indirectly, of matters relating to individual persons or institutions involved in these events. Almost invariably he opens his account of events with the remark, "One of the occurrences was. . . ." However, each event in his account is an illustration of certain moral truths or has a moral lesson. Abul Fazl generally prefaces his narration of each event with what may be called a preamble of which the event is meant to be an illustration. Failing that, he narrates the event and proceeds to draw one or another moral lesson from it. The effect of either prefixing or suffixing the lesson is practically the same for the content of the generalization is always the same. To take a few of the innumerable examples:

"Whenever from the good fortune of mankind, the time for collective worship of Truth arrives (the people) rapair to the king on account of his high dignity and (thus) he becomes their spiritual leader as well; for a king possesses, independently of any intermediate power, the ray of wisdom and every sign of duality is banished from his heart. At times (the king) observes unity in the diversity of things and at others the contrary of it, for he sits on the majestic throne and is equally detached to joy and sorrow. Now this is the case with the monarch of our age and this book is a witness of it."[1]

Or, referring to the corporal punishment awarded by Akbar to a leopard-keeper for having forcibly removed a man's shoes, Abul Fazl remarks, "This signified a warning to the men of the world and a lesson (literally sum or capital) in wisdom to the savages of the desert of ignorance. It became known in that region and (afterwards) no one thought of running away or suffering harm. Peace and tranquillity appeared in the empire."[2]

Or, "although the able ones may understand the importance of endeavour in the performance of duty, yet the far-seeing sage knows that in most cases the attainment of great objectives is associated with good intentions and appropriate actions of world-

[1]*Ain*, Vol. I, p. 159.
[2]*AN*, Vol. II, p. 157.

rulers. It is obvious to those who have been witness to the great deeds of the past that success does not embrace (one) without initial (unsuccessful) efforts, and until the second attempt the object is not attained. It is because of this that the sitter on the throne of fortune (Akbar) concentrates on every work, which calls for courage, in this delightful fashion and brings to a conclusion every hard job without tears. This is perfectly clear to anyone who knows the events and occurrences of this eternal reign. The conquest of Bhakkar is a fresh instance of this."[1]

Now these generalizations are not genuine generalizations, for each of them is related and therefore relevant to a single event. What appears to be a grandiose framework of general principles which forms the background to, or is a derivation from, an event is in reality an inference backwards. That is, Abul Fazl knows the event he is going to describe and makes generalizations on the basis of his knowledge of that particular event. The harangue about the spiritual leadership of the king, for example, is a prelude to Abul Fazl's description of the proclamation by Akbar of the Tauhid-i-Ilahi (or the so-called Din-i-Ilahi) as is clear from the subsequent pages. Thus this preamble has relevance only to Akbar. There is no evidence to suggest that Abul Fazl would have accepted just *any* king's spiritual leadership even in theory; but he accepts Akbar's both in theory and in practice.

Similarly, the formulation that success is achieved only after an earlier failure is relevant only to the taking of Bhakkar where an earlier attempt had failed.[2] As such, it is not a principle applicable to all situations at all times.

Significantly, whenever Abul Fazl deals with different kinds of situations, his generalizations are also different. Thus, when at one place he states that there are eight essential requisites of an Emperor—high fortune, rare courage, conquering power, administrative capacity, attention to the cultivation (development) of the territories, purity of intention in promoting the welfare of the holy men, cherishing of the army and restraining it form wreaking destruction,[3]—he generalizes on the basis of qualities he observed in

[1]*AN*, Vol. III, p. 90.
[2]*Ibid.*, pp. 90-91.
[3]*Ibid.*, Vol. I, p. 118.

or could attribute to Babur. But when he remarks that "Kingship is a gift of God" and that among the qualities of a king are inauguration of "universal peace" and "regarding of all sections of humanity and all sects of religions, not one as the mother and another as the stepmother, but with the single eye of favour,"[1] he is not propounding a general theory but is enumerating what he thought were Akbar's qualities as ruler.

Similarly, referring to his detractors and to himself, Abul Fazl divides mankind into four categories, "First, there are the darkened and the contumacious ones who do not listen to reproof and do not convey it from the ear-hole to the heart's chamber. . . . Second, those evil-natured, base ones who fancy their ignorance as knowledge and show off their incurable disease as excellence of health. Third, those seekers after light, with well-constituted nature, who have escaped from the demon castle of envy and the dark pit of ignorance and who seek after health, but who, owing to perverse fate and evil star cannot attain to lofty knowledge and to whom the veiled beauties of wisdom's seraglio but rarely show themselves. Fourth, that illustrious man of happy star, who, along with treasures of knowledge possesses loftiness of soul and great genius, and who, from profundity of perception ever fares forward."[2] But when he comes to describe the resistance by Akbar's nobles to the institution of the branding of horses, he groups humanity under a single head, "It is not hid under the veil of concealment from judicious observers that man is continually dominated by cupidity and anger . . . . The commander withholds from the followers what he has received from the court, and becomes more greedy and the follower sprinkles the dust of disloyalty on the head of his fortune and acts on all occasions as if he were his own master."[3]

In a number of cases Abul Fazl gives multiple explanations of the same event. For example, referring to Tardi Beg's flight from the fort of Delhi when it was besieged by Hemu, the author remarks, "some of the reckoners-up of registers of deeds regard the coming of Tardi Beg to such disgrace as a kind of expiation for

[1]*Ibid.*, Vol. II, p. 285.
[2]*Ibid.*, p. 382.
[3]*Ibid.*, Vol. III, p. 116.

the disloyalty which he showed to His Majesty Jahanbani Jannat Ashiani (Humayun) at the beginning of the journey to Persia. God forbid! that (merely) this be an expiation for disloyalty. Could a disgrace such as this be placed in the scales of justice as a counterpiece to the shameful act? Since he saw the Lord of the Age, who had been brought for the perfection of the visible and invisible, in the disguise of boyhood, he did not pay regard to him and, being arrogant, wanted to show off his greatness. The world-adorning God inflicted such a punishment on that self-approver. Alas! What a short-sightedness this was. Rather, the implementers of the Divine decree enhanced the arrogance and intoxication of Hemu, so that the intoxicated worshipper of conceit would appear great to the eyes of the short-sighted of whom this world is full, in order to show the majesty of the Emperor. Afterwards he was seized and cast down to the dust of shame so that his disgrace might become collyrium to the eyes of the short-sighted."[1]

Or, commenting upon the assassination of Bairam Khan, Abul Fazl remarks, "I do not know whether this event is a retribution of his past deeds or if his mind was still polluted by evil thoughts, or if his prayer had been answered or whether the favour of God had relieved that good man from the heavy burden of shame."[2]

Perhaps in most cases such explanations are mere literary embellishment to the hard core of historical events. But, as the first example above would show, at times they may be used as attempts to explain away inconvenient events or phenomena. This is particularly reinforced by the fact that such of the explanations offered are generally somewhat mystical rather than historical. Abul Fazl often resorts to this kind of mystical reasoning whenever he feels the need to explain, or explain away, inconvenient events or phenomena. He loyally and consistently sticks, for example, to a theory he has built up that during the first four years of his reign Akbar had drawn a veil over his face from behind which he silently judged each individual's character.[3] This explains his apparent political inaction during this period. At another place Abul Fazl relates an incident in which the elephant Akbar was

[1] *Ibid.*, Vol. II, pp. 30-31.
[2] *Ibid.*, p. 130.
[3] *Ibid.*, pp. 14-15.

riding fell into a ditch. As the animal sought to extricate itself, it tried to get rid of the Emperor's "sacred person." Akbar was saved by some "intrepid, loyal and alert men." Abul Fazl's conclusive remarks on this incident are, "I do not know if this beauty under the aspect of terror displayed itself without the intention of this chosen one so that the far-reaching thoughts of the wicked might be shortened by such (Divine) guardianship, or whether that sovereign of the apparent and the hidden, that king of the visible and the invisible, should, with Divine help and inspiration, knowingly and designedly, exhibit such glory so that by one act might be manifested the blindness of the malevolents and the illumination of the loyal."[1]

Now, although, as stated earlier, Abul Fazl does not formulate any fundamental concept of historical generalization, he does explain individual historical events within the framework of certain assumptions which are taken by him as self-evident and self-sufficient truths. He makes an assumption to explain a particular event and then places forward that event as its illustration which he also considers its proof. Alternately, he makes an assumption and elaborates it, the elaboration, to him, being the proof of the genuineness of the assumption. To take some examples:

"Since in the manner of the dispensation of justice and the law of the conquest of territories," he says, "it is necessary that whenever the ruler of a country or the governor of a province engages in his own pleasures and spends his valuable time in gratifying his own lusts and does not attend to the cherishing of his subjects and sympathizing with the oppressed and to overthrowing the oppressors, the Lord of the Age, whom the Almighty has given the power to conquer and has made the king of the world and its people, must, for the sake of thanksgiving to God, strive to uproot that tyrant and to make over the inhabitants of that country to the just-minded and the prudent and consider this as the preamble to elect devotion. Acting on this principle, which is founded upon Truth, an order was issued in this fortunate year (5th year of Akbar's reign), when the news of the disturbance and commotion of the intriguing Kashmiris and the injustice of Ghazi Khan, governor of Kashmir, reached the blessed ears (of Akbar), that a force be put

[1]*Ibid.*, p. 74.

under the command of Mirza Qara Bahadur. . . for the conquest of Kashmir. . . ."[1]

Or, "assuredly, dominion comes unsought to those rulers with whom increase of territory brings increase of devotion and humility. And what they desire is carried to the height of fulfilment in spite of thousands of obstructions on the way. The account of this great victory is another instance of this."[2]

Or, "if the majesty of royalty did not exist, how would various disturbances subside? And how would selfishness disappear? Mankind would, under the burden of passion and lust, fall into the pit of destruction; everywhere the world would lose its lustre and in a short time the prosperous world would be rendered desolate. But by the light of the King's justice some follow, with cheerfulness and freshness, the road of obedience, and others, out of fear of punishment, abstain from violence and willingly or unwillingly return to the path of lawfulness."[3]

Broadly, Abul Fazl makes two sets of assumptions. The first of these is that Akbar's is a semi-Divine personality; at least he is aided by Divinity whether in his action or non-action; that loyalty to Akbar is an essential virtue for everyone; and, that therefore the frustration of an act of rebellion or disloyalty or hostility to Akbar is predestined. This third assumption is, in fact, an inference from the first two.

Abul Fazl is practically obssessed with Akbar's proximity to Divinity. He feels no sorrow at the death of Humayun, for the Creator had so decided in order to give "rejuvenescence to the old world and new order to mankind,"[4] that is, to place Akbar on the throne. When Akbar promulgated the Ilahi era, that to Abul Fazl was the result of "Divine inspiration."[5] When "the feeble-hearted were depressed" for want of rain at a particular time, Akbar engaged in prayer and shortly afterwards there was a downpour."[6] When Akbar plunged his horse into a flooded river (the river

[1] *Ibid.*, pp. 128-129.

[2] *Ibid.*, Vol. III, p. 774. The victory referred to is the capture of the fort of Ahmednagar in the 45th regnal year.

[3] *Ain*, Vol. I, p. 2.

[4] *AN*, Vol. I, p. 365.

[5] *Ibid.*, Vol. II, p. 9.

[6] *Ibid.*, Vol. III, p. 578.

Mahindri in Gujarat), "by the fortune and miracle of his sacred person" the river became fordable.[1]

Abul Fazl pleads for unreserved loyalty to Akbar. In fact, any act not in complete conformity to it, and of course any act contrary to it, is bound to be visited by retribution.[2] Even among the loyal men there are two types—those who are loyal for the consideration of some expedience; and those who are "noble truth-seekers who illuminate their altruistic hearts with the light of love and stand at the head of the chosen ones of God."[3] The second of these types is naturally the superior of the two and, therefore, success comes to it unsought. It is to be noted that loyalty, to Abul Fazl, becomes virtuous only when owed to Akbar even if it involves deserting old friends and allies. Thus Shaham Khan, who had joined hands with the rebels in Bihar in 1580-81, "broke his promise and hoisted the flag of loyalty at Hajipur," and this he did out of "innate auspiciousness."[4]

The third assumption—predestined frustration of a rebellion or of an act of disloyalty or hostility to Akbar—is writ large on almost every page of the two later volumes of *Akbar Nama.* It is significant that, in Abul Fazl's view, only a rebellion against Akbar is bound to be frustrated and not against an Emperor as such, against Humayun, for instance. The success of Sher Shah—whom Abul Fazl insists on considering a mere rebel in that he never addresses him as Sher Shah but always calls him Sher Khan—would militate against the application of this notion to Humayun. But to rebel against Akbar "who has been made great by God and a ruler whom the inhabitants of the visible and the invisible world hasten to obey" is to "strike with one's hand the dagger of death into one's bosom."[5] Even as a pure logical inference, since Akbar is aided by divinity and since loyalty to him is absolutely essential, any thought or act to the contrary is bound to incur divine wrath. And in this, mere pretence of loyalty would not take one very far, for ultimately the pretence is bound to be detected and, therefore,

[1]*Ibid.*, p. 14.
[2]*Ibid.*, p. 20.
[3]*Ibid.*, pp. 449-450.
[4]*Ibid.*, p. 306.
[5]*Ibid.*, Vol. II, p. 84.

visited by retribution.[1]

The second basic set of Abul Fazl's assumptions concerns the nature of men to which he attributes their behaviour and it is to their behaviour that he attributes the causation of individual events in history. To this an exception is generally made where Akbar himself is directly involved in the occurrence of an event, for Akbar is a semi-divine person. Therefore his role falls beyond the pale of ordinary human reason. It must be stated here that Akbar's role in the occurrence of an event is not so explained in every instance without exception. There are examples where his role is explained in terms of his nature or volition.[2]

But it is only Akbar whose role in the happening of an event is explained in supernatural terms whenever it is so explained. Where an ordinary mortal is involved, his behaviour, to Abul Fazl, is the direct projection of his nature. An individual's nature comprises his innate traits along with his volition. A few examples may illustrate this point:

"At this time. . .a desire to kiss the threshold seized the collar of this fortunate one (Sultan Adam Gakkhar) also. But from his natural savagery he begged that when he is exalted by service he should not be taken to Hindustan along with the sublime cortege and that he should not, by marks of favour of the cherisher of the subjects, be made an exile from his own country."[3]

Or, "among the dominion-increasing events that occurred in Delhi at this time (the third regnal year of Akbar) was the execution of Musahib Beg, son of Khwaja Kalan Beg. The facts of this case in brief are that his soul was ever filled with hypocrisy and his disposition compact of wickedness. Both in the time of His Majesty Jahanbani Jannat Ashiyani (Humayun) and at the time of the rising of the world adorning sun, His Majesty the Emperor (Akbar), disagreeable actions of his came to light."[4]

[1]*Ibid.*, pp. 69, 97-98, 138.

[2]*AN*, Vol. II, pp. 68, 97, 141, 234-235; *ibid*, Vol. III, p. 50 where, in fact, the author theorizes that divine assistance notwithstanding, the ruler (the reference here is to Akbar) must depend upon "right design, just thinking and suitable action."

[3]*Ibid.*, Vol. II, p. 63.

[4]*Ibid.*, pp. 69-70.

Or, "when Adham Khan had become victorious by the good fortune of the Emperor, the intoxication of his innate lust increased and the cap of his pride was set awry by the wind of arrogance, the source of which is ignorance and folly. His brain deteriorated and whatever advice Pir Muhammad Khan, his disinterested mentor, gave him proved vain."[1] (Abul Fazl goes on to describe the steps Adham Khan had taken to treat himself as the independent ruler of Malwa after his victory there.)

The explanation of the causation of historical events in terms of human nature in *Akbar Nama* is based on the second set of assumptions which have been mentioned above. Abul Fazl divides men, from the point of view of their behaviour, into three categories:

Men who are good in every way.

Men who are wicked and invariably act wickedly.

Men who are essentially good but are surrounded by or are susceptible to evil influence.

This categorization is obviously a moral one. That is, Abul Fazl judges an individual's actions as moral actions. But a close examination of the basis of this categorization would bear out that in essence Abul Fazl equates political action with moral action.

Abul Fazl has written only of political events which have a direct or indirect relevance to Akbar's reign. Any reference outside the purview of political events is purely incidental and is subordinate to the latter. Thus he has written of men who have a positive or negative role to play in these events. Indirectly, it may be an individual's relation or attitude to the Emperor and his dominions. The basis of Abul Fazl's division of men into three moral categories is therefore their political behaviour and their attitude towards the Emperor (Akbar) and his empire.

It may be suggested that Abul Fazl's assumptions, though not logically proved by him as genuine, have a practical, historical validity in the context of the second half of the 16th century in India. This was the period when the Mughal empire was growing not only in territory but also in its intrinsic strength. The old administrative and political institutions were being so modified as to give to the Mughal empire a "steel frame"—the mansabdari system—

[1] *Ibid.*, pp. 137-138.

which sustained the growth of the empire both internally and externally in this formative period. This process of growth, supported as it was by the above-mentioned institutional structure, could be carried on only if political power was centralized in the hands of the monarch. Inversely, centralization of power would also be the result of this process.

In this context, when Abul Fazl, who had reason enough to align himself with Akbar intellectually as well as practically, places deliberate emphasis on Akbar's semi-divinity, it becomes understandable, for in essence it suggested wielding of unreserved political power. Abul Fazl could also understandably consider loyalty to Akbar essential and moral and hostility destructive and immoral. And on this basis he could categorize an individual's political behaviour as his moral behaviour.

Style

Abul Fazl believes that he has broken new ground in the style of history writing, distinct from the ornate verbosity and fantastic literary notions of most of the earlier authors and many others of his own day.[1] The claim is supported by the author of the *Ma'asir-ul-Umra*.[2]

Even a cursory reading of *Akbar Nama* would make it obvious that its author's claim to linguistic simplicity and easy style is untenable. If ornate verbosity there was, this book symbolizes it. Through the five revisions of his work[3] Abul Fazl appears to have selected each word very self-consciously and, with great diligence, constructed an elaborate literary edifice. Having done that, he sits back, as it were, to admire his own creation.

On the whole, Abul Fazl's style is very impersonal, unmodulated and uninteresting. Even the intermittent insertion of verses, apropos the medieval style, was made only in the fifth (and final) draft and that probably at the insistence, at least the suggestion, of others.[4] As

[1]*Ibid.*, Vol. II, p. 381.
[2]*Op. cit.*, Vol. II, p. 622.
[3]*Ain*, Vol. II, p. 256.
[4]*Ibid.*

such, the verses retain the character of a superimposition and fail to get integrated into the texture of the narrative.

Two of the translators of the *Akbar Nama* and the *Ain-i-Akbari* respectively are agreed in their evaluation of Abul Fazl's style. Beveridge is understandably impressed by the amount of industry that went into the writing of *Akbar Nama* and the accuracy of the information it contains. But, he remarks, "Abul Fazl is not a picturesque writer, nor are his reflections profound or affecting. Very seldom does he make an interesting remark. He has not the charm of Herodotus, nor the outspokenness and raciness of the crabbed, bigoted and sinful Badauni. He seldom tells a story without spoiling it."[1] Jarrett, writing in a similar vein, remarks that Abul Fazl's "annals have none of the pregnant meaning and point that in a few masterly strokes exalt or brand a name to all time and flash the actors of his drama across the living page in scenes that dwell for ever in memory.. . .His narrative affects a quaint and stiff phraseology which renders it often obscure and continues in an even monotone, never rising or falling save in reference to the Emperor whose lightest mention compels the adoring prostration of his pen, and round whom the world of his characters and events revolves as its central sun. Whatever its merits as a faithful representation, in a restricted sense, of a reign in which he was a capable and distinguished actor, it lacks the interesting details and portraiture of the life and manners of the nation which are commonly thought to be below the dignity of history but which brighten the pages of Eastern historians less celebrated than himself and are necessary to the light and shade of a perfect picture."[2]

Yet the division of *Akbar Nama* into two groups, the narrative part and the sort of gazetteer that the *Ain* is, did mark a new pattern in the style of history writing. Unfortunately, the *Ain* as a model was largely ignored by later historians, but the narrative part of *Akbar Nama* continued to provide a prototype for many of the later works.[3]

A significant feature of this work is the complete absence of encomia for the saints. Abul Fazl is aware of the convention of

[1]Beveridge's Introduction, *AN*, Vol. II. (*tr.*), pp. x-xi.

[2]Jarrett's Preface *Ain*, Vol. II (*tr.*), annotated by J.N. Sarkar, Bib. Ind., pp. vi-vii.

[3]*Supra*, p. 71, fn 3.

paying one's respects to them; still he refrains from following this convention, ostensibly because by praising Akbar, who was himself the personification of all that was noble and divine, he had praised the saints who had gone by.[1] This explanation, however, does not strike one as convincing. It is possible that, as in the later part of Akbar's reign, at the time when Abul Fazl was writing, the Emperor had given up many rituals and had abandoned even his earlier almost annual visits to Ajmer,[2] our author got the clue and refrained from recording any encomia for the saints.

A still more significant feature of the work is the complete absence of any religious fanaticism or what might today be called communal rancour. The explanation lies in part in the maturing of the state policy with regard to religion by the time Abul Fazl had started writing and in which he had played no small role himself. Unfortunately for today's historian, Abul Fazl accepts the policy in its mature form and applies it uniformly over the entire reign of Akbar, and this inhibits a reconstruction of the process of its evolution.[3]

One may be forgiven some speculation regarding another part contributing to Abul Fazl's "secular" stance. It is interesting to note that unlike the other medieval historians, who open their books with the praise of God, the Prophet and the Caliphs, gradually reaching down to the reigning sultan, Abul Fazl traces the descent of Akbar from Adam through a secular lineage—that of the rulers of Central Asia.[4] This is particularly significant in view of the fact

[1]*AN*, Vol. I, pp. 8-9.

[2]Narrating the events of the 18th regnal year of Akbar, Badauni tells us, "Since he (the Emperor), out of his excessive faith, considered the paying of annual visits to Ajmer essential. . . ." *op. cit.*, Vol. II, p. 173. Again, writing of the 24th regnal year he states, "On the 8th of September, 1579 he, Akbar, set out for Ajmer. After that to this day (when Badauni was writing) when fourteen years have passed he has not turned his rein towards that direction," *ibid.*, p. 272. Abul Fazl, writing of the 25th regnal year explaining why Prince Danyal was sent to Ajmer as Akbar's proxy, remarks, "The visiting of the tombs of the departed men of awakened heart he (Akbar) considers an instance. . .of shallowness," *AN*, Vol. III, pp. 316-317.

[3]A refreshingly new though still tentative attempt to explain the various phases in the evolution of Akbar's religious policy has been made by Iqtidar Alam Khan, "The Nobility Under Akbar. . . ."

[4]*AN*, Vol. I, pp. 48-49.

that Akbar's reign had witnessed the completion of the first millenium of Islam which could have created considerable temptation to associate Akbar with the revival and rejuvenation of the Faith. That Abul Fazl resists this temptation attests to his consciousness that Islam was not the only source of culture and that besides religion, whether Islamic or any other, there were other, secular, sources contributing to human thought and civilization. It is possible that his familiarity with contemporary Europe's emerging secular culture to an extent shaped his own thinking. He makes references to the discovery and capture of the New World (alam-i-nau) by the Europeans[1] and to European painting.[2]

Yet the fact that Abul Fazl's interpretation of Akbar's reign has a large semi-mystical element in it sharply brings forth the limitations of the new intellectual awareness at Akbar's court. The weaknesses of the Islamic heritage were recognized, but in the absence of any marked scientific and technological development in society,[3] the role of physical sciences as a component of any alternative ideology was missed altogether.

Beveridge began translating the *Akbar Nama* with the impression that Abul Fazl was a "shameless flatterer" of Akbar and the impression persisted with him to the end.[4] That Abul Fazl was conscious of the possibility of such a charge against him is obvious from his repeated attempts at denying it.[5] The very style of the *Akbar Nama*, whereby in the description of each event the author tries to build up a literary climax, is suggestive of his exaggerations in Akbar's favour. In most of the battles of Akbar or his men against rebels or other opponents (and the accounts of these form the bulk of *Akbar Nama*) Abul Fazl tries to exaggerate the strength and determination of the latter in order to inflate the significance and the glory of the Emperor's, or his agent's, victory. A more

[1]*Ain*, II, p. 26.

[2]*Ibid.*, Vol. I, p. 116. I owe this point to a discussion with Irfan Habib.

[3]For the rate of technological development in medieval India see Irfan Habib, presidential address, section II, *Proceedings of the Indian History Congress* (Varanasi session, 1969), Patna, 1970 and "The Technology and Economy of Mughal India" being the Dev Raj Chanana Memorial Lectures, Delhi, 1970 (mimeo).

[4]Beveridge's Preface, *AN* (*tr.*), Vol. III, p. ix.

[5]*AN*, Vol. I, p. 348; Vol. II, p. 114; Vol. III, p. 259.

interesting case is the author's own. In order to play up the light and guidance he had received from Akbar, he overly emphasizes his conceit and unsociableness before he came into contact with the Emperor.[1]

It must however be said to the credit of Abul Fazl that the exhaustive research which he had carried out for writing the *Akbar Nama* marks, up to his time in India, perhaps the most advanced attempt at writing a comparatively authentic history. To this day, even though his notions may appear extremely naive and his assumptions utterly invalid, his work remains a landmark in the history of medieval Indian historical writing.

[1]*Ibid.*, Vol. II, pp. 388-392; Vol. III, pp. 83-84, 113-114.

CHAPTER 3

I Mulla Abdul Qadir Badauni

Looking back at his life when he was well past his prime, Badauni expresses regret at having set his foot "into the street of illusory existence."[1] This pessimism, however, was punctuated with small mercies, one of which was that he was born during the reign of "so just a king as Sher Shah."[2]

Born at Todah and brought up at Bhusawar,[3] Badaun seems to have become his permanent home early in life.[4]

Badauni appears to have been remotely connected with the lower echelons of the imperial nobility. He mentions his maternal grandfather as having accompanied Farid Taran Panj Hazari on an expedition to Bajwara during the reign of Islam Shah Sur.[5] The fact that Badauni does not disclose his status perhaps suggests that it was not worth disclosing.

Badauni's father was also once engaged in a diplomatic assignment on Akbar's behalf.[6] When Sangram Khan, an amir of Adil Shah Sur, who was besieged by Akbar's forces at Ranthambhor, sought peace, Akbar sent Badauni's father, Muluk Shah, along with one Haji Bhikan, to negotiate the terms. Although Badauni attaches great importance to this mission, the negotiators do not

[1] Badauni, *op. cit.*, Vol. I, p. 364.

[2] *Ibid.*, p. 363. The date of his birth is 21 August 1540.

[3] *Ibid.*, Vol. II, p. 236. Both Todah and Bhusawar are situated in eastern Rajasthan.

[4] *Ibid.*, p. 87 where the author tells us that he moved from Badaun to Patiali; also p. 126 where he says that he went to Badaun where he got his brother married.

[5] *Ibid.*, Vol. I, p. 385. Bajwara, according to Badauni, was a dependency of Bayana.

[6] *Ibid.*, Vol. II, p. 31.

appear to have exercised much influence on either side.

Obviously, then, Badauni could not have greatly benefited from the status either of his father or his maternal grandfather in obtaining access to the imperial court. His career in Akbar's service carries the conviction of his own merit.

Regarding his education, Badauni does not appear to be very frank. Probably due to the hardened attitude at the time of writing the *Muntakhab*, he generally emphasizes the orthodox education he had received. His first teacher was his own maternal grandfather, Makhdum Ashraf, from whom he learnt the spellings and Arabic sciences.[1] Makhdum Ashraf, says our author, had many a claim on men of learning.[2] Later on Badauni went to Sambhal where he learnt to read the Quran from Mir Syed Muhammad Makki.[3] In 1552, at the age of twelve, he was introduced to Miyan Hatim Sambhali[4] at whose khanqah he learnt by heart the *Qasidah-i-Burdah* as also some lessons from *Kanz-i-Fiqh-i-Hanafi*.[5] The Miyan must have been greatly impressed by his young pupil, for he accepted him as one of his favourite disciples.[6] He gave Badauni, on behalf of his own mentor, Shaikh Azizullah, a cap and record of the line of his teachers and desired that he also acquire some esoteric knowledge.[7] Miyan Hatim Sambhali then entrusted his instruction to Shaikh Abul Fath Khairabadi.[8] In 1554 Badauni left Sambhal for Amroha in the company of his father.[9] There he was introduced to Mir Syed Muhammad (who later became Mir-i-Adl), who was their family friend.

Badauni's instruction at Agra under the guidance of Shaikh Mubarak is more significant. His association with the Shaikh and two of his sons, Faizi and Abul Fazl, lasted nearly 40 years.[10] Towards the later part of this period, the spectacular progress of

[1] *Ibid.*, p. 64.

[2] Meaning, he was a learned man.

[3] Badauni, *op. cit.*, Vol. II, p. 21.

[4] *Ibid.*, Vol. I, pp. 425-426; Vol. III, p. 2.

[5] *Ibid.*, Vol. III, pp. 2-3.

[6] *Ibid.*, p. 3.

[7] *Ibid.*

[8] *Ibid.*, Vol. I, pp. 425-426; Vol. II, p. 286.

[9] *Ibid.*, Vol. I, p. 426.

[10] *Ibid.*, Vol. III, p. 304.

Faizi and Abul Fazl in Akbar's favour filled Badauni with jealousy and bitterness, although the brothers continued to be considerate to him.

To Shaikh Mubarak's learning Badauni owed a considerable debt which he acknowledges ungrudgingly.[1] Although later on he accuses the Shaikh of vacillation in his fidelity to the creed, and of moulding his opinion to the needs of different circumstances, he never challenges Shaikh Mubarak's abilities as a scholar.[2]

At Agra, Badauni also studied under the guidance of Qazi Abul Ma'ali, with Naqib Khan as his classmate.[3] Naqib Khan was later to become an important noble in the imperial court under Akbar and Jahangir.

In the scattered references to the events of his life, Badauni leaves the impression that he was eager to converse with the most prominent theologians and scholars of his day and gather knowledge from them. In the third volume of his *Muntakhab* he writes that he actually had either visited or at least seen from a distance most of the learned men and Shaikhs of his age.[4]

In this there is little reason to disbelieve him. That he was well versed in the traditional sciences is proved by him in his numerous discussions with various persons,[5] as also by the fact that immediately on his introduction to the court he was able to vanquish in argument the Ulema "who beat the drums of their profundity."[6] His general acquaintance with orthodox Islamic literature is beyond doubt.[7]

[1]*Ibid.*, p. 75.

[2]*Ibid.*, p. 74 where he says, "A scholar of his general attainment is not to be seen. It is a pity that his avaricious love of the world and glory in the garb of holy poverty left no room for reconciliation with the Faith."

[3]*Ibid.*, Vol II, pp 30-31, 49.

[4]*Ibid.*; Vol. III, p. 157. Of the 38 Shaikhs of whom he writes biographical sketches in Vol. III, he had visited 26. Four of them he says he had never seen. Two he had seen only from a distance. About the rest he says nothing.

[5]*Ibid.*, Vol. II, pp. 216, 259, 262; Vol. III, pp. 14-15, 21, 50-51, 67-68, 71, 82-83, 121-125, 161-162.

[6]*Ibid.*, Vol. II, p. 172.

[7]Ranking believes that Badauni was not so thoroughly conversant even with the Quran, for at least twice he misquotes it, Ranking, *Muntakhab-ut-Tawarikh*, Vol. I, Bib. Ind. (*tr.*), p. 5, fn. Being ignorant of Arabic I cannot vouchsafe for Badauni's knowledge of the Quran. It is however possible that

However, Badauni does not tell us whence he acquired proficiency in other forms of intellectual and cultural activity which, if not strictly unlawful, was at least undesirable for a man of orthodox virtues. It is from Faizi that we learn that Badauni possessed this proficiency to a degree at least worth mentioning, probably more. "Mulla Abdul Qadir," he says, "has much aptitude and has studied those traditional sciences which the Mullas of Hindustan study . . . . In addition to his accomplishment in learning, he has an inclination towards poetry and taste in prose composition both Arabic[1] and Persian. He is also acquainted with Indian astrology and mathematics. He has knowledge of Indian and Persian music and is not ignorant of chess, both two-handed and four-handed. He has also made commendable practice on the *bin*."[2] Faizi's testimony is fully corroborated by the author of *Mirat-ul-Alam*: "Mulla Abdul Qadir Badauni was learned both in traditional and rational sciences. Along with learning he possessed to a degree of perfection skill in poetry, taste in Arabic and Persian prose-writing, knowledge of astrology and mathematics and acquaintance with Arabic and Persian music."[3]

In his *Muntakhab*, Badauni avoids making any reference to his knowledge of the rational sciences and music. It is unfortunate that he should have been so convinced of the antagonism between the "rational" and the "traditional" sciences that he had to try to suppress one part of his attainments in order to highlight the other. This attitude is clearly reflected in his writings, as we shall see later.

By 1562-63, when Badauni's formal education seems to have been

---

Badauni may have made some minor errors in quoting the Quran just by chance or oversight, or that the errors may have crept into the book at the hands of some copyists. Badauni, after all, was an imam, *Muntakhab*, Vol. II, pp. 226-227.

[1]Badauni's proficiency in the Arabic language is also attested to by the letter he wrote to Shaikh Salim Chishti, which he copies in the *Muntakhab*, Vol. III, pp. 12-14. Wolseley Haig remarks that the letter is more important for its style than substance, *Muntakhab*, Vol. III, (*tr.*), Bib. Ind., p. 22. Badauni also wrote verses in Arabic which he quotes in the *Muntakhab*, Vol. III, p. 145.

[2]Faizi's petition to Akbar interceding for Badauni's rehabilitation after his madad-i-ma'asli land had been resumed, *ibid* , p. 304.

[3]Bakhtawar Khan, *op. cit.*, f. 185 b.

completed, for he is silent about it thereafter, he also found himself at the head of his family. His father, Muluk Shah, had died a year earlier (in 1562).[1] Badauni's relations with his father appear to have been rather formal. In his not too-frequent references to him, Badauni is respectful, but he does not seem to have been greatly impressed by his learning; nor does he make references, usual in such cases, of great affection between them. He barely mentions the event of his death and states that he had the body buried at Bhusawar. However, Badauni, more out of courtesy perhaps, coins the chronogram of his death in the words, "A World of Learning."

Muluk Shah was followed by Makhdum Ashraf, the author's grandfather, whose death occurred in 1563 at Bhusawar.[2] Badauni learnt of it at Sahaswan (a town in western UP), and felt greatly distressed. The year 1563-64 must have been particularly hard on our author, for his "usually placid heart" begins to feel a strain.[3]

Badauni does not explain the circumstances that attended this strain. It may have been because suddenly he found himself faced with the responsibility of supporting his family with no definite source of income. He had his mother and younger brother, Shaikh Muhammad, to support. He might also have been married by then. Of this we cannot be sure, for Badauni mentions only his second wedding which took place in 1567.[4] His relations with his first wife were probably not quite to his satisfaction, which may explain the omission of any reference to her. Also, on the occasion of his second wedding, he quotes the Quran, "And verily the Future for thee is better than the Present" to mean that his second wife was better than the first.[5]

The chronogram of this second wedding is, "Conjunction of the Sun and the Moon."[6]

Badauni does not mention any source of his income except his service, first with Husain Khan, a noble who ultimately attained the

[1]*Muntakhab*, Vol. II, p. 53.
[2]*Ibid.*, p. 64.
[3]*Ibid.*, pp. 64-65.
[4]*Ibid.*, p. 105.
[5]Lowe, *Muntakhab-ut-Tawarikh*, Vol. II (*tr.*), Bib. Ind., p. 108.
[6]Badauni, *op. cit.*, Vol. II, p. 105.

mansab of 3000,[1] and later with the Emperor himself.

In 1565 our author moved from Badaun to Patiali.[2] He must have gone there in search of employment, for immediately afterwards we find him in the service of Husain Khan, jagirdar of Patiali and Shamsabad. Badauni must have been quite satisfied with this service, for, he says, any idea of leaving Husain Khan's company for another's made no appeal to him.[3]

Badauni praises Husain Khan for his orthodoxy. He was generous, true to the Faith, with the disposition of a darvesh. He had ordered the Hindu inhabitants of his jagir to wear a patch of cloth on their dress to distinguish themselves from Muslims. This had earned him the nickname of "Tukria" (the Patcher).[4] Constantly engaged in wars, mostly against Hindu chiefs and zamindars, he distributed the spoils among the poor and himself remained detached to money.[5] He died in debt of a lakh and a half of rupees, for which none of his creditors brought a suit out of deference to his memory.[6]

Badauni accompanied Husain Khan wherever his jagir was transferred—to Lucknow,[7] to Kant-&-Golah[8] and to Punjab (on an expedition).[9]

Before joining Husain Khan at Kant-&-Golah, our author took leave of him in 1569, and went to Badaun where he got his younger brother, Shaikh Muhammad, married.[10] Badauni was extremely fond of his brother for his learning and his courteous manners. But within three months of his marriage, Shaikh Muhammad passed away, followed soon after by Badauni's own first child, a son, "the pupil of my eyes. And I who was the prince of the age became at one stroke the pauper of the city."[11] Badauni

[1]Abul Fazl, *Ain*, Vol. I (*tr.*), p. 402.
[2]Badauni, *op. cit.*, Vol. II, p. 87.
[3]*Ibid.*
[4]*Ibid.*, p. 223.
[5]*Ibid.*, p. 225.
[6]*Ibid.*, p. 226.
[7]*Ibid.*, p. 124.
[8]*Ibid.*, p. 136. Kant-&-Golah was a very large paragana in Rohilkhand.
[9]*Ibid.*, Vol. III, p. 34.
[10]*Ibid.*, Vol. II, p. 126.
[11]*Ibid.*, p. 127.

expresses his anguish in a touching, pathetic marsia (elegy) which he has included in the book.[1]

In 1571, Badauni rejoined Husain Khan at Kant-&-Golah, and became the Sadr of his jagir,[2] which office he held till his separation from his patron in 1573-74. For nine years Badauni had enjoyed the patronage of Husain Khan, which had given him material stability but had also made him intellectually inert. During these years Badauni seldom expresses his disgust with the world, as he does later on, nor does he feel distressed in his personal life (except in consequence of the tragic death of his brother and his infant son). Yet he is not able to make any progress in creative intellectual activity. Nor does he feel the desire to. In Husain Khan's service Badauni perhaps found neither the stimulus of discussion nor the challenge of a contrary view which seem to have been so necessary for the activization of his genius.

At any rate, late in 1574, Badauni, for reasons unexplained, forfeited the patronage of Husain Khan.[3] That the estrangement of Husain Khan from our author must have been on account of some grave personal default of the latter seems certain, for besides laying the blame for this at the door of the heavens, Badauni is reticent in explaining the reason. Badauni also tried to plead with Husain Khan and secured the intercession of a few persons including his mother's.[4]

These efforts having proved vain, Badauni reached Agra where he was introduced to the Emperor by Jalal Khan Qurchi—a mansabdar of 500[5] and Akbar's personal friend[6]—and Hakim Ain-ul-Mulk, a court physician.[7] Jalal Khan recommended him to Akbar with the words, "I have discovered an Imam for Your Majesty whom you will be pleased with."[8]

[1]*Ibid.*, pp. 127-132.

[2]*Ibid.*, p. 136.

[3]*Ibid.*, pp. 87, 172.

[4]*Ibid.*, p. 87.

[5]Abul Fazl, *Ain*, Vol. I (*tr.*), p. 531.

[6]Badauni, Vol. II, *op. cit.*, pp. 172, 186. Abul Fazl calls him Akbar's nadim, *AN*, Vol. II, p. 271.

[7]Badauni, *Muntakhab*, Vol. III, pp. 164-165.

[8]*Ibid.*, p. 304.

Akbar, at this time, was engaged in his struggle against the supremacy of the Ulema. While it had been possible for the Emperor to overcome the challenge of Bairam Khan and of the Mughal nobles by force of arms, the power of the Ulema was more entrenched, based as it was on a long-established tradition. Shaikh Abd-un-Nabi, who, being the Sadr, was at the head of this group, enjoyed such absolute control over the grant of the madad-i-ma'ash as had not been enjoyed by any Sadr during the reign of any other ruler, so Badauni tells us.[1] Indeed, so formidable was his command that the Emperor himself, the imperial harem and a sizable section of opinion at the court dared not challenge him. It was when the Shaikh crossed the limits and confronted Akbar with an insulting challenge that Akbar decided to act—at the instigation of some of his courtiers—to suppress the Ulema.[2]

Akbar proceeded cautiously and gradually. He must have been aware of the dissensions with which the monolith was rent.[3] The two scions of this orthodox section, Shaikh Abd-un-Nabi and Makhdum-ul-Mulk, were "at loggerheads with each other, and had been responsible for the fall of people's faith in the scholars, past and present, amounting to a disinclination towards the Religion itself."[4] Akbar might have felt it politic, therefore, to further intensify these dissensions, thereby weakening the whole group and ultimately subjugating it to imperial authority.

Badauni could be of great use to Akbar, young and scathing

[1] *Ibid.*, p. 80.

[2] *Ibid.*, pp. 80-83. Badauni relates the story of a Brahman against whom the Qazi of Mathura preferred a charge before the Sadr that he had taken away the material of a mosque the Qazi was building, and had used it for a temple, and had uttered undignified words for the Prophet. The Sadr sentenced the Brahman to death in the teeth of opposition from Akbar, his harem and the Rajput nobles. Badauni traces the beginning of the fall of Saikh Abd-un-Nabi to this incident. It is significant that Akbar allows himself to be persuaded to deal with the "mullas" as such and not any particular mulla.

The *Zakhirat-ul-Khawanin* tells us how Akbar was once publicly bastinadoed by Shaikh Abd-un-Nabi for wearing a saffron coloured dress which was unlawful. All Akbar could do was to complain to his mother about the insult, Farid Bhakkari, *op. cit.*, p. 69.

[3] Badauni *op. cit.*, Vol. II, pp. 202-203, 255, 259.

[4] *Ibid.*, p. 267

critic that he was.[1] Immediately on his introduction to the court, he was encouraged to engage in discussions with the Ulema.[2] Akbar observed him keenly and was pleased to find him fit to encounter Haji Ibrahim Sirhindi.[3] "His Majesty desired that I should join the (imperial) service." Orders to that effect were issued.[4] From then onwards Badauni assumed an increasingly important role in these discussions until Akbar's design had materialized.

Badauni claims to have registered immediate victories in arguments with the Ulema.[5] It is these victories which later on became the cause of his disgrace. It is difficult to ascertain Badauni's ideological alignment. He considers Makhdum-ul-Mulk extremely bigoted.[6] For Shaikh Abd-un-Nabi he has many nasty words to spare.[7] He accuses them both of creating doubt in people's minds regarding the prophets and imams.[8] Sufism he holds in utter contempt,[9] though he may have respect for individual Sufis. Shias and Hindus—heretics and infidels, of course—he could not even barely tolerate.[10] And certainly, he was no partisan of the "liberalism" of Shaikh Mubarak and his sons. It is interesting that with Abul Fazl he shared great scorn for the Ulema; and with the Ulema—with Makhdum-ul-Mulk to be precise—he shared the hatred for Abul Fazl.[11]

Badauni's hostility to every prevalent opinion may have enhan-

[1]*Ibid.*, pp. 172-173.
[2]*Ibid.*, p. 172.
[3]*Ibid.*, pp. 172-173.
[4]*Ibid.*, p. 173.
[5]*Ibid.*, p. 172.
[6]*Ibid.*, Vol. III, p. 70.
[7]*Ibid.*, Vol. II, pp. 204-205.
[8]*Ibid.*, p. 273.

[9]The main Sufi doctrine of *Wahdat-ul-Wujud* is termed by Badauni "an engagement in falsehood which ultimately leads to license and open heresy," *ibid.*, p. 258. At another place he says, "In truth these wretched assemblies and the distressed condition (of the Sufis) and those hideous deeds, absurd ceremonies and those hypocritical Sufis—most of them are worthy of destruction," p. 279. *Muntakhab*, indeed, is full of such remarks.

[10]For two individual Shias, Badauni is full of praise—Bairam Khan and Nurullah Shustari, *ibid.*, Vol. III, pp. 190-192 and 137 respectively.

[11]Badauni on Abul Fazl, "The man who set the world in flames," *ibid.*, Vol. II, p. 198; Makhdum-ul-Mulk on Abul Fazl, "What injury will this man not cause to the Faith," *ibid.*, Vol. III, p. 72.

ced his value for Akbar. But his usefulness to Akbar could only be negative—he attacked everything without suggesting an alternative anywhere—whereas Akbar sought to rebuild an institutional framework within which the Ulema would be subject to his command. It was too late when Badauni realized this. He had himself helped Akbar to undermine orthodox Sunni opinion in the court—the opinion to which his own thinking could *broadly* be assigned. It was all running as if to a well calculated plan. He could not prevent the Emperor from implementing the latter part of it when the former had been so successfully carried through.

In a way it was Badauni's negative "independence" from all fixed opinions that helped him retain at least his source of income though in a remote corner he felt intellectually and emotionally frustrated.

Badauni had been appointed the imam for prayers on Wednesdays on account of his sweet voice.[1] And on his own choice he was given 1,000 bighas of land in madad-i-ma'ash instead of direct military service, contrary to the offer of the Emperor and the advice of his old well wisher Mir Syed Muhammad Mir-i-Adl [2]

Later on Badauni felt sorry for having made this choice. The reason for this is not clear. One thousand bighas could not have been a meagre source of livelihood for his small family. This, in fact, was the highest ever granted in charity till then.[3] In addition, Badauni was occasionally given handsome presents by the Emperor.[4] Indeed, it may easily be assumed that Badauni's total income must have been much larger now in the service of the Emperor than it was in the service of one of the Emperor's nobles. Yet, while Badauni felt no distress on this score when he was in Husain Khan's jagir, he complains against his condition in the service of the Emperor.

Badauni, in fact, views himself in relation to the steep rise of Abul Fazl in Akbar's favour, and his consequent material advance. Abul Fazl had, within a short space of time, followed Badauni to the court.[5] Akbar initially gave them both the same mansab of 20.

[1] *Ibid.*, Vol. II, pp. 226-227.
[2] *Ibid.*, pp. 206-207; Vol. III, pp. 75-76.
[3] *Ibid.*, Vol. II, pp. 206-207.
[4] *Ibid.*, pp. 229, 236, 368, 402; Bakhtawar Khan, *op. cit.*, f.185b.
[5] *Muntakhab*, Vol. II, pp. 172-173.

While Abul Fazl, on account of his "diligence, ingenuity and manoeuvring" ultimately attained the mansab of 2000 (up to the time Badauni was writing his *Muntakhab*), our author, due to his "innocence and inexperience," remained stuck at the initial rank.[1] It pained Badauni to reflect that the one man who had no merit of his own, who passed off his father's writings as his own,[2] and who was essentially dishonest even in his loyalty to Akbar,[3] held an office a hundred times superior to Badauni's own. It is significant that Badauni complains against his material circumstances immediately following such reflection.[4] It is therefore perhaps more out of jealousy of Abul Fazl than out of his own poverty, that "I saw what I saw and suffered what I suffered."[5]

In 1576 Badauni suddenly developed a strong desire to participate in a holy war. He persuaded the Emperor to allow him to join an expedition against Rana Kika (Rana Pratap).[6] The leader of this expedition happened to be an infidel, Raja Man Singh. But our author was ingenious enough to circumvent the dilemma—first, Man Singh was leading the armies to a Dar-ul-Harb[7]; secondly, what concern did Badauni have with Man Singh himself? They were all going on behalf of a Muslim Emperor. And, after all, what was important was the propriety of intentions.[8] In utter earnest Mulla Abdul Qadir joined the jehad. Man Singh fully reciprocated the Emperor's sense of humour in granting this permission to his imam by sending the letter of victory through Badauni's hands.[9] On Badauni's reaching the court with the letter, Akbar had a dig at him,[10] though he gave him 96 ashrafis as gift.

[1]*Ibid.*, p. 206.

[2]*Ibid.*, p. 198. At another place he says that Akbar entrusted Abul Fazl with the work of translating the *Hayat-ul-Haiwan* and Shaikh Mubarak translated it, *ibid.*, p. 204.

[3]*Ibid.*, p. 263.

[4]*Ibid*, pp. 206-207.

[5]*Ibid.*, Vol. III, p. 76.

[6]*Ibid.*, Vol. II, pp. 228-229.

[7]*Ibid.*, p. 228.

[8]*Ibid.*, p. 229.

[9]*Ibid.*, pp. 235-236.

[10]*Ibid*, pp. 236-237. Akbar jocularly asked Badauni to tell the truth as to which side he was on in the war, and whether he was barehanded or equipped

In 1577 Akbar allowed several courtiers to go on Haj. Badauni also sought leave to go. Shaikh Abd-un-Nabi made the permission conditional on the express consent of Badauni's mother who had no one else to stand by her. The mother could not give her consent and our author's wish remained unfulfilled.[1]

At this time Badauni received the news of the birth of a son, on whom the Emperor bestowed the name Abdul Hadi. Unfortunately the child died within six months of his birth. Badauni nearly holds Akbar responsible for his son's death—the bestowal of the name Abdul Hadi being the cause of it.[2] Some time later he had his third son. Badauni took no risk this time and named him Mohi-ud-din straightaway without consulting the Emperor.[3]

By 1578-79 the situation at the court had altered too radically for Badauni's liking. Up to this time, "His Majesty was genuinely seeking after the Truth. But doubts had been planted in his mind so that within five or six years Islam had all but disappeared."[4]

The discussions in the Ibadat Khana proceeded on lines Badauni had not anticipated. The participants now included learned men from various places professing various religions, and much common ground was being discovered among all religions. How was it necessary, then, that Islam, which was comparatively of recent birth, should claim pre-eminence at the expense of other religions? The Emperor "laid aside the doctrines of Resurrection and Judgment.. . .He became particularly convinced of the theory of metampshychosis."[5]

The ultimate result of this process, which had been started at the Emperor's initiative, was the eclipse of the chief Ulema, even their banishment, and subordination of the entire group to Akbar's authority. This latter end was achieved when the principle Ulema signed the Mahzar which made Akbar practically the arbiter in

---

with weapons. Replied the author, "I tremble even in telling the truth to Your Majesty, how can I tell a lie?" and related to him whatever had happened.

[1]*Ibid.*, p. 251.

[2]*Ibid.*, p. 252.

[3]*Ibid.*, p. 267.

[4]*Ibid.*, p. 255.

[5]*Ibid.*, pp. 255-264; *Dabistan-i-Mazahib*, pp. 323-326. The *Dabistan's* account of the developments of this period appears to be based mainly on Badauni himself.

theological and juridical disputes.[1]

At this point, says Badauni, "I read the Verse of Flight and fell out of the Emperor's favour. All that intimacy (now) turned into estrangement. I did not consider myself a fit recipient of His Majesty's favour, nor His Majesty worthy of my services . . . . And once in a while I used to go and prostrate myself from the line of the shoes and was a witness (to the truth of):

Companionship will not be
Unless dispositions are congenial."[2]

Badauni's "flight" may have been voluntary. At the same time the mulla in Abdul Qadir was of no more use to the Emperor either.

Yet Badauni could not give up the imperial service for reasons of sheer subsistence. Nor did Akbar throw him out. There was another branch of intellectual activity in which he could prove his worth—translation. Unfortunately Akbar showed supreme indifference to Badauni's religious susceptibilities, thrusting on him successively the task of translating the holy books of the infidels. Badauni feels disgusted with his new assignment. His desire to escape becomes more urgent; but there was no escape for him.

Badauni therefore translates them grudgingly, aware of the sinfulness of his undertaking, trying to convince himself that "relating the words of the infidels is not infidelity."[3] At the same time there was one place where he could give vent to his wrath in secrecy—the *Muntakhab-ut-Tawarikh.* From now onwards Badauni begins to view everything with contempt and bitterness and expresses himself in a language at times verging on obscenity.

Between the compulsion of service and the desire to escape, Badauni found a *via media:* He began frequently to absent himself from court. In 1579 he did so on the facetious plea that he considered himself among the forgotten ones of the court.[4] He nearly

[1]Badauni, *op. cit.*, Vol. II, pp. 270-272. Badauni remarks that this document raised the Imam-i-Adil "absolutely" above the Mujtahid, *ibid.*, p. 270.

[2]*Ibid.*, pp. 263-264.

[3]*Ibid.*, p. 366. At another place Badauni states that he wrote the *Muntakhab* as a penance for the writings he had been compelled to undertake, Vol. III, p. 394.

[4]*Ibid.*, Vol. II, pp. 275-276.

lost half his madad-i-ma'ash land in punishment; he was able to save it only on the intercession of Ghazi Khan Badakhshi and other courtiers.

Two years later he repeated the offence and overstayed his leave from the court. He had been granted leave for five months; he spent a full year at Bhusawar admiring the beauty of his "beloved," a young boy, Mazhar by name,[1] while his friend, Nizam-ud-din Ahmad, reported him sick to the Emperor.[2] Akbar may have believed the report of his sickness, for Badauni does not mention any punishment or even a warning.

The year 1588-89 was spent by him on leave.[3] He had wished to visit Nizam-ud-din Ahmad in Gujarat but was prevented by his "circumstances."

A second repetition of the offence of overstaying his leave in 1591-92 infuriated Akbar beyond repair. Badauni advanced the pretext of sickness. He might have been sick, but advancing the same pretext on more than one occasion had forfeited its credibility. Akbar cancelled his madad-i-ma'ash, despite all efforts of Abul Fazl and Nizam-ud-din Ahmad to conciliate him.[4]

This was the last straw for our author. Hurriedly he presented himself at the court, where he was deprived of attendance.[5] He was now out of his wits. He felt terribly aggrieved and to console himself kept reading the *Hisn-i-Hasin* (a prayer book) and repeating the *Qasidah-i-Burdah* every day, simultaneously trying to secure intercession with the Emperor. He kept "running about in Prince Daniyal's camp" which Akbar had left behind on the eve of his departure for Kashmir. He also approached Faizi, whom he maligns so much "in the interest of the Faith."[6] Faizi obliged him by writing "a model of a letter of recommendation"[7] to Akbar. Badauni, however, had been rehabilitated by the Emperor a little

[1] *Ibid.*, pp. 296, 297-298.

[2] *Ibid.*, pp. 296-297. He had been introduced to Nizam-ud-din only a year earlier.

[3] *Ibid.*, p. 368.

[4] *Ibid.*, pp. 383-384.

[5] *Ibid.*, p. 383.

[6] *Ibid.*, Vol. III, p. 305.

[7] *Ibid.*, pp. 303-305.

earlier than the receipt of this letter.

By then Badauni must have persuaded himself that it was prudent to adopt the ways of the world, like other men, and perform the sijdah before the Emperor.[1] He makes some cryptic remarks about himself wherein he talks of repentance. The chronogram of this repentance is "Rectitude."[2] Shaikh Faizi also composed a verse to commend Badauni's rectitude.

*

The grimness of Badauni's view of his life may appear rather morbid to us. But then, in not a very long span of life, he had witnessed many horrors and was the victim of many a personal tragedy. At the impressionable age of fourteen, he saw the devastations of war[3] and the desolation caused by famine when men ate their fellow men.[4] Of his own family he had laid at least seven members in the grave—his father, maternal grandfather, two sons, only daughter,[5] younger (and probably the only) brother and his mother.[6] Added to this was the death of the one man he had always looked upon as his most trustworthy friend and benefactor—Nizam-ud-din Ahmad.[7] On his death, says Badauni, "I decided never to get attached to another mortal being."[8]

However, these grim memories of Badauni's life were relieved by his sense of humour, and his occasional involvement in romantic escapades. His humour was generally caustic, but at times was delightfully innocent. His remarks on a physician, Saif-ul-Muluk, for instance, are devastating but subtle and light.[9] "It was one of the coincidences," he says, "that whenever this hakim went to attend on a patient, that unfortunate one surrendered his life to the messenger of death . . . . The following verses which have been

[1]Once Badauni had annoyed Akbar by refusing to prostrate himself before him, *ibid.*, Vol. II, p. 376. On p. 402, however, he states that he did perform the sijdah before him.

[2]*Ibid.*, pp. 395-396.

[3]*Ibid.*, Vol. I, p. 425.

[4]*Ibid.*, pp. 428-429.

[5]*Ibid.*, Vol. III, p. 39. Reference to the others has been made earlier.

[6]*Ibid.*, Vol. II, p. 376.

[7]*Ibid.*, pp. 396-398.

[8]*Ibid.*, p. 397.

[9]*Ibid.*, Vol. III, pp. 162-164.

composed in regard to Jalal, the physician, were as well applicable to him:

> *The Angel of Death last night complained to God*
> *regarding Jalal, the physician*
> *'Thy slave is helpless before the physician,*
> *Where I kill one, he kills a hundred,*
> *Either depose him from his office*
> *Or assign to me some other job'."*

Of his "affairs" Badauni confesses two—both with young boys. One of these occurred in a sacred shrine. Our author, who had become the Sadr of Husain Khan's jagir at Kant-&-Golah, visited the shrine of Shah Madar at Makanpur. Within the premises, he was suddenly overcome by passion for a young boy whose name he does not disclose. Badauni was caught by the relatives of the "beloved" and was belaboured rather harshly. He repents and praises God for having punished him for the impropriety and takes an oath of performing the "pilgrimage of Islam" (haj) on getting well,[1] a promise he was never able to fulfil.

A few years later, however, Badauni found himself so enamoured of another "beloved" that he overstayed his leave from the court.[2] He remained indifferent to the repeated reminders of his friends about his obligation as a servant of the Emperor and felt defiant and reckless. Seventeen years after he had met Mazhar, this lad, he still remembered the delight with a nostalgic longing: "Would that I had departed from the world during those moments, bare-headed and bare-footed and been relieved of the pains of separation."[3]

While hatred was Badauni's predominant passion, he responded equally to the finer human emotions. His concern for the romance of Shaikh Musa and Mohini was subtle and indirect in that, as he describes the story of this tragic love, he feels involved in it. All of a sudden his language assumes delicate form and flows uninter-

[1] *Ibid.*, Vol. II, pp. 136-138.
[2] *Ibid*, pp. 296-297.
[3] *Ibid.*, pp. 297-298.

rupted, with charming similes and metaphors.[1] Badauni confesses to this change in the language and obviously enjoys it. In a world which to him looked dismal, these were small mercies of which he made the most.

But in the final analysis it was Badauni's intense zeal for the Faith, as he understood it, that became the cause of his disillusionment. In what he thought was his zeal for the Faith, he adopted very rigid and orthodox attitudes in a period of turmoil, when conditions were moving towards a new flexibility, towards more liberal thinking. Badauni had entered the court with great enthusiasm; his immediate "victories" must have enhanced his confidence in himself. But he soon discovered that he and his thinking were a complete anachronism in the emerging set-up. Outwardly, by carrying out the Emperor's orders and by even performing the sijdah before him, he might appear to have compromised with these conditions. But—and to this extent he was being honest to himself—somewhere in the inner recesses of his heart, he refused to compromise. The dilemma before Badauni was nonetheless cruel for that it was of his own making. But somehow he went on performing his dual role, that of the courtier and the mulla.

It is significant that Badauni's orthodoxy is not directed against only the religious reforms of Akbar; it is all-pervading. He opposes not only Akbar's social reforms—from fixing the age for marriage[2] to the establishment of poor-houses[3]—but also the most important administrative measures—the branding of horses[4] and the mansabdari system.[5] He ridicules Akbar's views on language[6]; but he was especially hostile to the attempts to bring under the Emperor's supervision the grant of the aimah lands.[7]

For Badauni, the only means available for registering his protest

[1] *Ibid.*, pp. 109-118. "He threw a lasso strong as the covenant of the upright and the oath of the youth"; or, "She went with her lover as moonlight (goes) with the moon and shadow with the person"; or, "From that place they hurried off borrowing swiftness from the wind and speed from the water," etc.

[2] *Ibid.*, p. 305.

[3] *Ibid.*, p. 324.

[4] *Ibid.*, pp. 190-191, 218-219.

[5] *Ibid.*, pp. 189-190.

[6] *Ibid.*, p. 307.

[7] *Ibid.*, pp. 274-275.

was to write the*Muntakhab*. But occasionally he seems to appreciate more violent means of overcoming his opponents—physical annihilation. Faulad Khan Birlas, who assassinated Mulla Ahmed of Thatta, is made by our author into a hero, a martyr.[1]

Badauni often alleges that the Emperor had contracted certain rigid notions in his mind and would not listen to anything except what was derogatory to Islam.[2] It is difficult to vouchsafe for Badauni's veracity on most of the details he supplies. According to him, Akbar subjected Islam to a rational scrutiny along with other religions and accepted from each whatever he considerd were its best elements.[3] This had followed discussions at the court among the spokesmen of various religions. It is Badauni, on the other hand who refuses to discuss, for "it is well-known how little chance one has to adduce proofs before a man who is determined to reject them, and particularly when one's opponent can inflict upon one his wrath. Equality (of positions) is a condition of a debate."[4]

Very few of the collective discussions to which our author's contribution could be ascertained have been reproduced even in the *Muntakhab*, and these generally relate to some minor technicalities.[5] On a general, intellectual plane, Badauni only attacks his adversaries and ridicules their "innovations" and "heresies." He does not argue with them because they had all fallen from the Faith and had sold themselves to the Emperor for cheap worldly advantage.[6] It is impossible for Badauni to believe that one could disagree with him and yet be honest. For Truth for Badauni was absolute and this Absolute Truth was as Badauni understood it.

This logic lands our author into very unhappy dilemmas. He mentions, for instance, the sympathy and assistance he had received from Faizi.[7] Yet he maligns him, in fact hates him to the core of his heart. Perhaps Badauni feels guilty of insulting a man, particularly after his death, who had been so kind to him. "But

[1] *Ibid.*, p. 364.
[2] *Ibid.*, pp. 255-256, 259, 302, 307, 400.
[3] *Ibid.*, p. 256.
[4] *Ibid.*, p. 307.
[5] *Ibid.*, pp. 216, 259, 262-263.
[6] *Ibid.*, p. 269.
[7] *Ibid.*, Vol. III, p. 303.

what should I do? The claims of the Faith and of loyalty (to God) are greater than these claims (of courtesy and gratitude)."[1]

It is unfortunate that to Badauni's mind ordinary human courtesy and loyalty to the Faith were mutually exclusive phenomena in which he naively preferred one to the other. This attitude wrecked his nerves and wrought his disillusionment when he found his opponents riding the crest of hope and progress.

*

The versatility of Badauni's talent is attested to by the long list of his works on a variety of subjects.

The first work our author undertook at Akbar's command was a Persian translation of the *Singhasan Battisi*, a collection of thirty-two stories concerning Raja Bikramajit (Vikramaditya) of Malwa.[2] A learned Brahman was appointed to interpret the book to Badauni who, in turn, was to translate at least one page every day and present it to Akbar. Badauni began working on the project in 1574 and finished it in 1581-82. The translation was entitled *Nama-i-Khirad-Afza*.

Before this book was finished, Badauni had been asked to undertake the translation of the *Atharva Veda*.[3] Because the book was a difficult one and the assistance available to him incompetent, he gave up.

The *Kitab-ul-Ahadis* was the first original work that Badauni had actually completed; he presented it to Akbar in the year 1578.[4] It contains 40 hadises concerning the merit of waging holy wars and the advantage of archery. The book has most likely been lost to us.

In 1582, Akbar issued command for the writing of the *Tarikh-i-Alfi*.[5] This was to be a comprehensive history of the first millennium of Islam, then drawing to a close. The account of the first thirty-five years of Islam was to be written collectively by seven persons—Naqib Khan, Shah Fathullah, Hakim Humam, Hakim Ali, Haji Ibrahim Sirhindi, Nizam-ud-din Ahmad and Abdul Qadir Badauni.[6]

[1] *Ibid.*, p. 305.
[2] *Ibid.*, Vol. II, pp. 183-184.
[3] *Ibid.*, pp. 212-213.
[4] *Ibid.*, pp. 254-255.
[5] *Ibid.*, pp. 301, 318
[6] *Ibid.*, p. 318.

From the thirty-sixth year, the account was to be completed by Mulla Ahmed of Thatta. The Mulla brought the account up to the time of Changez Khan when he was assassinated by Mirza Faulad Birlas. The rest of the work was brought up to the year 1588-89 by Asaf Khan. In 1591, which marked the completion of a thousand years of Islam, Badauni was asked to revise the work and collate it with other histories.[1] He however confined himself to the correction of the arrangement of dates, etc., and that in the first two parts only. The third he entrusted to Asaf Khan, who, in fact, was its author.

Badauni had also been commanded to undertake a Persian translation of part of the *Mahabharata* and the whole of *Ramayana* in 1582 and 1583 respectively.[2] Our author abhorred the work, but had to do it nevertheless. The *Ramayana* he particularly disliked for all its "nonsensical tales." He translated it first into 70 parts and later into 120 parts, apparently abridging the book in the process rather than translating the whole of it. However, Akbar was pleased with the translation and suggested that Badauni, as its author, should write a Preface to it. Akbar was being too uncharitable to him, for Mulla Abdul Qadir would have had to write a Preface without the usual praise of God and the Prophet. He therefore quietly let the suggestion pass.[3] At any rate, he received from the Emperor a shawl, a horse and some cash in reward.[4]

The translation of the *Mahabharata*, which was named *Razm Nama*, nearly got our author into difficulties.[5] He had translated a certain passage from it wherein the counsels of a dying man (Bhishm?) are related and man is exhorted to forsake the path of ignorance and vice and take that of knowledge and virtue.

To the translation of this passage Badauni added a hemistich:

[1] *Ibid.*, p. 319.

[2] *Ibid.*, pp. 319-320 and 336-337 respectively. Abul Fazl, however, states that the *Ramayana*, just as the *Mahabharata*, was translated by Naqib Khan, Badauni and Shaikh Sultan Thanesari, *Ain*, Vol. I, p. 115.

[3] *Muntakhab*, p. 366. The work was finished in 1589.

[4] *Ibid.*, p. 368. Bakhtawar Khan says Badauni received 150 ashrafis and 10,000 black tankas in reward, *op. cit.*, f.185b.

[5] Badauni, *op. cit.*, Vol. II, pp. 399-400. The date of its completion is not mentioned.

Every action has its reward
And every deed its recompense.[1]

Akbar understood this hemistich to mean a reference to Munkir and Nakir, the Resurrection and the Last Judgment, etc., which, alleges the author, were contrary to his own notions of metempsychosis. Akbar therefore charged the author with bigotry and fanaticism in the presence of Abul Fazl. Badauni's explanation, that belief in the recompense of every action of every individual was a tenet of the religion of the Hindus, seems to have been accepted, for he remarks, "this affair passed off well."[2]

A minor job for our author was the rewriting, in an easy style, of the Persian translation of a history of Kashmir.[3] The earlier translation was by Mulla Shah Muhammad Shahabadi. Badauni finished the work in two months in 1591.[4] The book was placed in the imperial library and was read as a model (of translation?), so claims Badauni.

Soon after, Badauni translated part of the *Muajam-ul-Buldan*, a geographical dictionary, from Arabic to Persian [5] This he did in one month.

The translation of the *Jami-i-Rashidi* came as a blessing to Badauni.[6] The project was suggested to Akbar at the time when our author had fallen out of his favour and had been deprived of his madad-i-ma'ash land. Nizam-ud-din Ahmed mentioned Badauni's name in connection with the work. Orders for his attendance were issued. He was asked to make an epitome of the book under the supervision of Abul Fazl.[7] The condition attached may have been considered by Badauni his ultimate humiliation. But he did not express his feelings; he could not.

[1] *Ibid.*, p. 399.

[2] *Ibid.*, p. 400.

[3] Badauni does not tell us which history it was, but it was the *Raj Tarangini*, Rieu, *op. cit.*, Vol. I, p. 296; Ethe, *op. cit.*, Vol. I, pp. 201-202; Storey, *op. cit.*, Vol. I, p. 438.

[4] Badauni *op. cit.*, Vol. II, p. 374.

[5] *Ibid.*, p. 375.

[6] *Ibid.*, pp. 383-384. This was Rashid-ud-din's *Jami-ut-Tawarikh*, originally written in Arabic.

[7] *Ibid.*, p. 384. The year was 1591-92. Badauni does not tell us when he finished the work.

Perhaps the last of Badauni's works done at Akbar's behest was the completion of the translation of a work of the Hindus, which he does not specify, part of which had already been translated at Sultan Zain-ul-Abidin's instance.[1] Badauni was also asked to revise the already translated version, for its language was out of date and unfamiliar to the average reader.[2] He finished the first part of the work in five months and intended to take barely two or three months to do the second part in 1592-93. The Persian version of this book was called the *Bahr-ul-Ismar*.

Of the works written by Badauni on his own, the first was a treatise on the astrolabe comprising twenty chapters.[3] He showed a part of it to Mir Taqi, son of Farighi Shirazi, a poet of Akbar's court.[4] Nothing else, however, is known about it.

The second was the *Najat-ul-Rashid*.[5]

The third and the last was the *Muntakhab-ut-Tawarikh*. Badauni tells us that he received the stimulus for writing the *Muntakhab* from his re-translation of the history of Kashmir.[6] This work he did in early 1591.[7] Therefore, it would have taken him nearly five years to complete the *Muntakhab* which he finished in 1595-96.[8]

By 1595-96, Badauni seems to have grown weary of life. All that he had cherished had slipped out of his hand with little hope of redemption. He then looked forward to eternal rest, to his watan.[9] For this Badauni did not have to wait long. From all accounts he died in the same year, 1596.[10]

[1] *Ibid.*, pp. 401-402. Lowe suggests this may have been the *Raj Tarangini*, *Muntakhab*, Vol. II, (*tr.*), p. 415 fn.

[2] Badauni, *op. cit.*, Vol. II, pp. 401-402.

[3] *Ibid.*, Vol. III, p. 293.

[4] *Ibid.*, pp. 292-293.

[5] *Najat-ul-Rashid* deals with problems of theology, mysticism, ethics and the propriety of certain ceremonies. It also contains a number of historical anecdotes. The title, read as a chronogram, suggests 1590-91 as the date of its completion.

[6] Badauni, *op. cit.*, Vol. I, p. 5.

[7] *Ibid.*, Vol. II, p. 374.

[8] *Ibid*, pp. 406-407; Vol. III, pp. 398-399. There is a discrepancy of four months in these two references.

[9] *Ibid.*, Vol. II, p. 402; Vol. III, p. 90.

[10] H., Blochmann, "Badaoni and His Works," *J.A.S.B.*, Vol. 38, Part I, 1869, pp. 142-143.

II. TREATMENT OF HISTORY IN THE *MUNTAKHAB-UT-TAWARIKH*

Basic Form

Badauni's *Muntakhab-ut-Tawarikh* is, literally, history written with a vengeance. His disgust with the "heresies" and "innovations" of Akbar's reign, against which he could openly register only limited protest, compelled him to resort to the writing of this book secretly.[1] Here he could record the "true" version of events for the benefit of the virtuous ones among posterity.[2] "I have no other object," he says, "in writing this (book) except (to express) my grief for the Faith and heart-burning for the deceased community of Muslims, which. . .became a nonentity and (still) is so. And to God I look for refuge from reproach, hatred, jealousy and persecution."[3]

From this point of view, Badauni looked back on the past of Islam since the day it had made its appearance in India and from where it was never to disappear until that fateful age of Akbar and our author. It is significant that he does not begin the book with the Muslim conquest of Sind; for, according to him, "Islam could not be stabilized in this region" after the death of Muhammad bin Qasim[4]; on the other hand, since it was "Nasir-ud-din Subuktgin whose son was Sultan Mahmud of Ghazni, who led annual expeditions to India with the intention of waging holy wars, and Lahore became the capital during the reign of his descendants, and moreover (since) Islam was never (thereafter) eliminated from this land," Badauni considers it proper to begin his history with Subuktgin.[5]

One could, perhaps, expect that the first volume of the *Muntakhab*, dealing with the history from Subuktgin to Humayun, would have been written in a manner so as to stand as an embodiment of

[1] *Muntakhab-ut-Tawarikh*, Vol. III, p. 398.
[2] *Ibid.*, pp. 393-394.
[3] *Ibid.*, Vol. II, p. 264.
[4] *Ibid.*, Vol. I, pp. 7-8.
[5] *Ibid.*, p. 8.

the glory of Islam in India in contradistinction to the deliberate annihilation of it during the reign of Akbar, the subject matter of the second volume.

Badauni however does not make it so. For his treatment of history in the first volume is merely formal—he deals mainly with accessions, wars, rebellions and expeditions, etc. of the Sultans. Of these, also, there is hardly an integrated account. If these alone signified the glorification of Islam to our author, there were enough of them during Akbar's reign. Therefore, that which should contradistinguish the period before Akbar's reign from Akbar's reign itself is not established by him.

The very arrangement of Volume I of the *Muntakhab* is suggestive of a formal political history. It is written in the form of reigns, though initially Badauni had, perhaps, decided to break it into dynastic units. After the formal praise of God and the Prophet,[1] he opens the work with an account of the Ghaznavide dynasty[2] and follows it up with that of the Ghori dynasty.[3] For each of these two accounts he uses the word tabqa (section).[4] This word, however, is not used subsequently. He mentions the total length of the rule of the Ghaznavides,[5] but not of any other dynasty. However, even within the accounts of these two dynasties, the basic division is in terms of the reigns of individual rulers.

Badauni does not treat each reign comprehensively. That is, he does not narrate all the known events pertaining to it. In fact, sometimes he would pass off fairly long reigns in a few sentences.[6] The events narrated by him are selective. The basis of his selection of events, however, is not to be looked for in the first, but in the second volume. For, the impulse which made him write the *Muntakhab* was a response to the contemporary circumstances[7]; it was also negative (in that Badauni condemns Akbar's heresies, but

[1] *Ibid*., pp. 1-8.

[2] *Ibid*., pp. 8-46.

[3] *Ibid*., pp. 46-127.

[4] *Ibid*., pp. 8, 46 respectively.

[5] *Ibid*., p. 8.

[6] The six-year reign of Sultan Farrakhzad, grandson of Mahmud Ghaznavi, is given half a page, *ibid*, pp. 34-35; the 16-year reign of Ala-ud-din Masud of the same dynasty is dismissed in one short sentence, p. 38.

[7] *Ibid*, Vol. III, pp. 393-394.

does not suggest any alternative, not even a return to the past);[1] and therefore, while the impulse, born of certain contemporary circumstances, made a "true" record of Akbar's reign his main objective, his negative approach disabled him from placing Akbar and his reign in the perspective of history. Thus, the selection of events in the first volume of the *Muntakhab* is random and haphazard.[2] It does not form either a background or a contrast to Akbar's reign.

Badauni generally adheres to a chronological order in his narration of the selected events, although at times he does transgress the rule. For example, he deals with all the Mughal attacks on India during the reign of Ala-ud-din Khalji at one place,[3] but returns to the narration of the intermediate events immediately after. Or, he places the massacre of the neo-Muslims during the same reign before the expedition to Gujarat.[4] He however realizes that the massacre had followed, and not preceded, the expedition, but places the blame on historians "who have not been particular as to the order (of the occurrences)."[5] The rebellion of Gurshasp, during Muhammad Tughlaq's reign, is placed after his so-called transfer of the capital,[6] this time without an apology.

Badauni generally begins a chapter with the accession of a ruler and ends it with his dethronement or death. At the end of the narrative of events, the length of the reign is stated. It is only rarely that he gives the early life of a Sultan—in the case of Iltutmish, for example[7]—or refers to some events of a ruler's life prior to his accession—Sher Shah in this case.[8]

Of special significance, however, are the lists of the poets of a reign which Badauni appends at the end of each chapter coinciding

[1]This point will be discussed later.

[2]The only incident of Qutb-ud-din Aibak's reign mentioned is his occupation of Ghazni for forty days, *Muntakhab*, Vol. I, p. 55; more pages are devoted to an account of the reign of Kaiqubad than to that of Balban, pp 127-131, 155-157 and 157-165 respectively; at times more pages are given to the poets of a reign than to the account of the reign; Balban's reign is a case in point.

[3]*Ibid.*, pp 183-186.

[4]*Ibid.*, pp. 187-190.

[5]*Ibid.*, p. 190.

[6]*Ibid.*, pp. 226-227.

[7]*Ibid.*, pp. 62-63.

[8]*Ibid.*, pp. 357-363.

with the end of the reign of a Sultan. These lists are attached to a large number of chapters, though not to all.[1] Occasionally he also quotes verses of some of the poets and gives his own evaluation of their life and art. Amir Khusrau and Amir Hasan are understandably given the pride of place.[2]

Badauni makes no formal assessment of the reign of a Sultan, or a dynasty, or a period as a whole. However, individual events, or acts, or persons, are frequently the subject of his incidental remarks. Often these remarks are succinct and crisp and to an extent are indicative of the author's mind. Referring to the massacre of the Mughals by Ala-ud-din Khalji, for example, our author remarks, "Many poor and unfortunate Mughals were killed by the sword of injustice. . . .The name Mughal no longer remained in Hind. However, this tradition of massacring the poor has survived since that time."[3] The death of Muhammad Tughlaq is followed by the comment, "The Sultan was relieved of the people, and the people were relieved of the Sultan."[4] Mentioning the arrival of the pretentious Shaikh Shah Muhammad Dehlavi, from Persia to India, during the reign of Sher Shah, Badauni inserts a verse

What is expected of a Shaikh are miracles and attainment of a spiritual order;
What we see in them are the ravings of an ecstatic, and hypocrisy.[5]

As stated above, these remarks are incidental and limited to individual entities and as such they do not reflect the author's broader view of history. Nor can an inference to that end be derived from them. In fact, even the arrangement of the narrative sometimes loses its proper proportion and becomes disorganized. Thus, while the narrative of Nasir-ud-din Mahmud's reign is given five to six pages, the qasidahs written during his reign claim thirty-three.[6]

[1]No such lists are attached, for example, to his accounts of the reigns of Qutb-ud-din Aibak, Aram Shah, Razia, Ghiyas-ud-din Tughlaq, Tughlaq Shah (grandson of Firuz Shah), etc.

[2]*Ibid.*, pp. 138-154, 200-201.

[3]*Ibid.*, p. 188.

[4]*Ibid.*, p. 238.

[5]*Ibid.*, pp. 391-392.

[6]*Ibid.*, pp. 89-94 and 94-127 respectively. This and some of the following

The events of Balban's reign are described in just over five pages, while those of Kaiqubad take over eight.[1] More than these two combined are devoted to the elegies written on Prince Muhammad, Balban's son, and other poems.[2] He generally eschews description of administrative measures of the Sultanate and pre-Akbar period. He refers to the economic and administrative measures of Ala-ud-din Khalji but for details directs the reader to Barani's *Tarikh-i-Firuzshahi.*[3] He completely skips over the reforms of Sher Shah, whom he otherwise admires so much, without so much as an explanation. It is only of Islam Shah's reign that he gives the administrative reforms in comparatively more detail,[4] but without his own evaluation.

The second volume of the *Muntakhab* marks a clear distinction from the first in form, substance and treatment. It comprises the events of the first 40 years of Akbar's reign set in the form of an annual chronicle. The events have generally been narrated under the head of the year of their occurrence. If the occurrence of certain events extended to more than one year, the narration is split into as many places as the number of years involved. Thus, Badauni describes Akbar's first march for the conquest of Gujarat in the year 1572 at one place[5] and the second the following year at another.[6] Subsequently, the affairs of Gujarat are taken up again for narration.[7] He tells us at two places how Akbar twice turned down the request of Shaikh Abd-us-Shahid, grandson of Khwaja Ahrar, for the release of Sharf-ud-din Husain. The request had been made in 981 H. and 982 H. respectively.[8] Akbar's dealings with Daud, ruler of Bengal, are spread over a number of years and therefore the narration of events in Bengal is broken up repeatedly.[9]

---

points were first suggested by M. Mujeeb in his article on Badauni in *Historians of Medieval India*, M. Hasan (ed.), Meerut, 1968, pp. 106-112.

[1]Badauni, *op. cit.*, Vol. I, pp. 127-131, 155-157 and 157-165 respectively.

[2]*Ibid.*, pp. 138-155.

[3]*Ibid.*, p. 195.

[4]*Ibid*, pp. 384-385.

[5]*Ibid.*, Vol. II, pp. 139-142.

[6]*Ibid.*, pp. 166-167.

[7]*Ibid.*, pp. 327-334.

[8]*Ibid.*, pp. 171, 184.

[9]*Ibid.*, pp. 173-181, 227, 229-230, 237-238, etc.

Accordingly, we frequently come across phrases like, "as will be related later" or "as shall be recorded in its proper place" or "as has been stated earlier," etc.[1] At the same time it is significant that Badauni generally establishes the date of an event by beginning its narration with the words, "In this year" such and such an event took place.

Within the framework of the annual chronicle the order of precedence of events has been maintained. Badauni however does not go to the length of breaking the continuity of an event to describe another if the latter took place between the beginning and the end of the former within the same year. That is, he describes one event at a time, then takes up the next, irrespective of whether the second event may have intervened during the time the first one was in the process of happening.

It is not as if there are no instances contravening the order of the annals or the precedence of events. In fact, Badauni himself confesses at places to defaulting in the matter of the order[2] and the precedence.[3] On the other hand, this confession attests to the author's awareness of the significance of chronology.

An interesting feature of the book is the intertwining of biographical notes with the narrative of events. In a number of cases Badauni interrupts the narration of an event to give personal notes on the men involved in it. Thus, mentioning the capture of Nagarkot, he gives a short story of Birbal's life, who was given charge of the fort.[4] Or, referring to the arrival of Sharif Amli at the court, he gives a long account of his personal life.[5] His account of Shaikh Abul Fazl's life, when he joined the imperial court, is a classic in literary abuse.[6]

Badauni treats events individually, just as his other contemporaries do. He generally opens the narration of an event with the

[1] *Ibid.*, pp. 28, 55, 58, 71, 78, 92, 101, 141, etc.

[2] *Ibid.*, p. 264 where he states that it had not been possible to maintain the chronological order of the events that took place in the private sittings of Akbar where matters of religion were discussed.

[3] *Ibid.*, p. 321 where he craves the indulgence of the reader for not having observed the precedence of events of the year 1582.

[4] *Ibid.*, pp. 161-162.

[5] *Ibid.*, pp. 245-248.

[6] *Ibid.*, pp. 198-200.

words, "Among the events of this year was" or "In this year" such and such an event took place, etc. Thus the basic form of Badauni's history is similar to that of Abul Fazl's work (excepting the *Ain-i-Akbari*) although the treatment of history is different.

The events described in the *Muntakhab* had necessarily to be selective. Badauni was not writing a complete history either of the entire period from Subuktgin to his own day, or even of the reign of Akbar for "that was the assignment of others."[1] Utterly distressed by what he thought was a devastation that had been wrought on Islam by Akbar and his courtiers, and realizing that there was no one who would give a faithful account of the relevant events, he wrote the *Muntakhab* as an alternative to the contemporary histories.[2] Therefore, he recorded only "events of a general importance" and omitted "the minor ones."[3]

The third volume is in the form of a *Tazkira.* In this volume, Badauni writes short biographical sketches of the Mashaikh and the Ulema of Akbar's age and of the physicians and the poets of Akbar's court. The Mashaikh include those whom Badauni had personally attended upon, or had seen from a distance as well as those of whom he could bear no personal testimony.[4]

Badauni follows no particular order of precedence in placing the Mashaikh, the Ulema[5] and the physicians in a sequence. The poets, however, are placed in the alphabetical sequence (except the first three).

The nobles of Akbar's court are excluded from the *Tazkira* for two good reasons[6]—because Nizam-ud-din Ahmad had already treated them in his *Tabaqat-i-Akbari*; and Badauni would not give those "fallen" men the honour of independent treatment. He also excludes some "obscure Muslim" and other "accursed Hindu" physicians, of whom his heart did not prompt him to write.[7]

[1]*Ibid.*, Vol. I, p. 449.

[2]*Ibid.*, Vol. III, pp. 393-394.

[3]*Ibid.*, Vol. II, p. 18.

[4]*Supra*, p. 91.

[5]Badauni confesses that he did not observe the proper order of precedence in placing the Ulema and the Mashaikh, *Muntakhab*, Vol. III, p. 159.

[6]*Ibid.*, p. 1.

[7]*Ibid.*, p. 170. However, Badauni includes one Hindu, Manohar, in the list of poets, *ibid.*, pp. 201-202.

Badauni does not merely narrate the events of the lives of his subjects, but passes his judgments on their piety, knowledge, accomplishments and, above all, on their religious views. In fact, very frequently even the physicians are judged by our author more for their theological disposition than their professional expertise. Of the one and a half pages given to Hakim-ul-Mulk Gilani, for example, exactly nine words are devoted to his medical accomplishment, the rest to his postures in disputes between the Ulema and the physicians.[1] About Hakim Ahmad Thattavi, similarly, Badauni is more concerned with describing his efforts to turn him (the Hakim, who was a Shia)[2] into a true (Sunni) Musalman than with his proficiency as a physician.[3] Incidentally, medicine being one of the "rational" sciences, our author thoroughly distrusts its efficacy. "If knowledge of medicine could prolong life," he says, "physicians should never die."[4] He would rather repose his trust in God, and that would keep him alive, than in Aristotle,[5] which was sure to bring death to him.[6]

The notices on the poets of Akbar's court include Badauni's evaluation of their life and art, their views and morals. The narrative of their lives is seldom a straight one; Badauni often tries to highlight one or the other aspect of their life, judging them, of course, by their posture (or what he thought was their posture) *vis-a-vis* our author's own. Of Halati, for example, he writes, "He was a sincere and orthodox person."[7] A similar judgment is passed on Mulla Sadiq Halwai Samarqandi.[8] On the other hand, Shaikh Faizi is given a very abusive and bitter life sketch.[9] So bitter indeed is Badauni with Faizi that he grossly underrates even his poetical skill. He says, The "diwans of Urfi and Husain Sanai were

[1] *Ibid.*, pp. 161-162.

[2] *Ibid.*, Vol. II, p. 317.

[3] *Ibid.*, Vol. III, pp. 168-169.

[4] *Ibid.*, p. 165.

[5] Symbolizing Reason on which medical science is based.

[6] *Muntakhab*, Vol. III, p. 162. Badauni quotes Arabic verses to this effect. I have taken them from W. Haig's translation of the *Muntakhab*, Vol. III, p. 225.

[7] *Muntakhab*, Vol. III, p. 221.

[8] *Ibid.*, pp. 255-256.

[9] *Ibid.*, pp. 299-310.

very popular and were sold at every street corner. Faizi, on the other hand, spent considerable money from his jagir to have his book copied which no one would purchase. The only copy that sold was the one Faizi himself purchased to send abroad."[1]

Following the author's notice of a poet, he quotes some sample verses from his poetry. The quotations extend from one verse[2] to more than four pages.[3] At times Badauni points out technical flaws in the works of contemporary poets.[4] At others, he makes an overall qualitative evaluation of the literary output of poets.[5]

At times Badauni antedates his terms. That is, he applies terms of his own day to the past when these had not been coined. However, such instances are rare. He makes Iltutmish the amir-ul-umra of Qutb-ud-din Aibak,[6] although this nomenclature of office is not found in that period. The term "rupia" (rupee) is used in the context of the reign of Muhammad Tughlaq.[7]

CONTENTS

Unlike the *Akbar Nama* and the *Tabaqat-i-Akbari* the *Muntakhab* does not proceed as a straight, continuous narration. History, for Badauni, "had many bylanes"[8] and fortunately he strays into them quite frequently.

The formal tenor of the *Muntakhab* being that of political history, information on accessions, rebellions of nobles, wars, conquests, battle arrays, etc. is abounding. In the second volume Badauni gives considerable information on the administrative organization of Akbar's empire. He deals in some detail, for example, with the introduction, working and subsequent failure of the karori system.[9] Similarly, the institution of the branding of

[1] *Ibid.*, p. 285.
[2] *Ibid.*, p. 361.
[3] *Ibid.*, pp. 306-310.
[4] *Ibid.*, pp. 210, 340.
[5] *Ibid.*, pp. 170, 285, 295, 361, etc.
[6] *Ibid.*, Vol. I, p. 63.
[7] *Ibid.*, p. 230.
[8] *Ibid.*, p. 449.
[9] *Ibid.*, Vol. II, pp. 189-190.

horses has been given in sufficient detail.[1] The author also gives his own version of how this system affected the concerned interests. That the widespread rebellions in Bengal and Bihar were linked with this measure is established by him.[2] Similarly, the various experiments for the control of the aimah grants have been discussed.[3] These points of information, however, are piecemeal, for Badauni does not prefer to make any comprehensive study of the whole administrative organization as such. For this reason there is no discussion of the mansabdari system in all its aspects or of the revenue administration as a whole or even the Ten-Year Settlement.

On the discussions in Akbar's Ibadat Khana, Badauni is our chief contemporary source of information.[4] He was himself a participant in the discussions and therefore his is a firsthand account. This, however, is not sufficient testimony to the authenticity of the details. Yet, but for him, the details would have been much fewer. From Badauni we know that ordeal by fire was put forward as a means of establishing the truth or otherwise of a religion.[5] Or, that the Sufic doctrine of Wahdat-ul-Wujud was not universally accepted. It is Badauni alone, among contemporary authors, who discusses in detail, of course from *his* point of view, the circumstances that had preceded the proclamation of the Mahzar.[6] Abul Fazl furnishes only a cursory account and gives only a summary of the document,[7] while Nizam-ud-din Ahmad's narration of the preceding circumstances[8] is inadequate and even incorrect.

It is however Badauni's digressions into the bylanes of history and other incidental details that form his most interesting contri-

[1]*Ibid.*, pp. 190-191, 218-219. M. Mujeeb in his article on Badauni referred to above unfortunately makes a slip in saying that our author dismisses momentous decisions like the branding regulations and the karori system in one brief sentence. The brief sentence quoted by Mujeeb is followed by Badauni's remark that details would follow, *Muntakhab*, Vol II, p. 173.

[2]*Muntakhab*, Vol. II, pp. 280-284.

[3]*Ibid.*, pp. 204-205, 274-275, 295-296, etc.

[4]*Ibid.*, pp. 200-204, 255-264. Our only other contemporary informants are the Jesuit Fathers at the court.

[5]*Ibid.*, p. 299.

[6]*Ibid.*, pp. 270-273

[7]Abul Fazl, *Akbar Nama*, Vol. III, pp. 268-270.

[8]*Tabaqat-i-Akbari*, Vol. II, pp. 344-345.

bution to our information. He tells us of famines[1] and earthquakes[2]; gives us details of the jauhar committed by the Rajputs at Chittor[3]; describes in detail some of the buildings he had seen.[4]

Above all, Badauni does not merely mention individuals, but also presents their mode of behaviour and thinking. This presentation may not be entirely objective, for our author was out to stamp "on the forehead of each human being of his age his judgment on whether he was a Muslim or an infidel and consequently assign each to God's forgiveness or to perdition."[5] Yet even his subjective reflection on the modes of thought and deed is significant, for that represents a contemporary viewpoint.

In the third volume, while Badauni discusses the views of some of the Mashaikh and the Ulema on various aspects of religion, and gives sample verses from the compositions of the poets, he is silent about the contemporary state of medicine, although a list of biographical notices of the physicians has been included in the book. Thus, whereas some information may be derived from the *Muntakhab* in regard to the cultural level of Akbar's age, for a reconstruction of the state of scientific achievement of the time, we shall have to depend entirely on other sources.

ATTITUDE TOWARDS THE SOURCES OF INFORMATION

Badauni states that he had derived his information for the *Muntakhab* from the *Tabaqat-i-Akbari* of Nizam-ud-din Ahmad and the *Tarikh-i-Mubarakshahi* of Yahya Sirhindi, and to this he had "added something of his own."[6] In this, however, he is being very modest. In the course of his book, he shows easy familiarity with numerous works. Even a cursory examination of some of the passages would show that his sources are more numerous and diverse than the ones he has acknowledged. His story of the early

[1]*Muntakhab*, Vol. I, pp. 428-429; Vol. II, p. 186.
[2]*Ibid.*, Vol. I, pp. 319-320.
[3]*Ibid.*, Vol. II, p. 104.
[4]*Ibid.*, Vol. I, pp. 182, 222, 244; Vol. II, pp. 74, 78, etc.
[5]*Ibid.*, Vol. III, pp. 390-391.
[6]*Ibid.*, Vol. I, p. 7.

life of Iltutmish is based on Minhaj's *Tabaqat-i-Nasiri.*[1] His references to Balban's hostile disposition towards the low born[2] and to Ala-ud-din Khalji's reforms[3] as also his treatment of the reign of Ghiyas-ud-din Tughlaq[4] are based on Barani's *Tarikh-i Firuzshahi.* His statement, that Muhammad Tughlaq punished those soldiers who returned alive from the abortive expedition to Qarachil, is obviously taken from Isami.[5] A five-page quotation from Amir Khusrau's *Ashiqa* follows the reference to Dewal Rani being brought to Mubarak Khalji's harem.[6] From Abbas Sarwani's *Tuhfa-i-Akbar Shahi* he reproduces the remark that an old woman could sleep anywhere in security with a basket full of gold during the reign of Sher Shah.[7] In his third volume, while writing many of his biographical sketches, he has drawn heavily upon the *Nafais-ul-Ma'asir* of Ala-ud-daula, written earlier in Akbar's reign.[8]

These are merely random instances. It is neither possible, nor necessary to compare each passage of the *Muntakhab* with the sources that Badauni has or has not mentioned. Many of these have, in fact, been lost to us. But Badauni's occasional quotations from various books and his references to these for certain points[9] leave the impression that his reading was much wider than he casually mentions.

Badauni's main object in writing the *Muntakhab* was to record *his* reactions to the events of Akbar's reign and to the persons involved in them, from a certain point of view.[10] This object naturally

[1]*Ibid.*, pp. 62-63; Minhaj, *op. cit.*, Vol. I, pp. 599-604.

[2]*Muntakhab*, Vol. I, pp. 127-128; Barani, *Tarikh*, pp. 33-39.

[3]*Muntakhab*, Vol. I, p. 195; Barani, *Tarikh*, pp. 282-289.

[4]*Muntakhab*, Vol. I, pp. 221-251; Barani, *Tarikh*, pp. 425-453.

[5]*Muntakhab*, Vol. I, pp. 229-230; Isami, *op. cit.*, pp. 448-449.

[6]*Muntakhab*, Vol. I, pp. 204-208; Amir Khusrau, *Ashiqa*, pp. 273-280.

[7]*Muntakhab*, Vol. I, p. 363; Abbas Sarwani, *Tuhfa-i-Akbar Shahi*, I.O.L. Pers. MSS Ethe 219=I.O. 218, Rotograph, Research Library, Deptt. of History, Aligarh Muslim University.

[8]Ala-ud-daula Qazwini, *Nafais-ul-Ma'asir*, Subhanullah collection, Maulana Azad Library, Aligarh Muslim University, MS No. 920/45. This MS contains notices on 224 poets though there are some other MSS accounting for as many as 350, see Storey, *op. cit.*, p. 801.

[9]*Muntakhab*, Vol. I, pp. 167, 195, 197, 250; Vol. III, pp. 10, 113, 161-162, 170, etc.

[10]*Ibid.*, Vol. II, p. 264.

determines his use of the sources and his attitude towards them. He was writing neither an official history, as Abul Fazl was, nor a bare, detached narrative of political events, as Nizam-ud-din Ahmad was. Indeed, the *Muntakhab*, particularly its second volume, which is also the most significant of the three, often reads more as Badauni's memoirs than history. As such, for his account, particularly in the second volume, Badauni depends more on his personal testimony than on any documentary research. He makes scarce use of official documents anywhere.[1] It is significant that while in Volume I he at times challenges the facts and views of his sources on a rational, historical basis,[2] the second volume bears little evidence of it. He writes in it mostly of what he had seen or heard or what he had himself been a party to or had dissociated himself from, and not what he had found out after due investigations. And, to what he had seen or heard he adds his own colour and comments. In fact, Badauni goes further than that—he uses for his information not only his own eye-witness, or hearsay, or conversations, but even the thoughts of men, or the thoughts that he could attribute to them. In this respect Badauni does not merely adapt information to conform to his object; he *creates* it.

TREATMENT OF HISTORY AND HISTORICAL CAUSATION

"Among the branches of knowledge, history is a noble science and an instructive art," remarks Badauni.[3] No one will grudge the science of history this little eulogy. But the operative implications of

[1]He summarizes Islam Shah's letter to his brother, Adil Khan, when the former ascended the throne, *ibid.*, Vol. I, p. 375; at another place he gives a copy of the Mahzar in full; Vol II, pp. 271-272. However, instances like these are quite rare.

[2]He disputes the *Tabaqat-i-Mahmud Shahi's* establishing Jalal-ud-din Khalji's descent from Qulij Khan, son-in-law of Changez Khan, *Muntakhab*, Vol. I, p. 167. He refuses to believe that there was a causal connection between the execution of Sidi Maula and the subsequent drought during the reign of Jalal-ud-din Khalji. It may have been a mere coincidence, he asserts, *ibid.*, p. 172. He believes that Muhammad Tughlaq was responsible for his father's death and says that Barani omits this allegation perhaps in order to flatter Firuz Tughlaq, *ibid.*, p. 225.

[3]*Muntakhab*, Vol. I, pp. 2-3.

history do not recommend themselves as fully to our author as this general encomium. For, while "it is a source of examples for the wise, and worthy of the experience of the learned and the discriminating,"[1] taken as a rational science, history and the established beliefs would become mutually antagonistic, resulting in the undermining of the latter. This was what had happened in the case of Akbar who had "based religion on reason rather than on tradition,"[2] and in the cases of "some other people from amongst the lukewarmly faithful and the (constantly) doubting, people who are shortsighted," who were led by their "study and contemplation of history into deviation from the straight path of the *Shariat* of Muhammad."[3]

In writing the *Muntakhab*, therefore, Badauni addresses himself to "people who possess sound character and excellence of mind and a natural disposition towards justice; and not to such people who transgress the *Shara* and deny the fundamental and the derivative (law)."[4]

Thus, at the very outset, Badauni places important limitations on his conception and treatment of history.

But what precisely were the detailed implications of these limitations? What did Islam signify to him in relation to the various state policies? Who were the people he would address as true believers and why? Did Badauni represent any organized section of opinion like the orthodox Ulema or the Sufis or the "liberals" led by Shaikh Mubarak and his sons? Why precisely does he oppose all that he does and what was his alternative model? What was his conception of the ideal state?

To these questions Badauni has few answers. He wrote the *Muntakhab* under intense emotional stress, created by what he thought was the organized undermining of Islam during the reign of Akbar. And he wrote from the point of view to which he had settled down at the time of writing. Quite frequently we come across his comparison of the past with the situation in his own day.[5]

[1] *Ibid.*, p. 3.

[2] *Ibid.*, Vol II, p. 211. The reason for this given by Badauni is that "since history was read out to him. . . ."

[3] *Ibid.*, Vol. I, p. 3.

[4] *Ibid.*

[5] *Ibid.*, Vol. I, pp. 187-188; Vol. II, pp. 29-30, 65, 71, 239, 343.

Badauni's conception of Islam is very naive and personal. His discussions on religion are generally on trivial, technical points.[1] Nowhere does he show any understanding of the historical development of Islam from the primitive Arabia of the 7th century to the highly organized empires of the 16th. Islam does not provide our author with a world view whereby to judge and interpret history in a cosmic order. He does not even feel that Islam needed to adapt itself, at the level of the state, to ever changing conditions for its sheer survival. Nor does he treat the history of India from Subuktgin to his own day as the history of a part of the Muslim world. That he begins the *Muntakhab* with "the establishment of Islam in India,"[2] (with the first Ghaznavide invasion of India) is not sufficient evidence to prove that he does treat the five and a half centuries of Indian history as a part of Islamic history. This is so because Badauni does not show a historian's understanding of the dynamics and growth of Islam into a world order, and therefore his choice of the date whence to commence the *Muntakhab* becomes a very subjective one.

Elaborating his most basic assumption, that Islam was being undermined by the state in his age, in terms of his own personal experience, he writes a very impressionistic account, basing his information mostly on the evidence of his own eyes and ears[3] (particularly in the second volume, the most important of the three). Events and developments of no personal concern to him tend increasingly to recede into the background. He does not treat history as an organic whole; instead, he equates it with "stories and biographies"[4] which he proceeds to write.

It may be suggested here that it is Volume II of the *Muntakhab* which is truly representative of Badauni's genius, and also the most valuable of the three for the historian of today. Therefore, the analysis of his modes and methods may best be done mostly in relation to this volume, to be supplemented by the two others wherever necessary.

[1] *Ibid.*, Vol. II, pp. 187-188, 216, 259, 262-263, 306, 307-308; Vol. III, pp. 66-70, 70-73, 121-125, 137-138.

[2] *Ibid.*, Vol. I, pp. 5, 7-8.

[3] *Ibid.*, Vol. III, pp. 393-394.

[4] *Ibid.*, Vol. I, p. 3.

Now, Badauni's highly personal interpretation, devoid of a historical perspective, leads him to treat events and individuals as atomic entities. Individuals, in fact, are central to his treatment of history. It is not that he makes any conscious attempt at delineating the role of the individual in history. On the contrary, he refuses to judge an individual against the background of a particular historical situation, or a situation against the background of history in general. The historical personale, to him, are suspended in a vacuum, as it were, where they act entirely according to their will. There is a constantly running thread of an implicit assumption in the book that the historical personale might as well have acted completely differently than they did. The choice, indeed, was theirs to make. If ever Badauni goes further than that, he finds the cause of an individual's behaviour in his nature, or his motives. Thus, it was Shaikh Mubarak's nature to "converse with men according to their understanding,"[1] or Akbar welcomed Abul Fazl to his court because he expected to find in him a man "capable of teaching the Mullas a lesson,"[2] or the men who became Akbar's disciples were motivated by temptations of worldly gain,[3] etc. It is in human volition that Badauni establishes historical causation. Human volition, consequently, assumes the form of an independent and articulate entity; as such, for Badauni, it is *the* subject for evaluation and passing of moral judgment. It is for this reason that Badauni is so bitter against Akbar and against all those who had been instrumental in corrupting his mind, and all those who had sold themselves off to Akbar's whims, preferring transitory to eternal, salvation. For, according to Badauni's assumption, they could all have acted differently than they did. He, in fact, simply presumes that all those men who, according to him, had "corrupted" Akbar's mind were dishonest men.[4] That is, they chose to be dishonest, otherwise without doubt they would have conformed to our author's ideas. On the basis of this presumption Badauni is able to unite men like Shaikh Abd-un-Nabi and Makhdum-ul-Mulk with those like Abul Fazl and Faizi who all were motivated by their

[1]*Ibid.*, Vol. III, p. 74.
[2]*Ibid.*, Vol. II, p. 198.
[3]*Ibid*, pp. 269, 404-405.
[4]*Ibid.*, pp. 211, 256-264.

personal gain, and consequently were not worthy of our author's approbation. It is significant that Badauni's attack on his adversaries is invariably of a very personal nature.[1] He would not challenge their ideological stand at an ideological level, obviously because if they were just honest, there could have been no ideological controversy. To this end Badauni takes note not only of what those men did but of what they thought, or, rather what he thought they thought or what he wished them to have thought. This transsubstantiation of the product of his own mind into the thinking of others is the most subtle bias which Badauni imparts to his *Muntakhab*.

Badauni narrates the events individually, as they are made to happen by the men at the helm of affairs. Though the events are strung in the chronological sequence of their occurrence, Badauni does not establish either their rationale in the perspective of history, or their interrelationship. Thus, for example, although he narrates the events in relation to the evolution of Akbar's religious policy at every stage—founding of the Ibadat Khana,[2] discussions with the Ulema,[3] the subsequent participation by the professors of other religions,[4] Akbar's desire to unite the spiritual with the temporal authority under his own direction,[5] the attestation of the Mahzar[6] the emergence of the new "religion,"[7] etc.—he does not study these events as part of the totality of change in the policies and institutions of Akbar's state, nor does he study each event as the logical outcome of the cumulative effect of previous events. Similarly, he gives accounts of many campaigns for the subjugation of near and distant territories. These campaigns are all treated individually, in detail. But, for Badauni, they are all, individually, the manifestation of the ruler's will to conquer new territories; he does not relate them to the nature of the contemporary state, nor does he treat one as even remotely an extension of another.

[1] *Ibid.*, pp. 29, 173, 199-204, 206, 209-210, 211,245-248, 255-264, 272, 277-278, 285-287, 306, 312-313, 364, 404-405.

[2] *Ibid.*, p. 198.

[3] *Ibid.*, pp. 200-204, 255-256.

[4] *Ibid.*, pp. 256-264.

[5] *Ibid.*, p. 268.

[6] *Ibid.*, pp. 270-272.

[7] *Ibid.*, p. 291.

It is not that Badauni merely narrates events and mentions individuals. He evaluates them in his own light. As he describes the instituting of the karori system,[1] for example, or the branding of horses[2] or the resumption and reallotment of the madad-i-ma'ash lands,[3] he adds his own judgment on each. Or, when he mentions persons, such as Shaikh Abd-un-Nabi,[4] or Shaikh Mubarak,[5] he evaluates their life and work and so on. (These two names are random but not isolated examples. The *Muntakhab* is full of them.) Unfortunately, however, Badauni's value-world is entirely negative. His hostility to all that Akbar does—from founding the Ibadat Khana to making administrative changes—is intense. But he does not base this hostility on a study of history. Nor does he ever offer a rational alternative either piecemeal or total, that is, either for each measure of Akbar individually, or an entire alternative basis of state. He does not suggest the maintenance of the *status quo*. He does not suggest a return to the past. Nor does he advocate any fundamental change in the state structure of the 16th century in order to return to the days of Islamic puritanism—of the days of the Prophet and his immediate successors. In this respect the first volume of the *Muntakhab* is not very helpful either, for Badauni does not exactly glorify the period dealt with, or the reign of any particular ruler which could have provided us with a clue to our author's choice.

Thus Badauni's hostility to Akbar's reign is emotional and personal, and he makes no attempt to rationalize it. His professed orthodoxy is not exactly a new factor in medieval Indian history writing. Barani is his most distinguished predecessor. But whereas Barani insists on offering an alternative political theory and institutions to the state of his day, Badauni concentrates merely on demolishing all that had emerged after a long historical process without suggesting any positive choice. The reason is that whereas Barani studies history as a changing process capable of yielding certain general lessons,[6] and whereas in the light of historical

[1]*Ibid.*, p. 189.
[2]*Ibid.*, pp. 190-191.
[3]*Ibid.*, pp. 274-275.
[4]*Ibid.*, pp. 270, 272, 388, etc.
[5]*Ibid.*, pp. 71, 173, 204, 208, etc.
[6]Barani, *Tarikh*, p. 13.

experience he was prepared to rationalize even Islam,[1] for Badauni history was equivalent to stories and biographies and at best a source of examples to the virtuous men, and a study of history as a rational science would destroy his basic assumption of loyalty to the Faith.

STYLE

Badauni does not pretend to have written the *Muntakhab* as a masterpiece of literary style.[2] His pride in leaving behind for posterity "a priceless jewel"[3] lay not in the style but in the substance which would prove that Truth was on the side of the true Muslims as against the works of those who glorified infidelity for the sake of some worldly gain.[4]

Conforming to this, Badauni's style is naturally informal and unaffected. His hatred of men, as his love, was too intense to be bound within any established frame of literary style. It may do him no credit that his hatred of certain honourable men carried him to the verge of obscenity[5]; but he needed to express himself exactly as he felt. Consequently the *Muntakhab* vibrates with life and emotion and is a very readable, if not an equally reliable, work.

The entire *Muntakhab* is interspersed with verses—with couplets, quatrains, long elegies and short excerpts from poems. The insertion of verses appears to be a mere formality, for it is seldom that the verses yield any additional information (except in the section of Volume III dealing with the poets of Akbar's court) or take the narrative further. At times, indeed, the narrative is hindered by what appears to be a misplaced insertion of verses. The short narrative of Balban's reign, for example, is cut into two by the intervening elegies of Prince Muhammad and sundry other poems.[6] Or,

[1]Barani, *FJ*, pp. 34, 39-40.

[2]*Muntakhab*, Vol. III, p 394.

[3]*Ibid.*, p. 398.

[4]*Ibid*, pp. 393-394.

[5]Birbal is called a bastard, *ibid.*, Vol. II, p. 211; a son of Mulla Mubarak is also called a bastard, p. 306; Raja Dip Chand is called a buffoon, p. 211.

[6]The narrative, *ibid.*, Vol. I, pp. 127-131 and 155-157; the poems, pp. 131-155.

the death of Pir Muhammad Khan or Daud Khan's execution of his amir-ul-umra, or the author's first meeting with Husain Khan,[1] etc. are all followed by verses which interrupt the flow of the account. More than the verses, the abounding chronograms in the *Muntakhab* are valuable both for identifying the dates of the occurrence of events as well as for ascertaining the author's value judgment regarding persons and events. There are charitable chronograms like "A World of Excellence," for the death of Badauni's father,[2] and not so charitable ones like "The Carcass of a Great Swine," for the death of Shaikh Gadai.[3] For Shaikh Faizi's death Badauni mentions as many as seven chronograms, all of them extremely abusive.[4] One of these places the occurrence 200 years ahead of time[5] but Badauni apparently considered any stick good enough if it could be employed to beat Faizi with.

Some of the chronograms give wrong dates even otherwise,[6] but since most of the events (in the second volume) have been recorded under the head of the year of their occurrence, the two, when they coincide, reinforce the chronological authenticity of these events. It is possible, of course, that some of the chronograms were coined by Badauni as he wrote along, and the slightest lack of care could result in wrong dates.

An interesting feature of the *Muntakhab* is that the author's invocation of God's blessings for persons has been used by him as a reflection of his attitude towards the individuals concerned. For some Badauni invokes these blessings,[7] for some others he wishes damnation[8]; towards still others he is indifferent.[9] "My blessings and curses," he says, "are in accordance with the established *Shara*

[1] *Ibid.*, Vol. II, pp. 51, 174-176 and 225 respectively.

[2] *Ibid.*, p. 53.

[3] *Ibid.*, p. 119.

[4] Two chronograms in *ibid.*, p. 406 and five in Vol. III, pp. 300-301.

[5] "Bachar mazhab-i-nar" (the four religions of hell-fire), *ibid.*, Vol. III, p. 300. Its numerical value is 1204, while Faizi died in 1004 H./A.D. 1596.

[6] For example, *ibid.*, Vol. II, pp. 98, 106, 245, 304.

[7] For Miyan Hatim Sambhali, *ibid.*, Vol. III, p. 3; Shaikh Daud Jhanniwal, p. 39; Nizam-ud-din Ahmad, Vol. II, p. 99; and Shaikh Jalal Thanesari, p. 312.

[8] For Todar Mal and Bhagwan Das, *ibid.*, Vol. II, p. 371.

[9] For example towards Shaikh Badr-ud-din son of Shaikh Salim Chishti, *ibid*, p. 334.

and praise and censure I have apportioned according to my zeal for the Faith."[1]

From this, however, it cannot be inferred that Badauni's invocation of blessings or damnation can serve as an absolute criterion to ascertain his predilections and prejudices towards individuals. There are instances where he is just being formal.[2]

Badauni narrates incidents or mentions persons and follows them up with some anecdote or another But he is a master, in particular of chronograms which enliven almost every alternate page of the book. Add to this his very frequent citation of sayings and phrases. The style is more akin to that of Barani than to that of the writers of Badauni's day. He interrupts his narrative to relate some sundry incident away from the rebellions of nobles or expeditions to territories. The incident may be a story of frustrated love, like that of Mohini and Syed Musa[3]; or the story of the trickery of a fake magician.[4]

Badauni tells us that he did not write the *Muntakhab* for securing the favours of any important person, as those "who could write two connected sentences" did.[5] Indeed, he had to keep his "priceless jewel" concealed for obvious reasons. Even when both Akbar and Badauni were dead, the discovery of the MS entailed punishment to the author's children at Jahangir's hands.[6] To that extent, therefore, Badauni is true to his word and his conscience. But he reserves the last laugh for his readers when he says, "It was not my habit to record the faults of others."[7]

[1]*Ibid.*, Vol. III, p. 391.

[2]*Ibid.*, Vol. II, p. 63 where he quotes a kindly chronogram on the death of Shaikh Ghaus, of whom he is otherwise so critical, pp. 34, 63; he also maligns Shaikh Salim Chishti, p. 109, but the chronograms of his death are in a different tenor, p. 136.

[3]*Ibid.*, pp. 109-118.

[4]*Ibid.*, pp. 366-368. The story runs as follows: a certain Shaikh Bayabani would cross over from one bank of a river to the other within the twinkling of the eye. What really used to happen was that this gentleman would take leave of his spectators on his side of the river at an appointed moment towards dusk, and a second later his son, who had similar looks, would appear on the other side and shout some words, affecting his father's voice. When his bluff was called and Akbar threatened to punish him, he pointed to his stomach and said, "All this I have done to fill this hell."

[5]*Ibid.*, Vol. III, p. 393.

[6]Bakhtawar Khan, *op. cit.*, f. 185b.

[7]*Muntakhab*, Vol. III, p. 347.

CHAPTER 4

I Khwaja Nizam-ud-din Ahmad

It is unfortunate that for a reconstruction of Nizam-ud-din Ahmad's life we have to depend on extremely scanty detail. Perhaps out of modesty, Nizam-ud-din Ahmad avoids referring to himself in his *Tabaqat-i-Akbari* except where necessary to complete his account of events. Even his contemporary authors are not very obliging in this respect. Whatever has been noted by his contemporaries, like Badauni and subsequent writers like Shah Nawaz Khan, author of the *Ma'asir-ul-Umra*, is more or less based on the meagre information given by Nizam-ud-din himself. With the author's modesty may have been combined the want of anything spectacular in his life, which, at best, appears to be the story of his graduated promotion in the imperial service.

There is no direct evidence for the date or the year of Nizam-ud-din Ahmad's birth. We are however told by his intimate friend Badauni that at the time of his death, 28 October 1594, he was forty-five years of age.[1] That places his birth in 1549.

Almost nothing is known about Nizam-ud-din Ahmad's early youth and education. We have only Dowson's statement that he was a pupil of Mulla Ali Sher, a learned man and father of Faizi Sirhindi, author of the *Akbar Nama*.[2] One can only conjecture that the kind of education imparted to him may not have been different from the prevalent pattern. However, from a perusal of his work it would appear that he had not been trained into adopting any rigid orthodox attitude in religion.

Nizam-ud-din's family background must have played an important part in his education as well as his career. He belonged to a

[1] Badauni, *Muntakhab*, Vol. II, p. 397.

[2] Elliot and Dowson, *History of India*, Vol. VI, p. 116.

family with a long record of service under the Mughals. His father, Khwaja Muqim Harawi, served under Babur as the diwan-i-buyutat.[1] Nizam-ud-din tells us in some detail about his father's role in frustrating Mir Khalifa and Mahdi Khwaja's conspiracy to prevent Humayun's succession to Babur's throne.[2]

When Humayun conquered Gujarat and appointed Mirza Askari its governor, Khwaja Muqim was the Mirza's vazir.[3] The next we hear of him is when he, with a few others, accompanied Humayun to Agra after the latter's defeat at Chausa.[4] Subsequently, Shah Nawaz Khan tells us, he was "honoured with serving the Emperor during the reign of Arsh Ashiyani (Akbar)."[5] Nizam-ud-din also reports him in attendance at Akbar's court at Agra in the twelfth regnal year.[6] What the nature of his employment was at Akbar's court is not stated. In the nineteenth regnal year, however, he is reported to have gone to Bhakkar as amin where he, "by wise counsels, prevailed upon Muhibb Ali Khan to abstain from misplaced strife and improper commotion."[7]

Nizam-ud-din Ahmad informs us that his maternal uncle, Sultan Ibrahim Ubhi, was also in Akbar's service. He had brought under imperial control the territory of Kumaon.[8]

Nizam-ud-din himself appears to have joined Akbar's service early in his life, though the date and circumstances of his formally joining it are not known. However, that he had done so at a comparatively young age seems certain, for gradually he rose to the important post of the bakhshi of the empire in his early forties.

In what capacity Nizam-ud-din began his career is not quite certain. The *Zakhirat-ul-Khawanin* tells us that he was Akbar's

[1]Nizam-ud-din Ahmad, *Tabaqat-i-Akbari*, Vol. II, p. 28; *Ma'asir-ul-Umra*, Vol. I, p. 660.

[2]Nizam-ud-din Ahmad, *op. cit.*, Vol. II, pp. 28-29.

[3]*Ibid.*, p. 37; *Ma'asir-ul-Umra*, Vol. I, pp. 660-661. Neither of these informants tells us when exactly this appointment (of Khwaja Muqim) took place.

[4]*Ma'asir-ul-Umra*, Vol. I, p. 661.

[5]*Ibid.*

[6]Nizam-ud-din Ahmad, *op. cit.*, Vol. II, p. 211.

[7]Abul Fazl, *Akbar Nama*, Vol. III, p. 91. "Misplaced strife and improper commotion" refers to the projected imprisonment of Mir Gesu who had been sent by Akbar to take charge of the fort of Bhakkar from Sultan Mahmud.

[8]Nizam-ud-din Ahmad, *op. cit.*, Vol. II, p. 449.

diwani-i-huzur to start with.[1] The author of the *Ma'asir-ul-Umra* is rather sceptical of the authenticity of this piece of information for, he says, "no other writer supports it."[2] Nizam-ud-din's first formal appointment came in the twenty-ninth regnal year as the bakhshi of the province of Gujarat.[3] However, long before this appointment he was associated with Akbar's court though in capacities unspecified. When, for instance, in the twelfth year of his reign Akbar marched out to attack Ali Quli Khan, Nizam-ud-din Ahmad remained at Agra where he spread rumour, in good humour, that the heads of the Khan-i-Zaman and Bahadur Khan had been brought to the capital.[4] In the twenty-seventh regnal year Nizam-ud-din Ahmad mentions himself again as having been sent on the Emperor's errand to Prince Murad.[5] Akbar at this time was on his march against Mirza Hakim and had crossed the Sind Sagar and the Prince was seventy-five kos away at Jalalabad.

The author claims to have covered the distance in a single day and night and soon returned with the Prince's reply. He accompanied Akbar from Sind Sagar to Kabul and must have been in some position of influence. For this we have Badauni's testimony alone. Somewhere near Kabul, Badauni tells us, the Emperor had ordered the sadr-i-jahan to prepare a list of all those pious people who were then present in the camp and of those who were absent. When Badauni's name came up among the absentees, Nizam-ud-din Ahmad, "with all his kindness and consideration which he showed to his friends in general and to me in particular, reported me sick."[6] Even the fact of his appointment two years later to the crucial post of bakhshi of the most turbulent province of the

[1]Farid Bhakkari, *op. cit.*, p. 208.

[2]*Ma'asir-ul-Umra*, Vol. I, p. 661.

[3]Nizam-ud-din Ahmad, *op. cit.*, Vol. II, p. 368; Abul Fazl, *Akbar Nama*, Vol. III, p. 403; *Ma'asir-ul-Umra*, Vol. I, p. 661.

[4]Nizam-ud-din Ahmad, *op. cit.*, Vol. II, p. 211; also Badauni, who bases his account of this incident specifically on Nizam-ud-din's authority, *Muntakhab*, Vol. II, pp. 99-100. Abul Fazl makes it not a rumour but a prognostication emanating from his father who performed a Sufic service to make the prognostication at Munim Khan's request, *Akbar Nama*, Vol. II, p. 296.

[5]*Op. cit.*, Vol. II, pp. 360-361; Badauni, *op. cit.*, Vol. II, p. 294.

[6]*Muntakhab*, Vol. II, pp. 296-297. Badauni was then at Bhusawar in the company of his "beloved."

empire suggests that he must have risen to his post from only a slightly less important one.

In Gujarat, Nizam-ud-din Ahmad proved his worth as a soldier. Whereas earlier the indecision of Aitmad Khan and the intrigues of Shihab-ud-din Ahmad had resulted in a very difficult situation, Nizam-ud-din Ahmad, along with his newly appointed colleagues, was able to make an immediate impact on the affairs of the province, ravaged as it was by one of the most serious rebellions during Akbar's reign. Nizam-ud-din began by defeating Sher Khan Fauladi, an important partisan of the rebel, Muzaffar Gujarati, at Jutanah.[1] He then arranged to attack Muzaffar himself on two sides—from Bharoch and Baroda (under the command of Mirza Abd-ur-Rahim, who was soon to be awarded the title of the Khan-i-Khanan) and from Sarkhej (under Nizam-ud-din's own command). This two-pronged attack resulted in Muzaffar's defeat.[2] Some time later, Muzaffar was again routed in the hills of Nadot, thanks mainly to Nizam-ud-din's efforts.[3]

In 1587 the Khan-i-Khanan was recalled to the court with the order to leave the charge of Gujarat to Nizam-ud-din Ahmad with Azd-ud-Daula and Qulij Khan to assist him in the discharge of his duties.[4] The rebellion of Muzaffar Gujarati had not till then been suppressed. His partisans had besieged the fort of Radhanpur, a dependency of Patan.[5] Nizam-ud-din Ahmad, in concert with Syed Qasim, Daulat Khan Lodi, Mir Masum, Husain Khan and others not only relieved the fort but launched a counter-attack by crossing the waters of the Kutch and plundering the territory. Soon afterwards he "ravaged and devastated" about fifty villages of the Kolis and the Girasias and constructed seven forts in that territory[6] because the Kolis and Girasias had earlier assisted Muzaffar Gujarati.[7] For his services in Gujarat our author was honoured by the Emperor with the award of a horse, a robe and

[1]Nizam-ud-din Ahmad, *op. cit.*, Vol. II, pp. 372-373.
[2]*Ibid.*, pp. 375-376.
[3]*Ibid.*, pp. 377-378.
[4]Abul Fazl, *AN*, Vol. III, p. 517.
[5]Nizam-ud-din Ahmad, *op. cit.*, Vol. II, p. 389.
[6]*Ibid.*, p. 390.
[7]*Ibid.*, p. 381.

enhancement of his salary.[1]

In 1589 the governorship of Gujarat was conferred upon Azam Khan and Nizam-ud-din Ahmad was recalled to the court.[2] Soon afterwards we hear of him as holding charge of a part of the khalisa (lands assigned to the king's own revenue) in the provinces of Ajmer, Gujarat and Malwa.[3] Akbar had divided the khalisa of the empire into four parts on account of the territory having become very large, and each of these parts was given over to the charge of one person. Towards the end of 1591 Nizam-ud-din was favoured with the grant of the pargana of Shamsabad as his jagir.[4]

It was in the thirty-seventh regnal year, 1592, that Nizam-ud-din reached the pinnacle of his career when he was nominated to replace Asaf Khan Mirza Jafar Bakhshibegi in the post of the bakhshi of the empire.[5] As bakhshi, he accompanied the Emperor to Kashmir soon afterwards.[6]

What precise services Nizam-ud-din rendered to the Emperor in that post we do not know. He was, however, destined not to reach the capital again. On the return of the Emperor's camp to Lahore, he contracted high fever which proved fatal. His death took place on 28 October 1594.[7] In his death Nizam-ud-din Ahmad appears to have united Badauni and Abul Fazl in paying him homage in a similar vein. "He took nothing with him," remarks Badauni, "except a good name. A host of his friends and companions, who, having been witness to the excellence of his qualities, had great hopes of him. . .poured tears of regret from their eyes and beat their bosoms with the stone of despair. . . .There was hardly any one, high or low, in the city who did not weep over his bier and recall his gracious qualities and gnaw the back of the hand of regret."[8]

[1] *Ibid.*, p. 379.
[2] *Ibid.*, p. 390; Badauni, *op. cit.*, Vol. II, p. 372.
[3] Abul Fazl, *AN*, Vol. III, p. 605.
[4] Badauni, *op. cit.*, Vol. II, p. 376.
[5] Nizam-ud-din Ahmad, *op cit*, Vol. II, p. 415.
[6] *Ibid.*, p. 419.
[7] Badauni, *op. cit.*, Vol. II, p. 397.
[8] *Ibid.*, p. 397.

"Strangers and acquaintances mourned," says Abul Fazl, "and honesty sate in grief."[1]

*

At Akbar's court, during a period of hectic controversies of various natures, Nizam-ud-din appears to have remained a largely noncontroversial figure. It is possible that there were small personal feuds between him and some others. Badauni refers to a "continual hostility" between him and Qulij Khan.[2] As Nizam-ud-din Ahmad gained the Emperor's favour and confidence, "Qulij Khan and other courtiers who had never been separated from the court were appointed to outlying areas." Badauni does not dwell upon the reasons why the rise of one in Akbar's favour led to the exclusion from it of another.

This minor, and presumably personal, dispute apart, there appears to have been little ideological conflict between Nizam-ud-din Ahmad and others. He is never mentioned by Badauni as taking part in the great discussions. Nor does he appear to have made use of controversies in Akbar's court for his personal aggrandizement. Even in the *Tabaqat* he avoids all controversies and, to the best of his judgment, sticks to a bare sketch of events. Consequently it is difficult to assess his personal views on the prevalent controversies in Akbar's court.

In a study of Nizam-ud-din Ahmad's life, Beni Prashad believes that the author's interest in Sufism and theology is "indicated by his association with Sufis, Shaikhs and religious people in general. He may thus be assumed to have had a religious frame of mind, and his writings and the regard in which he was held by such bigoted Muhammadans as al-Badauni seem to indicate that he must have been quite orthodox in his views and observances."[3]

Beni Prashad has referred to Badauni only for one instance of Nizam-ud-din's association with a Sufi, namely, Shaikh Abdul Haqq of Delhi.[4] Badauni's passage in question is: "On account of his (Shaikh Abdul Haqq's) long-standing friendship with them he was for some time the companion, in Fathpur, of Shaikh Faizi and

[1] *Akbar Nama*, Vol. III, p. 655.

[2] Badauni, *op. cit.*, Vol. II, pp. 396-397.

[3] *Tabaqat-i-Akbari* (*tr.*), Bib. Ind., Vol. III, pt. II, p. x.

[4] The reference is to W. Haig's *tr.* of Volume III of the *Muntakhab*, Bib. Ind., p. 167.

Mirza Nizam-ud-din Ahmad." This one instance in which Shaikh Faizi shares the friendship of Shaikh Abdul Haqq with Nizam-ud-din Ahmad is not sufficient evidence of "association" with the Sufis, Shaikhs and religious people in general. In his book Nizam-ud-din Ahmad does not show any extraordinary respect for the Shaikhs and the Ulema. In fact, it is only on exceptionally few occasions that, while mentioning a Shaikh or a theologian, he invokes God's blessing for him,[1] which was the most common method of showing one's respect for pious people. At any rate, association with Shaikhs and Sufis, a common practice, particularly among the higher officers of the state, does not necessarily indicate any deep-rooted religiosity, much less orthodoxy, just as its absence cannot be taken for an inclination towards secularism.

Similarly, the fact that Badauni holds Nizam-ud-din Ahmad in high respect is no sure testimony to the latter's orthodox frame of mind. If their respective works are any guide, there is very little in common, as far as their viewpoints are concerned. This is in spite of Badauni's statement that his *Muntakhab-ut-Tawarikh* is only an abridgement of Nizam-ud-din Ahmad's *Tabaqat-i-Akbari*.[2]

It is not suggested here that Nizam-ud-din Ahmad conformed to any high abstract ideal of secularism, or indifference to religion. He may have been deeply religious in his personal life, but this did not colour either his career or his historical work.

Nizam-ud-din Ahmad's interest in history had developed at a young age. He had been initiated into this branch of knowledge by his father.[3] His proficiency in the study of history appears to have been considerable by contemporary standards. Apart from his study of history he appears to have been conversant with literature. He was a patron of poets. Badauni tells us that during the seven years that Nizam-ud-din Ahmad was in Gujarat he had invited and patronized poets like Amani, Baqai, Hayati, and Sarafi Sawaji.[4]

In the writing of the *Tabaqat*, Nizam-ud-din Ahmad was assisted

[1]No blessings are invoked for any of the Ulema and the Mashaikh in the section of the *Tabaqat* where the author gives their brief life sketches, Vol. II, pp. 458-480.

[2]Vol. II, pp. 389-390.

[3]Nizam-ud-din Ahmad, *op. cit.*, Vol. I, pp. 1-2.

[4]*Muntakhab*, Vol. III, pp. 187-188, 196, 221 and 260 respectively.

by Mir Masum Bhakkari,[1] who was a poet and a historian, and Shaikh Muhammad Ishaq Taghai.[2] This assistance was necessary on account of the scarcity of time which his office forced on him. Nizam-ud din was also entrusted, along with six others, with the task of compiling the *Tarikh-i-Alfi*.[3] What precise contribution he made to this work it is difficult to ascertain.

There is one more work, the *Tarikh-i-Irich*, presumably a local history of Erach in central India, which is ascribed to him by Sarup Chand, author of *Sahih-ul-Akhbar*.[4] However, there is no other supporting evidence among our present sources in favour of this ascription and if Nizam-ud-din Ahmad did write this book, it has been lost to us.

II. TREATMENT OF HISTORY IN NIZAM-UD-DIN AHMAD'S *TABAQAT-I-AKBARI*

Basic Form

The *Tabaqat-i-Akbari* comprises its author's account of the history of nine regions, each designated by him as a separate tabqa.[5] These regions are Delhi (the seat of the imperial government), the Deccan, Gujarat, Bengal, Malwa, Jaunpur, Sind, Kashmir and Multan. At the outset is an Introduction which is an account of the Ghaznavides from 977 to 1186-87. The book ends with a Conclusion in which the length and breadth of Akbar's empire have been described. The Conclusion also tells us that there were then 3,200 towns in the empire, of which 120 were great cities. The author had intended writing a separate account of the three thousand-odd towns, "the great God willing."[6] This part of the

[1] *Ma'asir-ul-Umra*, Vol. I, p. 663.

[2] *Zakhirat-ul-Khawanin*, Vol. I, p. 209.

[3] Badauni, *op. cit.*, Vol. II, p. 318.

[4] Elliot and Dowson, *History of India*, Vol. VIII, p. 314.

[5] The tabqa is construed by Nizam-ud-din Ahmad not as a geographic but as a politico-geographic unit, which had, at some time or another been (in the not too-distant past with which the author shows no familiarity) an independent state finally brought under imperial control during Akbar's reign.

[6] Nizam-ud-din Ahmad, *Tabaqat-i-Akbari*, Vol. III, p. 546.

work, however, he was unable to do.

Within this regional framework he writes dynastic history. That is, he writes the history of a dynasty or dynasties ruling in each of these regions to the time of its conquest by Akbar. Within this dynastic framework, each reign forms a separate unit. The break-up of Akbar's reign, however, is in the form of an annual chronicle. This treatment of history naturally precludes any explicit suggestion of a causal relationship between the events of the reign of any one Sultan and another, even if one be consecutive to the other.

The chronological sequence of reigns has, however, been adhered to with at least one exception in favour of convenience—the reigns of Sher Shah, Islam Shah and Adil Shah have been dealt with subsequent to that of Humayun though chronologically the three fall within the compass of the period of Humayun's rule.[1]

The account of each reign opens with the enthronement of the ruler concerned and closes with the end of the reign. It is very rare that the author chooses to give a biographical sketch of a ruler, or an account of life prior to his accession. Iltutmish[2] and Farid[3] (later Sher Shah) have, however, been accorded a special consideration. The reasons in the case of the first are not clear and in the second, they can be assumed safely. To have given an account of Sher Shah's rule without his long and eventful career—which ultimately won him the crown—would have made no sense. Sher Shah had not inherited the empire, unlike most others, nor had he won it in a single battle. Obviously, Nizam-ud-din must have realized that a bare account of the five years of Sher Shah's reign would be utterly incomplete.

With these two exceptions, Nizam-ud-din Ahmad generally conforms to the pattern he had set before himself. Even Babur's career in the Central Asian region has been excluded from the *Tabaqat*, for within the strict limitations of writing the history of India, the author considered it irrelevant.[4]

[1] *Ibid.*, Vol. II, pp. 27-85 for Humayun's reign and pp. 86-125 for the Afghan rulers.

[2] *Ibid.*, Vol. I, pp. 56-57, 61-62.

[3] *Ibid.*, Vol. II, pp. 86-101.

[4] *Ibid.*, Vol. II, p. 1. The author adds that another reason for this exclusion was that Abul Fazl's *Akbar Nama* and the *Waqiat-i-Baburi* and "other histories" have dealt with it.

The end of each chapter is equally prosaic. In most cases Nizam-ud-din merely mentions the length of the reign he has dealt with. As far as possible he tries to be accurate in details of the length of each reign and gives the years, the months and the days.[1] It is only in very few cases that he either tries to evaluate the personal qualities of a Sultan, or adds a list of the important nobles of a particular ruler. Babur's death, for instance, puts our author in a pathetic mood and he inserts in his account a few verses to give vent to his complaints against the conduct of the heavens.[2] He then mentions, almost casually, Babur's cultural ccomqmlpiasents. At another place he closes his account of Sultan Mahmud Gujarati's reign with a few words of praise for the dead ruler.[3] He also mentions some of the buildings constructed at his command and some of the edicts issued by him to suppress immorality which had become common in his kingdom.

At list of amirs of a particular ruler is supplied only in two cases—for Sultan Bahlul Lodi[4] and Sultan Sikandar Lodi.[5] Why did the author abruptly decide to adopt this form, which is a common feature in Minhaj's *Tabaqat-i-Nasiri* and an invariable feature in Barani's *Tarikh-i-Firuz Shahi*, it is difficult to say. However, Nizam-ud-din Ahmad drops it as abruptly as he had adopted it.

The account of the forty years of Akbar's reign that have been dealt with in the major part of the second volume of the *Tabaqat* is largely in the form of an annual chronicle. An exception has, however, been made in the case of events in Gujarat. The events in that province, during the seven years that our author was on duty there, have been described at one place.[6] Within the confines of the annual chronicle, Nizam-ud-din meticulously maintains the chronological order of the events. If a particular event was spread over more than an year, he would break the thread of his narration at one place and pick it up later under the head of the later year.

[1] *Ibid.*, Vol. I, pp. 65, 68, 70, 242; Vol. III, pp. 19, 26, 198, etc.

[2] *Ibid.*, Vol. II, p. 27.

[3] *Ibid.*, Vol. III, pp. 241-242.

[4] *Ibid.*, Vol. I, pp. 298-299.

[5] *Ibid.*, pp. 314-315.

[6] *Ibid* , Vol. II, pp. 370-391, Nizam-ud-din is aware of this small deviation, for he states, "The events of seven years in Gujarat, when this humble one was there, have been narrated at one place," p. 391.

Even within a year he adheres to the chronological precedence of events.

The account of each tabqa (region, province) begins at a separate date not far removed from the time when Nizam-ud din Ahmad was writing, when the particular region could be assumed to have had (or to have attained) the status of an independent kingdom. In cases of regions where this status was acquired by breaking away from the imperial government, the author opens his account with the reign of the particular ruler who had established the independent identity of the regional state. Thus, the history of Malwa begins in the *Tabaqat* with the reign of Dilawar Khan Ghori who became the sovereign ruler of that region after the death of Sultan Firuz Tughlaq.[1] Or, the account of Gujarat opens with the reign of Azam Humayun Zafar Khan who similarly broke away from the Delhi Sultanate during the reign of Sultan Muhammad, son of Sultan Firuz Tughlaq.[2] In other instances, however, like that of Kashmir, where the particular region had never been subjugated to imperial authority until the reign of Akbar, Nizam-ud-din Ahmad begins with the establishment of an independent Muslim dynasty.[3]

Nizam-ud-din's account of each of these tabqas practically synchronizes with that of the others in that each of these accounts is brought to a close in the reign of Akbar when the particular region became part of Akbar's empire. The effect of it is a picture depicting the unification of the various regions under the imperial standard. That this was so desired by the author is explicitly stated by him.[4] As a history of the various regional kingdoms, Nizam-ud-din Ahmad's work is a substantial achievement, but the severe limits he had set to its framework prevent his book from conceptually rising to anything higher than mere narration.

CONTENTS

The contents of the *Tabaqat* are, in comformity with its nature as

[1] *Ibid.*, Vol. III, p. 289.
[2] *Ibid.*, p. 82.
[3] *Ibid.*, p. 424.
[4] *Ibid.*, Vol. I, pp. 2-3.

dynastic history, confined to information on accession of rulers to the throne, their wars, rebellions of the nobles, etc. Even within this limited field Nizam-ud-din Ahmad does not traverse his ground vertically, as it were. That is, he does not go into details of administration, political policies or other aspects; on the contrary, he tries to briefly narrate a large number of events of a similar type. This makes the work singularly monotonous both in content and style. Even the story of the grant of the Bahmani kingdom, prior to its establishment, by Shaikh Nizam-ud-din Aulia to Hasan Gangu[1] and another of Nizam-ud-din Ahmad's spreading a rumour about the death of the Khan-i-Azam Ali Quli Khan,[2] are related essentially to political events, lacking an identity of their own.

At times, however, the author refers to extra-political phenomena such as the occurrence of a disastrous earthquake[3] or the plan of a city (Ahmedabad).[4] But such instances are rare.

It is towards the end of the book that Nizam-ud-din Ahmad gives us some information about the land, the number of towns in Akbar's empire, the revenues of the empire,[5] etc. As noted earlier, he had wished to write a separate volume on the towns and cities of Hindustan in an alphabetical order,[6] a wish which he did not live long enough to fulfil.

ATTITUDE TOWARDS THE SOURCES OF INFORMATION

For writing his *Tabaqat*, Nizam-ud-din Ahmad appears to have utilized more sources than he has mentioned in a list at the outset in his work.[7] This list consists of twenty-eight works. These are:

Tarikh-i-Yamini
Tarikh-i-Zain-ul-Akhbar
Rauzat-us-Safa
Ma'asir-i-Mahmud Shahi Gujarati
Tarikh-i-Muhammadi
Tarikh-i-Bahadur Shahi

[1] *Ibid.*, pp. 5-6.
[2] *Ibid.*, Vol. II, p. 211.
[3] *Ibid*, Vol. I, pp. 325-326.
[4] *Ibid.*, Vol. III, pp 97-98.
[5] *Ibid*, pp. 545-546.
[6] *Ibid.*, p. 546.
[7] *Ibid.*, pp. 3-4.

Taj-ul-Ma'asir	*Tarikh-i-Bahmani*
Tabaqat-i-Nasiri	*Tarikh-i-Nasiri*
Khazain-ul-Futuh	*Tarikh-i-Muzaffar Shahi*
Tughlaq Nama	*Tarikh-i-Mirza Haidar*
Tarikh-i-Firuz Shahi (of Zia Barani)	*Tarikh-i-Kashmir*
Futuhat-i-Firuz Shahi	*Tarikh-i-Sind*
Tarikh-i-Mubarak Shahi	*Tarikh-i-Baburi*
Tarikh-i-Futuh-us-Salatin	*Waqiat-i-Baburi*
Tarikh-i-Mahmud Shahi Mandawi	*Tarikh-i-Ibrahim Shahi*
Tarikh-i-Mahmud Shahi-i-Khurd Mandawi	*Waqiat-i-Mushtaqi*
Tarikh-i-Mahmud Shahi Gujarati	*Waqiat-i-Humayun Padshah*

Apart from these twenty-eight works, Nizam-ud-din Ahmad refers to the *Akbar Nama* of Abul Fazl in the body of the text.[1] Reference is also made there to the *Siraj-ut-Tawarikh* of Khwaja Muhammad Lari which covers the history of the Bahmani Sultanate,[2] to the *Qiran-us-Sadain* of Amir Khusrau[3] and to the *Malfuz-i-Khwaja Qutb-ud-din Bakhtiyar*.[4] However, such references to works not included in his list are rare.

Evidently, among the specified sources, our author does not propose to go beyond utilizing what may loosely be called court histories. These sources suffice for his limited objective of writing yet another court history.

Among the notable omissions from the list of Nizam-ud-din Ahmad's sources are Afif's *Tarikh-i-Firuz Shahi*, Barani's *Fatawa-i-Jahandari* and some of Amir Khusrau's works like the *Ashiqa* and the *Miftah-ul-Futuh*. Of these, Barani's *Fatawa-i-Jahandari* was probably not known to the historians of Akbar's day, for none of them refers to it.

Besides the chronicles, Nizam-ud-din Ahmad at times makes use of hearsay, individual informants and his personal observation. We are told on the basis of hearsay, the story of a yogi's offer of the transmigration of his soul into the diseased body of Sultan

[1] *Ibid.*, p. 3.
[2] *Ibid.*, Vol. III, p. 3.
[3] *Ibid.*, Vol. I, p. 107.
[4] *Ibid.*, p. 61.

Zain-ul-Abidin of Kashmir.[1] Nizam-ud-din tells us, again on the basis of hearsay, how Shaikh Usman Sarmadi refused to accept the grant of some villages from Prince Muhammad, son of Balban.[2]

It is not often that Nizam-ud-din Ahmad includes in his account information supplied by individuals. However, whenever he does so, the information concerned is never questioned. Thus, for example, he relates the story of how his father helped frustrate the attempt of Mahdi Khwaja to succeed Babur to the throne,[3] obviously basing it on information supplied by the father. Similarly, he informs us of an attack on Mirza Askari by the local Gujarati forces after Bahadur Shah had fled his kingdom. His informant in this case also was his father.[4]

The account of the events in Gujarat during 1580-87,[5] when our author was himself present in that province, is presumably based on his personal observation and experience. Nowhere in the *Tabaqat* does he himself intrude so much into his narrative of events as he does here.

Nizam-ud-din Ahmad's attitude towards his sources is particularly slavish. While for the limited scope of his undertaking it was extremely easy, apart from being necessary, to be somewhat critical of his sources, he betrays an astonishing lack of any examination, or questioning, of the information he receives. In general, his account is not a reflection of his or his informants' *impression* of men and events; it is on the whole a bare structure, a mere narration, of a certain type of event. It was therefore possible for him to check the authenticity of the events narrated through collation, corroboration or sheer logic. Nor were these elementary methods unknown in his day. The *Akbar Nama* of Abul Fazl is a fairly convincing attempt at using these methods.

On the contrary, our author appears merely to copy his sources, in the process, however, summarizing them. This copying is confined not merely to an uncritical acceptance of information but is extended to borrowing the style and language also. The part of his *Tabaqat* dealing with the period of the early Turkish empire in

[1] *Ibid.*, Vol. III, pp. 441-442.
[2] *Ibid.*, Vol. I, p. 88.
[3] *Ibid.*, Vol. II, pp. 28-29.
[4] *Ibid.*, pp. 37-38.
[5] *Ibid.*, pp. 367-391.

India up to the accession of Balban to the throne is unmistakably an abridged version of the corresponding portion in Minhaj's *Tabaqat-i-Nasiri*. It is a prosaic narration of mainly the various expeditions of the Sultans. Where Minhaj departs from his normal style of commencing his account of a Sultan's reign with his enthronement, and briefly describes some salient features of the early life of a prospective Sultan—Iltutmish, for example[1]—Nizam-ud-din follows suit.[2]

Up to the accession of Balban to the throne our author shows no interest in anything except the various battles. No notice is taken of a Sultan's policies, or his thinking, or even his personal virtues and vices. With Balban's enthronement, the language, the scope and the style of the *Tabaqat* change *a la* Barani's *Tarikh*. Dealing with the reign of Balban, for example, Nizam-ud-din reproduces the counsels supposedly given by the Sultan to his two sons.[3] The four principles on which Balban based his administration are also described.[4] More remarkable than these is the long sentimental account of the death of Prince Muhammad.[5] Similarly, the burden of emphasis in the author's account of Kaiqubad's reign is on the intrigues of Malik Nizam-ud-din, with a fairly clear picture of the inner conflicts within the nobility.[6] Prior to this our author had shown no interest in such conflicts and intrigues except where a clear case of armed rebellion against the Sultan was involved. Dealing with the reign of Ala-ud-din, again, Nizam-ud-din reproduces in some detail the market control regulations including the prices fixed by the Sultan[7] and the administrative measures to curb the rebellious tendencies in his subjects.[8] For all this Nizam-ud-

[1]Minhaj, *op. cit.*, Vol. I, pp. 599-605.

[2]*Op. cit.*, Vol. I, pp. 56-57, 61-62.

[3]*Ibid.*, pp. 89-92.

[4]*Ibid.*, p. 81.

[5]*Ibid.*, pp. 97-102. While Barani's grief in describing the death of the Prince is understandable, for he was the patron of two of his greatest friends—Amir Khusrau and Amir Hasan—Nizam-ud-din Ahmad could not have felt it with the same intensity 300 years later.

[6]*Ibid.*, pp. 104-107, 114-116.

[7]*Ibid.*, pp. 158-162.

[8]*Ibid.*, pp. 151-153.

din Ahmad borrows information as well as style from Barani's *Tarikh*.

At times Nizam-ud-din Ahmad summarizes his sources without discrimination; he reproduces two different, even mutually contradictory, versions of the same event as he describes it at two places, obviously borrowing from a different source for each version. The conquest of the fort of Kherla, for example, by Muhammad Shah, son of Humayun Shah Bahmani is described in the tabqa dealing with the Sultans of the Deccan and also in the tabqa of the Sultans of Malwa. The earlier version is: "He (Sultan Muhammad Shah) gave a special robe of honour to Malik Nizam-ul-Mulk, governor of Junair, and appointed him to conquer the fort of Kherla which belonged to the rulers of Mandu. Malik Nizam-ud-din, after arraying the soldiers, crossed the various stages with a large number of men and encamped on the bank of the river which flows in the vicinity of the fort. The Mandu army sallied out of the fort and fought a battle, after which they fled back into the fort, pursued by Nizam-ul-Mulk's soldiers up to the gates. The garrison, having discovered the grandeur of Nizam-ul-Mulk, prayed for safe conduct. Nizam-ul-Mulk, having granted it, had them brought out of the fort and to every individual he gave pan (betel) with his own hands. At this time, one person, having taken the pan, struck Nizam-ul-Mulk with his dagger and made him a martyr. Adil Khan and Darya Khan, the accomplished sons of Nizam-ul-Mulk, killed the thanadar and the entire garrison, and having placed a trusted man in the fort, they left for doing homage to Muhammad Shah carrying with them the dead body of their father. After (they had) the good fortune of service, the mansab and the iqta of their father was conferred on them."[1]

In the other tabqa he gives the following version of this event: "In the year 1462 . . . the petition of Siraj-ul-Mulk, thanadar of the fort of Kherla, arrived with the information that Nizam Shah Deccani had despatched Nizam-ul-Mulk with a large host of soldiers to Kherla and they would reach in a few days. When (Sultan Mahmud Khalji) heard this news he immediately set out for assisting the thanadar. On the way the news arrived that Nizam-ul-Mulk Turk, having arrived, had assaulted the fort and at

[1]*Ibid.*, Vol. III, pp. 45-46.

the time when Nizam-ul-Mulk was nearing the vicinity of the fort, Siraj-ul-Mulk was busy getting intoxicated and had lost awareness of himself. The son of Siraj-ul-Mulk had come out of the fort, engaged in battle and fled. Nizam-ul-Mulk, out of his pride and haughtiness, did not occupy himself in arranging the affairs of that place. On hearing this news Sultan Mahmud despatched Maqbul Khan with four thousand horsemen towards the fort, and himself marched towards Daultabad to take his revenge."[1] What was the result of these efforts on the part of the Khalji ruler Nizam-ud-din Ahmad does not tell us.

More interesting is our author's description of the conquest (?) of Chanderi by Sultan Sikandar Lodi. In the tabqa of the Sultans of Delhi he writes, "At this time Bahjat Khan, governor of Chanderi, whose ancestors had for generations been obedient to the rulers of Malwa, on account of the weakness of Sultan Mahmud Malwi and the disturbed condition of his kingdom, joined (the service of) the Sultan (Sikandar Lodi) by sending presents. The Sultan sent Imad-ul-Mulk Bidah, whose name was Ahmad, towards Chanderi that he, in concert with Bahjat Khan, might have the khutba read in the Sultan's name in Chanderi and its neighbourhood. After this the Sultan returned from Dholpur to Agra, and by sending firmans containing the good news of the submission of Bahjat Khan and the reading of the khutba (in his name) in the territory of Chanderi and the gaining of fresh victories, raised his prestige in all sides and directions."[2]

Later on, referring to the same event in the tabqa dealing with the Sultans of Malwa he narrates, "Sayid Khan Lodi and Imad-ul-Mulk sent a massage to Bahjat Khan that the understanding that had been reached was that as soon as the victorious armies of Sikandar arrived in the territory of Chanderi the khutba would be read in the great name of the Alexander of the age (Sikandar Lodi) and that dirhams and dinars would also be struck in, and impressed with, the Emperor's name. But, to this day, no sign of these has manifested itself. And since they did not get a suitable reply, they marched from the mauza of Sahrai and halted fourteen krohs further back, and from there they reported the matter to Sultan

[1] *Ibid.*, pp. 343-344.
[2] *Ibid.*, Vol. I, p. 332.

Sikandar. The Sultan had them recalled."[1]

That this approach of summarizing diverse sources of information incidentally confers an advantage on the present-day student of history—in that it presents more than one contemporary view of events—cannot be denied. Yet this fact would not entitle the work to an explicit commendation. The *Tabaqat* in substance being largely a straight narrative of political events, collation and authentication of information was the least claim that a reader could make on the author even by medieval standards.

TREATMENT OF HISTORY AND HISTORICAL CAUSATION

Nizam-ud-din Ahmad's entire approach—the scope and method of his work, the treatment of the subject and the reliance on a very selective bibliography for his information—is fundamentally related to the objective of his writing the *Tabaqat*. The objective was to demonstrate through his writing the unification of diverse regions in India under the imperial banner during the reign of Akbar. "Now that all the districts and provinces of Hindustan," he says, "have been conquered by the world-opening sword of His Majesty the Viceregent of God, and the many have been unified into one and various provinces from amongst those which are outside (the territory) of Hindustan, such as had never been acquired by the great Sultans, have been included in His Majesty's dominions . . . it came to the dull mind (of the author) that he should write a complete account of the events of the entire Hindustan in a very lucid style from the reign of Subuktgin. . . to the year 1001 H., the thirty-seventh regnal year of His Majesty,[2] tabqa by tabqa—and the end of (the account of) each tabqa should coincide with (the account of) a victory of His Majesty's glorious army . . . . Then he should give a compendium of all the victories, events and occurrences of His Majesty's reign. These should be described in brief, each in its own place. Their details are recorded in . . . the *Akbar Nama*."[3]

[1]*Ibid.*, Vol. III, p. 391.

[2]He actually records the events up to the thirty-eighth year of Akbar's reign, 1002 H. (1594), *ibid.*, Vol. II, p. 424.

[3]*Ibid.*, Vol. I, pp. 2-3.

Having limited himself thus, Nizam-ud-din confines his treatment of the subject to the *narration* of what is known as political history. By and large the emphasis in the *Tabaqat* is on the enthronement of a ruler, his conquests, rebellions against him, and the suppression of these rebellions. Indeed, the nearly twenty-year reign of Sultan Muhammad Shah bin Mahmud bin Bahman Shah of the Bahmani kingdom has been disposed of by the author in just a few sentences, for he "could find nothing of interest in it."[1] The only event he takes note of in this reign is a rebellion which was suppressed. There are cases where he barely mentions the name of the ruler and the length of his reign.[2]

While Nizam-ud-din Ahmad is conscious of the objective of his writing the *Tabaqat*—to record the integration of various regions into a single entity that was Akbar's empire—this objective, for him, is not the end result of any *process* directed either by a force (or forces) within history or outside it. That is, he does not treat history as a self-impelled force, with the events as the manifestation of this force, moving in any particular direction, nor does he introduce any supernatural elements directing a predetermined plan of historical events. History, for him, has no such logic, nor any inherent or supernatural design, nor, indeed, any lesson except that its study "sharpens the intellect and is a source of examples to the meritorious."[3] History, in short, is for him a narration of events rather than a study of their causes.

Consequently, Nizam-ud-din Ahmad treats history as a collection of individual, atomized events. Even the selection of events for narration in the *Tabaqat* is not based, explicitly or implicitly, on any theoretical understanding of history. Whatever selection he

[1] *Ibid.*, Vol. III, p. 11. He says, "for 19 years the administration of the territory of the Deccan was under his control. There is nothing worthy of mention among the events of his reign. Towards the end, the thanadar of the fort of Sagar became rebellious.The Sultan went to quell his rebellion and was successful. In this expedition itself he died. The duration of his reign was 19 years, 9 months and 24 days."

[2] *Ibid.*, pp. 81-82 where, for example, he disposes of the reigns of four rulers in such a manner. The summary treatment of a reign as in the following instance, "Jamshed succeeded his father and ruled for seven years," (*ibid.*, p. 81) is nothing exceptional.

[3] *Ibid.*, Vol. I, pp. 1-2.

makes appears to be arbitrary and at times influenced more by his personal consideration of avoiding controversies of all kinds rather than by an intellectual position. This becomes particularly clear when events are described without going deep into the details of the process of their development that precedes their actual occurrence.

Thus, for example, the story of Bairam Khan's fall is narrated in considerably over-simple terms.[1] As our author describes that event, it was Maham Anaga, her son Adham Khan, and Shihab-ud-din Ahmed, who, out of jealousy of Bairam Khan, poisoned the mind of the young Akbar against him. Akbar's firman, issued from Delhi, which for the first time informed Bairam Khan of the Emperor's changed disposition towards him, was apparently received by the Khan rather casually, for he, without much astonishment or ado, expressed a wish to proceed to Mecca.

Now, what escapes Nizam-ud-din Ahmad is that it was Akbar himself who was growing conscious of his authority and of Bairam Khan's encroachment on it, and that Akbar's assertion of his authority, with which Bairam Khan's position came into conflict, was the beginning of the development of a new system of polity. The import of this event is missed by the author.

A more interesting instance, however, of such descriptions of events is the account of the signing of the Mahzar in Akbar's court.[2] In all, our author devotes about half a page to the process which culminated in the emergence of the important document and naively informs us that once, during some discussions, the question of ijtihad[3] and the position of the mujtahid came up. Upon that, all the important Ulema, including Shaikh Abd-un-Nabi and the Makhdum-ul-Mulk, and others like Shaikh Mubarak presented the said document to the Emperor with their signatures inscribed on it. The text of the document then follows.

It is obvious that Nizam-ud-din is trying to avoid entering into a controversy or making a value judgment. The signing of the Mahzar has only one significance for him for which it deserved inclusion in the *Tabaqat*—it had been signed. What considerations,

[1] *Ibid.*, Vol. II, pp. 142-147.
[2] *Ibid.*, pp. 344-345.
[3] Interpretation of questions of theology.

tensions and attitudes were involved in the process, do not concern him, nor do the consequences of it.

Similar is his treatment of the introduction of administrative measures. He mentions, for example, the introduction of the karori system just as a result of an imperial command issued in the nineteenth regnal year (of Akbar)[1] without relating it to the administrative and institutional changes it inaugurated. Indeed, like a battle somewhere, this measure has been "narrated" and done with in barely half a page.

Yet, within these limitations, Nizam-ud-din Ahmad's subordination of personalities to events is a significant departure from history writing during the period of the Sultanate and, to an extent, even during his own period. The acceptance of the basic (regnal) form is a continuation from the earlier times, but the burden of his emphasis within these accepted limits is on events and not on personal biographies of the *dramatis personae* including the rulers. That is, the events are not treated in the *Tabaqat* as the outward manifestation of the unfolding of the lives of the rulers or their supporters or adversaries, but as events that occurred at the hands of these persons.

It is significant that in the main body of the *Tabaqat* we rarely find personal biographies of men, though it is not completely devoid of them.[2] Nizam-ud-din Ahmad seldom formally "introduces" an individual, in that he seldom gives details of his personal life before describing his role in some event or other. He would refer to him, even if for the first time, as part of his description of some event without otherwise yielding any information about his life including the author's own. It is therefore only logical that when Nizam-ud-din Ahmad comes to the treatment of men exclusively,[3] he shows himself at his weakest. His pages on the umra, the Ulema and the hakims, etc., of Akbar's court are perhaps a necessary paraphernalia of a book of history written during the 16th century, rather than a source of detailed information on the

[1] *Ibid.*, pp. 300-301.

[2] There are some details, for example, of the personal lives of Iltutmish and Sher Shah prior to their accession to the throne, *ibid.*, Vol. I, pp 56-57 and Vol. II, pp. 86-101 respectively. Similarly, Shah Mansur, once Akbar's Diwan, has been treated to this rare favour, *ibid.*, Vol II, p. 327.

[3] *Ibid.*, Vol. II, pp. 425-520.

lives of the persons concerned. He might, indeed, have been aware of it, and therefore at times in this portion of the book he abandons even the half line for each and just recounts their names.[1]

STYLE

Nizam-ud-din Ahmad's conception of writing regional (or provincial) histories at one place, in the third volume, is his single great contribution to the form of history writing in the 16th century. Apparently he conceived of this plan because no other work of this model was available.[2] The purpose of his writing the *Tabaqat* was therefore to fill this lacuna and write a compendious history of the "whole of Hindustan."

The *Tabaqat* has for long been considered one of the most reliable sources of our information. It would appear that its narrative style and the absence of value judgments in it have been construed to be its strongest points, for these provided a stable prototype for writing political history. The narration of individual events rather than their evaluation, individually or collectively, may have been taken for objectivity. For the present-day historian, however, this may prove to be its chief weakness.

[1]*Ibid.*, pp. 468, 469, 470, 478, 479, 480, etc.
[2]*Ibid.*, Vol. I, pp. 2-3.

CHAPTER 5

Some Minor Historical Works Written During Akbar's Reign

An attempt has been made in this chapter to analyze some of the minor historical works written during the reign of Akbar. These are Bayazid Biyat's *Tazkira-i-Humayun-wa-Akbar*, Abbas Sarwani's *Tuhfa-i-Akbar Shahi* (or *Tarikh-i-Sher Shahi*), and Jauhar Aftabchi's *Tazkirat-ul-Waqiat*. These works have been selected out of a considerably long list for the reason that a common thread binds them together in the diversity of their styles and the nature of information. All the three were written as memoirs to serve as sources for the *Akbar Nama*.[1] Yet all these books are used today

[1]Of these authors only Bayazid specifically states that the work he had undertaken was meant to furnish information to Abul Fazl. He begins, however by making a general statement: "Akbar had asked all the servants of the court, who had an aptitude for (writing) history to write (one). In fact, if anyone remembered anything about the reign of Humayun, he was to write it down and submit it for the Book of Akbar's Name (the *Akbar Nama*)," *Tazkira-i-Humayun-wa-Akbar*, Bib Ind., pp. 1-2.

Abbas Sarwani tells us that he had been asked by Akbar to write down whatever he remembered of the events to which he had borne personal witness or about which he had reliable information, *Tuhfa-i-Akbar Shahi*, I.O.L. Persian MSS. Ethe 219=I.O 218, Rotograph, Research Library, Deptt. of History, Aligarh Muslim University, f. 2b.

Jauhar however states that he had written his *Tazkirat-ul-Waqiat* on his own so as to leave behind his memorial in the world, *op.cit.*, f. 3b. Nevertheless, his treatment of the subject shows that like the others, it is a memoir and as such it might also have been written at Akbar's command.

I have not included a study of the *Humayun Nama* of Gulbadan Begam in this chapter though it falls in the same class of works as the three mentioned above. The reason is that I feel I have practically nothing to add to what its translator, Mrs Beveridge, has said in her introduction to the translation.

as independent sources of information. Hence a separate analysis.

BAYAZID'S *Tazkira-i-Humayun-wa-Akbar*

The Tazkira comprises events of half a century, from 1542-43 to 1590-91. In the former year Bayazid had entered Humayun's service in Persia.[1] Since he was to write an eye witness account of events, he commences his work from 1542-43. The other date signifies the year of writing.[2]

Bayazid did not write the book himself on account of paralysis of his left side.[3] Instead, he dictated it to a scribe appointed by Abul Fazl.[4] Nor had our author prepared any rough draft for the purpose.

As a result, the whole work is disjointed. The facts given are of "a rambling character."[5] Bayazid would suddenly remember some events, as it were, and dictate them to his scribe even if it meant disturbing the whole sequence of his narrative.

Although Bayazid claims to have written (or dictated, to be precise) everything from memory,[6] there is inferential evidence to believe that he might have used some records at some points of his narration. For example, he has given in full Shah Tahmasp's firman to the governor of Khurasan in which the minutest details regarding the reception to be accorded to Humayun on his entry into Persia have been mentioned.[7] At another place Bayazid gives three lists of men who were attached to Humayun, Prince Akbar and Bairam Khan on their return from Kabul to Hindustan.[8] The list of those accompanying Humayun contains the names of singers

[1]Bayazid, *op. cit.*, p. 106.

[2]*Ibid.*, pp. 2, 373. The chronogram for the completion of the work.Rashk-i-Jannat-i-Javed, p. 374, yields 997 H., 1588-89. However, year 999 H. 1590-91 is the correct date, for Bayazid refers to the events of that year, pp. 373, 374.

[3]*Ibid.*, p 373.

[4]*Ibid.*, p. 2.

[5]H. Beveridge, "The Memoirs of Bayazid (Bajazet) Biyat," *J.A.S.B.*, Vol. LXVII, Part I, No. 4, 1898, p. 297.

[6]Bayazid, *op. cit*, p. 1.

[7]*Ibid.*, pp. 12-31.

[8]*Ibid.*, pp. 176-187.

and musicians also which Bayazid specifies. The three lists together contain 333 names—Humayun's list, 226; Akbar's, 56; and Bairam Khan's, 51; and they include everyone from princes and amirs to watermen and singers and painters. It may be suggested that to dig out 333 names 40-years old from memory and with so assured an exactness as to divide them into three separate lists is implausible and the existence of written lists in Bayazid's hands must be assumed. This is particularly so, for Bayazid's memory was not entirely reliable as is attested to by his extensive confusion of dates.[1] It is quite possible, therefore, that the author *was* using some records to substantiate some specific parts of his narrative. He might possibly have obtained access to these records on account of his intimacy with Munim Khan Khan-i-Khanan.[2]

Perhaps the most valuable information that this book yields consists of the various lists of nobles (given in different contexts) and the details of administration. There is, for example, a list of the amirs who accompanied Humayun to Shah Tahmasp.[3] Similarly, there is a list of the Persian nobles deputed by the Shah to assist Humayun.[4] There is a list of nobles who were with Humayun on the eve of his departure for Kabul after the conquest of Qandhar[5]; and there is another of those who accompanied the Emperor from Kabul to Hindustan.[6]

These lists can obviously be of immense help for identifying persons as also for reconstructing the organization of the nobility and its composition in terms of various groups and, possibly, interests.

The information on administration contained in the *Tazkira* is more incidental and, there is reason to believe, fairly authentic. Bayazid had been in the service of one or another noble or in the imperial service itself for nearly five decades.[7] Generally he had

[1]This point will be discussed later.

[2]For his closeness to Munim Khan, see Bayazid, *op. cit.*, pp. 220-221, 224-225, 232-233, 302-303, 312-313, etc.

[3]*Ibid.*, pp. 4-7.

[4]*Ibid.*, pp. 35-36.

[5]*Ibid.*, pp. 52-53.

[6]*Ibid.*, pp. 176-183.

[7]*Ibid.*, p. 376 where Akbar is reported to have stated that Bayazid had been in the imperial service for two *qarns*. At the time of writing (1590-91) Bayazid

served as a minor functionary ultimately reaching, after this long service, the mansab of 300.[1] At times he was also given fairly important jobs like administering Chunar[2] and Dipalpur[3] or the superintendence of the imperial mint at Fatehpur,[4] etc. This, plus his closeness to Munim Khan, of which he is ever so boastful, must have given him an insight into the actual working of the administrative system. Thus, even the incidental details about the administration given in the *Tazkira* are important for this reason. It is Bayazid, for instance, who tells us, of course casually, that the khalisa did not signify merely the crown lands, or lands held under the direct administration of the crown—even an amir could hold khalisa lands to himself, which is obviously different from saying that an amir could be granted or assigned land out of the crown's reserve. Unfortunately, however, no more details of this phenomenon are available. In fact, even this is an inference drawn from a remark made by the author.[5]

It is in Bayazid's book, and probably there alone, that we find the minutest details of the actual procedure of the escheat of a dead amir's property.[6]

Bayazid, however, confuses dates very generously. This is not entirely unexpected, for he was speaking to his scribe from his

---

had completed 50 years in the service of two Mughal emperors, Humayun and Akbar, having joined it in 1542-43, pp. 373 and 106 respectively.

[1]Abul Fazl, *Ain*, Vol. I (*tr.*), p. 563.

[2]Bayazid, *op. cit.*, p. 352.

[3]*Ibid.*, p. 353.

[4]*Ibid.*, p. 373.

[5]Bayazid tells us that he was once imprisoned for twenty-nine days at the orders of Munim Khan, who, he says, had been instigated by some people to that end. Then he was released and rehabilitated in the Khan-i-Khanan's favour. Indeed the Khan-i-Khanan profusely apologized to him for the unfortunate happening, and asked him to return to Banaras where he was managing his (Mu[illegible]m Khan's) jagir. Our author then reminded himself of an oath he had taken never to go to Banaras again. He therefore requested Munim Khan to turn Banaras into *his* khalsa where the author would be the shiqdar. In this manner the oath could be kept. The request was accepted, *op. cit.*, pp. 302-303.

[6]*Ibid.*, pp. 349-351. Bayazid tells us how he managed the escheat of Munim Khan's property after his death. Even the expense incurred on the ceremonies of mourning was not to be met out of the late amir's property. In this case it was Bayazid himself who met the expense.

memory of events, sometimes half a century or so after their happening. Nor did he have any training in historical method; nor, indeed, was it expected of him for he had not been asked to write history. Thus, he dates Humayun's departure from Tabriz to Mashahad in March 1534.[1] The correct date is given by Abul Fazl as July 1544.[2] Bayazid's date of Akbar's birth is the night of Monday, 6th (month not given) of the year 946 H./1539.[3] This adds three years to Akbar's actual age, for he was born in 1542.[4] Bayazid places the first encounter between Humayun and Kamran (on the former's return from Persia) in 1535.[5] Abul Fazl correctly places it ten years later.[6]

The language of the *Tazkira* is entirely devoid of any polish. At times the impression becomes inescapable that Bayazid was speaking Persian but thinking in Hindustani. One could spot out passage after passage to show that the author's language was grammatically as well as idiomatically deficient and that what he said made sense only in Hindustani. He uses Hindustani words like "jhakkar" Persianized into "jakkar."[7] At times the Hindustani word "chaar" replaces the Persian "chahar."[8] The phrase "baad yak ghari"[9] would be intelligible only to one conversant with the Indian divisions of time. The phrase "jhak zadah" is obviously a literal translation of the Hindustani "jhak maari."[10] On the whole, Bayazid displays a gross departure from the literary idiom of the Persian language.

One very noticeable feature of the *Tazkira*, particularly in the latter part of it, is the author's desire to emphasize his own importance. He practically makes himself the hero of the book, whose counsel is sought by everyone from the Emperor and the Khan-i-Khanan

[1] *Ibid.*, p. 37.

[2] Abul Fazl, *Akbar Nama*, Vol. I, p. 216.

[3] Bayazid, *op. cit.*, p. 46.

[4] Abul Fazl, *Akbar Nama*, Vol. I, p. 18; Gulbadan Begam, *Humayun Nama*, Mrs A.S. Beveridge (ed.), London, 1902, p. 59; Jauhar Aftabchi, *op. cit.*, f.55a.

[5] Bayazid, *op. cit.*, p. 58.

[6] Abul Fazl, *Akbar Nama*, Vol. I, p. 244.

[7] Bayazid, *op. cit.*, p. 246.

[8] *Ibid.*, pp. 283, 285.

[9] *Ibid.*, p. 283.

[10] *Ibid.*, p. 287.

downwards. And his advice always turns out to be the most appropriate. His narration of events about the march of the imperial armies under the leadership of Munim Khan to Kabul in the eighth regnal year of Akbar is so framed as to prove that Haidar Muhammad Akhtabegi's advice to the Khan-i-Khanan, which was contrary to Bayazid's, proved disastrous. And, ultimately, the Khan-i-Khanan eagerly sought our author's counsel once again which, of course, he tendered most willingly. As a result, "the advice of Haidar Muhammad Akhtabegi was no longer heeded to."[1] It is possible that all these counsels may have been simply an afterthought. At any rate, this ascription of an exaggerated importance to himself may be an indication of the mentality of a petty official who had been able to obtain the mansab of 300 at the most.

A feature Bayazid has in common with the other memoirists is the relation of less formal incidents than those included in the political histories of the period. The story of Emperor Humayun greatly enjoying a very meagre meal of horse flesh and afterwards remembering it as the most delicious one he had ever had, is very interestingly told by Bayazid.[2] No less interesting is the story of our author winning a game of cards and making his opponent, Muqim, mortgage his garments, much to the delight of Akbar.[3] There is then the story that Kamran wanted the Sunnis' hatred of Ali ibn Abu Talib to be as big as a pumpkin instead of an orange.[4] Beveridge's remark that Abul Fazl had taken this story from Bayazid and had rather spoiled it[5] is fully borne out by a comparison. Finally, Bayazid has reproduced a very interesting exchange of courtesies between Shaikh Abd-un-Nabi, Makhdum-ul-Mulk, and Mirza Muflis. In one of the sittings in the Ibadat Khana Shaikh Abd-un-Nabi and Makhdum-ul-Mulk, having found Mirza Muflis alone, tried to harass him. They put very intricate questions to him. As Makhdum-ul-Mulk had placed one problem before him, and he had not yet replied to it, Shaikh Abd-un-Nabi, from

[1] *Ibid.*, pp. 253-264. For some other pieces of advice, pp. 214-216, 275-276, 324-326, etc.

[2] *Ibid.*, p. 124.

[3] *Ibid.*, pp. 241-242.

[4] *Ibid.*, p. 100.

[5] H. Beveridge, *Akbar Nama* (*tr.*), Vol. I, p. 537 fn.

the other side, gestured to place another. Mirza Muflis, in response to the Shaikh, said, "Thou little slave! Have patience until I have answered the question of the big slave; after that I shall answer you." And this remark of Mirza Muflis became known throughout India and holy Mecca.[1]

ABBAS SARWANI'S *Tuhfa-i-Akbar Shahi*

The *Tuhfa-i-Akbar Shahi*, as its author, Abbas Sarwani, had named it,[2] originally comprised three chapters. The first two chapters dealt with the reigns of Sher Shah (whom, in courteous recognition of the Mughal feelings on the Sur claims to sovereignty, he calls Sher Khan throughout the book) and Islam Shah (Islam Khan) respectively. The third chapter had not been assigned to any individual monarch; it deals with "The Affairs of the Amirs Who Claimed the Sultanate after Islam Khan and Struck Coins and Read the Khutba in Their Name and Who Removed the Son of Islam Khan From the Throne."[3] Of these three only the first chapter has survived. I have used the Aligarh Muslim University rotograph of the copy that is preserved in the India Office Library. It is dated 1620-21.[4] The colophone of the MS tells us that it belonged to Adil Shah's Library where it was entered in 1654-55.

The book opens with a description of the situation that obtained with the establishment of the Lodi empire at Delhi, surrounded by various other provincial kingdoms.

The *Tuhfa* is frankly a panegyric of Sher Shah. The loyalty of the author rests unreservedly with the founder of the second Afghan empire in India.

Abbas Sarwani was an Afghan himself and claimed a distant relationship with Sher Shah.[5] He also claimed contacts in the

[1]Bayazid, *op. cit.*, pp. 307-308, Beveridge has missed the bitter irony by reading "ghulam-i-khurd" (little slave) as "ghulam-i-kor" (blind slave) which also he translates merely as "slave," "The Memoirs of Bayazid Biyat," p. 314.

[2]Abbas Sarwani, *op. cit.*, ff. 2a, 33a.

[3]*Ibid.*, ff. 2a-b.

[4]*Ibid.*, f. 121b.

[5]*Ibid.*, f. 33a.

highest places of the second Afghan empire. He was married to the daughter of Muzaffar Khan who was, in turn, the nephew of Isa Khan.[1] He also proudly states that he and Isa Khan belonged to the same tribe.[2] At another place he states that when Sher Shah got burnt at Kalinjar, and the important nobles waited upon him, Sher Shah called Abbas's uncle (whom he does not identify) and said that they should capture the fort before he died.[3] At still another place Abbas claims descent from a respectable family of Roh. He was the grandson of Shaikh Bayazid Sarwani, head of the Sarwani tribe of Roh.[4] One of his ancestors, Shaikh Bayazid, was welcomed by Sher Shah by standing up and escorting him a few steps.[5] Our author's father, Shaikh Ali, was similarly received by Islam Shah.[6]

Abbas Sarwani's pride in being an Afghan, and such a respectable one at that, occasionally manifests itself in various incidental remarks. The irony, for instance, in the following statement of his is ill-concealed: "When His Majesty Humayun Padshah reached Lahore, some Mughals, who had recently arrived from Central Asia and had not witnessed a war with the Afghans, appealed to Humayun that they be sent to fight the Afghans. They boasted (like this), 'What are those Afghans that they should become our adversaries on the day of battle?' Humayun set the Mughals in array . . . . The Mughals were routed and returned to Lahore."[7] Similarly, Abbas remarks that Humayun had once been warned by Khan-i-Khanan Yusuf Khaila, the Afghan, to beware of Sher Khan who was very seditious and who fully knew the methods of (establishing) an empire, and that all the Afghans had collected under him. "But His Majesty Humayun Padshah, in excessive pride of his kingship, ignored Sher Khan."[8] After stating this Abbas explains how Humayun was entrapped in Bengal which finally led to his rout at Chausa.

[1] *Ibid.*, ff. 83a-b.
[2] *Ibid.*
[3] *Ibid.*, ff. 102a-b.
[4] *Ibid.*, f.85b.
[5] *Ibid.*, ff. 85a-86a
[6] *Ibid.*, f.86b.
[7] *Ibid.*, ff.84a-b.
[8] *Ibid.*, f. 54a.

Abbas Sarwani's pride in and commitment to the Afghan cause are inherent in the very system of his analysis and narration of history. The basic premises of his work are that the Afghans were far superior to the Mughals in the field of battle, and that the disunity of the Afghans was their greatest curse which had caused the collapse of the first Afghan empire. Against this background Sher Khan's attempt at uniting them and re-establishing the second Afghan empire was a cardinal achievement.[1]

This historical analysis leads our author into writing an euology of Sher Shah. Unfortunately for him, writing as he was during the reign of Akbar and at his behest, he had to refer to Sher Shah merely as Sher Khan, for he was treated merely as a rebel by the Mughal state.[2] Only thrice does he call him Sher Shah, once for stating the fact of his assumption of that title[3] and twice again, which, perhaps, were slips.[4] His reverence for Sher Shah in a style that is due to an Emperor is, however, reflected in other incidental remarks. He refers to Sher Shah's falling ill thus: "Fever overtook his blessed person."[5] He goes on to say, "God the Almighty granted him relief from that fever and gave him health." At another place he refers to one of Sher Shah's firmans as "firman-i-ali shan" as if it was an imperial rescript.[6] His remarks on Sher Khan's occupation of Bihar following the defeat of Ibrahim, ruler of Bengal, are significant: "Since Almighty God had willed at the beginning of Time that He will grant the country of Hind to Sher Khan and that the people of God would live in peace and tranquillity in the shadow of his justice, and that the ruler would be powerful and just, his (Sher Khan's) empire was on the increase day after day and he moved himself to consolidating and cultivating any territory that came under his control."[7]

[1]*Ibid.*, ff.121a-b, where he remarks, "During the period of his rule, Sher Shah completely eliminated from amongst the Afghans of Roh and Hind the mutual animosity and conflicts that are innate to their nature; in astuteness and effectiveness, Sher Khan was unique in his age." See also ff.51a, 66b.

[2]Abul Fazl, Nizam-ud-din Ahmad, Badauni all refer to him as Sher Khan,

[3]"Sher Shah Shah Alam," Sarwani, *op. cit.*, f.74a.

[4]*Ibid.*, ff.82b, 121a.

[5]*Ibid.* f.92b.

[6]*Ibid.*, f.80b.

[7]*Ibid.*, f.43a

Sher Shah's success after the earlier failure of the Afghans appears to have overwhelmed our author, particularly as, at the time of his writing, the empire had been eliminated again, presumably for the same reasons as earlier.[1] Between these two failures, Sher Shah's success appeared to him a glorious achievement on which he looks back with nostalgia.

This nostalgic approach to Sher Shah's achievement made him overlook any shortcomings in the career of Sher Shah, at any period in his life, in any sphere of activity, personal or political. The administrative system of Sher Shah appears to him perfect in every detail,[2] the empire stable and the prestige of the Afghans high.

Against this background it is possible that Abbas may have added something of his own to the details, apart from colouring whatever details were factual. The possibility is all the more strongly inherent in the style of his writing. A large part of the book is in the form of reproduction of either dialogues or discourses of the men concerned with the events. It is possible to argue that these dialogues and discourses might be as much the author's own explanations or those of his informants as of the principal persons.Thus, for example, when Humayun set out on his march back from Bengal, we are told that Sher Khan sought the counsel of his amirs as to the alternative courses open to him. "Azam Humayun Sarwani, who was one of the great amirs of Sultan(s) Sikandar and Ibrahim said, 'Regarding a conflict with the Mughals, you should not seek the advice of the sons of the amirs of Sultan(s) Bahlul and Sikandar because whatever method we had thought of failed on account of (our) misfortune, and whatever battle we joined with the Mughals we were defeated on account of the hostility of our own amirs. Fortune has been kind to

[1]The chapter dealing with this period of the second Afghan empire has been lost to us. Some idea, however, of what Abbas Sarwani might have discussed in this chapter can be formed from its title which has survived, "The Affairs of the Amirs who Claimed the Sultanate After Islam Khan and Struck Coins and Read the Khutba in Their Name and Who Removed the Son of Islam Khan from the Throne," *ibid.*, f.2a.

[2]*Ibid.*, f.43a where he writes, "In a short time. . .it became known that Sher Khan pays the soldiers their due and does not oppress the peasant nor does he allow others to oppress (them),"

you that the Afghan soldiers are with you with all their mind and heart and have become bold enough for a war with the Mughals. The wise have spoken thus to me, that the Afghans are not inferior to the Mughals in wielding the sword; but on account of their mutual hostility they flee from the battle. The moment the Afghans have one leader and they are with him, they would be able to drive the Mughals out of Hind. You are that fortunate one and you should consult your own new amirs. Whatever advice they tender, act upon that and you will be blessed with victory'. After listening to the words of Azam Humayun Sarwani, Sher Khan inquired of his own amirs. The new amirs of Sher Khan, Qutb Khan Naib, Haibat Khan Niyazi, Jalal Khan bin Jallu, Shujaat Khan and Sarmast Khan Sarbani, etc., unanimously suggested that war be waged on the Mughals and that they would never get a chance like that again."[1]

That the amirs of the eminence of Azam Humayun Sarwani would have surrendered their importance so willingly and that Sher Khan would be equally anxious to accept their resignation is not an ordinary occurrence. What has been attributed to Azam Humayun may have been the author's own interpretation or that of his informant. It might even be what he wished to have happened.

Similarly, Abbas tells us that after Humayun had formally granted the fort of Chunar to Sher Khan, the Afghan leader started organizing his followers. He brought into the army some of the Afghans who had taken to retirement on account of "tragic accidents of Time," and killed the others who did not adopt the profession of a soldier and had become mendicants. He said, "I shall kill every Afghan who did not become a soldier."[2] In the background of Abbas's repeated emphasis on Sher Khan's attempts at uniting and reorganizing the Afghan forces, could it be that the above statement was the author's wish (or that of his informants) or his interpretation of what may have been Sher Khan's attempt at a general mobilization of the Afghans (or the interpretation of his informants)?

It is significant that the circle of Abbas's informants was very

[1] *Ibid.*, ff.66b-67a.
[2] *Ibid.*, ff.50b-51a.

narrow. He tells us that he had derived his information from "reliable Afghans" who were proficient in the knowledge of history and who had been with the Afghan empire from its beginning to its end.[1] At another place he states that he had obtained information for a large part of what he had written from his father-in-law, Khan i-Azam Muzaffar Khan, whose ancestors had been great amirs of Hind.[2]

It is not surprising then that Abul Fazl, for whose assistance the book had been written, found it of little use to him.[3] The respective points of view of the two authors were mutually too antagonistic to admit of any compromise.

JAUHAR AFTABCHI'S *Tazkirat-ul-Waqiat*

The distinction of Jauhar Aftabchi's *Tazkirat-ul-Waqiat* rests on the intimate and unaffected style which lends it an aura of sincerity.

Jauhar had been in attendance upon Humayun for over two decades[4] and was a witness to some of the most confidential consultations by the Emperor.[5]

"It therefore occurred to me," he says, "that I should write down the events from the beginning of (Humayun's) reign to its end when His Majesty the Emperor regained the empire."[6] This book he wanted to leave behind as his memorial in this world. He named it *Tazkirat-ul-Waqiat*.[7]

The *Waqiat* consists of thirty-three chapters. The chapters have been arranged in a chronological sequence though the chronology is not strictly annual. There are at times gaps of the events of an year

[1] *Ibid.*, f.2b.

[2] *Ibid.*, f.83b.

[3] A comparison between Abul Fazl's and Sarwani's treatment of Sher Shah's life and reign would show that Abul Fazl had borrowed little from his source.

[4] Jauhar, *op. cit.*, f.122b where referring to the events of 1554 he states that he had completed nineteen years in Humayun's service till then.

[5] *Ibid.*, f.63a where the author tells us that Humayun had no objection to his staying on in the Presence even as a stranger was informing the Emperor of the evil designs of Askari.

[6] *Ibid.*, f.3b.

[7] *Ibid.*, f.3a.

or more between two chapters.[1] However, this obviously implies that Jauhar had done some amount of planning before be gave his work its final shape. It is also to be noted that the author makes use of some official documents in the course of his writing. He quotes, for example, a letter of Humayun to Shah Abu Ma'ali in regard to his complaint that many of the amirs had deserted him and joined Bairam Khan; and another to Bairam Khan in response to his petition in connection with the same incident.[2] He also gives the substance of a letter written by Humayun to all his relations announcing his personal safety after the battle of Qipchaq.[3]

The main significance of Jauhar's work rests on two scores—some very intimate and enlivening details of some of the events of the period which he describes in his own full knowledge; and an impression of the general atmosphere during the reign of Humayun, particularly after his defeat at Kanauj, which Jauhar conveys perhaps unwittingly.

We are told, for example, how insolently Zahid Beg behaved with the Emperor when Humayun expressed his desire to nominate him to the governorship of Bengal prior to the battle of Chausa. In the private assembly Zahid Beg said to Humayun, "Could you not find another place to kill me in that you are leaving me in Bengal?"[4] This remark infuriated the Emperor immensely. He was not conciliated even on the intervention of Bega Begam whose sister was wedded to Zahid. Zahid Beg then fled and instigated Haji Muhammad Koka and Dindar Beg also to flee. The three of them fled to Agra where they "deluded Mirza Hindal into rebellion."[5]

When Humayun was defeated at Kanauj, some flag bearers tied their turbans to help the Emperor climb the steep bank of the river and brought him a horse on which he rode back to Agra. On reaching safety, Jauhar tells us, Humayun remarked, "the persons who commanded the flag bearers were two brothers who seemed so

[1]The second chapter, for example, deals with the events of 1533 (ff.5a-12a) and the third with those of 1537 (12a-15a); the 23rd chapter deals with 1548 (ff.101b-106a) and the 24th with 1550 (106a-112b).

[2]*Ibid.*, f.143a.

[3]*Ibid.*, f.109b. The battle took place in 1550 between Humayun and Kamrān at Qipchaq Pass on the northwestern frontier.

[4]*Ibid.*, ff.18a-b.

[5]*Ibid.*, f.18b.

affectionate to each other that it aroused sympathy in my heart and I became anxious for the safety of my brother Hindal and my other relatives." When Hindal arrived shortly afterwards and paid his respects, Humayun felt greatly relieved.[1]

When Humayun reached Lahore, on his way out of his empire, Mirza Hindal and some other amirs, according to Jauhar, "suggested to Humayun that Kamran may be done away with so that the armies should become united and their division may disappear. His Majesty did not accept this suggestion that for the sake of this ephemeral world his brother be deprived of his life. He also remembered the advice of Babur: 'Beware Humayun, a thousand times beware! Never bring in killings amongst brothers and never adopt evil intentions'. Humayun was therefore not prepared to do that kind of unworthy thing."[2]

We are told that Humayun, as he was wandering in the deserts of Sind, paid off his huge debt to a Mughal merchant through mutual agreement by allowing him to drink as much water as he could.[3]

Jauhar gives the impression that Humayun took the decision to blind Kamran rather suddenly, and passed on the order rather indifferently without even nominating the person to perform the operation. The amirs were in great confusion as to who should do the job. Sultan Ali Bakhshi asked Ali Dost Ishak Agha to do it. Ali Dost said, "whenever you give one ashrafi to anyone, you report it to His Majesty. How can I, without his orders, do this on your asking? If tomorrow His Majesty asks (me) why did (I) do this and why was his brother uprooted, shall I, at that moment, say that Sultan Ali Beg had suggested it? This I cannot do."[4] Jauhar also gives in detail the actual proceedings of the operation at which he was himself present.[5] He felt extremely depressed after the event and returned to sit down in a melancholy mood.

It is from Jauhar that we get the true date of Akbar's birth as

[1] *Ibid.*, f.29a.
[2] *Ibid.*, f.35a.
[3] *Ibid.*, f.46b.
[4] *Ibid.*, ff.123a-b.
[5] *Ibid.*, ff.124a-b.

has been convincingly argued by Vincent A. Smith.[1] All other sources give a wrong date in order to avoid the evil consequences of an enemy's manipulating the Prince's stars if the correct date and time of his birth were known.

No less important than these details is the general impression of the immense decline in Humayun's prestige, particularly after he had lost the empire to Sher Shah. We are told, for example, that Princes Askari and Yadgar Mirza once abused and then whipped each other and earned only a mild reproof from Humayun.[2] Humayun once ordered his men to lay siege to the fort of Sehwan, but his amirs, having been bribed by Shah Husain, ruler of Thatta, would not make a move. Even when one amir, Ali Beg Jalair. offered to surprise Shah Husain's camp and the Emperor was favourably inclined towards this proposal, the others would not agree to it and nothing was done.[3]

Not infrequently, the amirs, and even lesser men, showed complete indifference to etiquette and obtained only a reprimand in return and that too not always. Fakhr Ali once preceded the Emperor on horseback and had to be harangued to return to position.[4] While crossing the Indus, Tardi Beg occupied the last available boat even as the Emperor and the royal family waited for one, and refused to surrender it to them.[5] One Champati Bahadur forcibly took away the horse of a Mughal soldier and refused to return it to the owner even when ordered by the Emperor to do so.[6] Twice Tardi Beg withdrew his horse from Hazrat Begam and Humayun surrendered his own horse to the Begam and himself walked on foot until he was given a horse by another person.[7] Jauhar also relates the story of an oath taken both by Humayun and his amirs pledging allegiance to each other, in spite of Mirza Hindal's protest against the impropriety of the Emperor being

[1] *Ibid.*, f.55a; V.A. Smith, "The Date of Akbar's Birth," *Indian Antiquary*, Vol. XLIV, 1915, pp. 233-244.

[2] Jauhar, *op. cit.*, f.31b.

[3] *Ibid.*, ff.40b-41a.

[4] *Ibid.*, f.32b.

[5] *Ibid.*, ff.41b-42a.

[6] *Ibid.*, ff.33b-34a.

[7] *Ibid.*, ff.53a, 64a.

administered the oath by the amirs.[1]

The situation changed later on when Humayun had regained the possession of Qandhar and Kabul and was on a stronger footing. Jauhar tells us that once Humayun descended into a stream on horseback near the Qipchaq Pass, and not a single one of the horsemen accompanied him into the water. Humayun said to them, "O impertinent ones! When Shah Ismail had dropped one handkerchief from the peak of a hill, twelve thousand soldiers followed it and broke themselves into pieces. Not one of you soldiers accompanied me. I am your Padshah, and I crossed the water alone. Not one of you followed me. How will progress be made with soldiers like these?"[2]

Jauhar relates a very interesting story of how Humayun once offered a deal to Haji Muhammad Khan and his brother. The Haji was to write down the services he had rendered (to Humayun) and Humayun was to write down his offences. If the two lists were even, he was to be pardoned for his offences. If the offences, on the other hand, outweighed the services, he was to be executed. This was done and his offences far outweighed his services. Humayun sent Haji Muhammad to prison and later on the two brothers were executed.[3]

[1] *Ibid.*, f.113b.
[2] *Ibid.*, f.106b.
[3] *Ibid.*, f.127a.

CHAPTER 6

Conclusion

A significant fact regarding the historians we have just reviewed is that they were all either courtiers, or, like Yahya Sirhindi, aspirants to such position. Within the court, they were not infrequently aligned with one faction or another—Minhaj, Barani, Abul Fazl, Badauni. Else, they might seek to rise above the narrow divisions and represent the interests of the entire nobility in their historical outlook, as Afif, Isami and to an extent Nizam-ud-din Ahmad tried to do. At any rate, the works they have left to us are court histories written by courtiers who both shared a number of attributes in their approach to history and yet differed widely from one another on important issues. The common elements in their approach, as well as their differences, arose in consequence of the position they occupied. As members of the ruling class at some level or the other, they were not only indifferent to the conditions of the common people, except in so far as the latter were ultimately the source that sustained the ruling class, but they were greatly concerned with the stability of the state system. It is no accident that more often than not they condemned rebellions and rebels of every kind, and that they were all agreed on denouncing the zamindars as a class. For it was this class which created so much tension for the ruling class and in the end contributed greatly to the disruption of the state structure that had been worked out since the inception of Turkish rule in India.

Within this framework, the historians had their differences. Thus, for example, while Minhaj is full of praise for Sultan Nasir-ud-din Mahmud's resignation and piety, Barani contemptuously refers to him as "incompetent" and holds him responsible for the near-disintegration of the state during his reign. Similarly, to Barani,

Ala-ud-din Khalji was a wholly irreligious Sultan; Isami gives him more credit than to any other, except Mahmud of Ghazni, for bringing glory to Islam in India. To Abul Fazl, the reign of Akbar is the most glorious period in all human history; Badauni considers it a dismal age in every detail.

The main features of the works of these historians may be recapitulated here. The basic form of these works is dynastic and within the dynastic whole each reign is treated as a unit. From the Sultanate period to the reign of Akbar there is a pattern of development in some elements of history writing, particularly in the contents and the attitude of the historians to their sources of information. In contents the growth is vertical rather than horizontal. That is, while generally the focal point of the histories remains the court, the accession of rulers, wars, etc., there is increasing information on allied subjects such as administration, imperial policies and composition of nobility. Similarly, while in the earlier period, the histories are more or less impressionistic, by the time Abul Fazl began writing his book, some elements of what is today called research methodology were beginning to be used.

The historians generally treat historical events as single, individual events, unrelated to one another, and their narrative style reinforces the singularity of the events. There is, however, a very keen sense of chronological precedence of events in most of our historians. They establish the cause of the occurrence of these events in human volition, or, at best, in human nature which, in turn, determines human volition. In particular the rulers' nature or will is treated as the major causal factor in the events of his reign. This is not surprising in view of the fact that the historians, as courtiers and at times even as participants in some of the events, were often eye-witnesses to the occurrence of many of the events they were describing and would therefore be aware of human will operating as the cause of those events. And in the light of their current experience, they explained the occurrence of similar events in the distant or near past also in terms of the operation of human volition.

The treatment of historical causation in terms of human volition had the effect of focusing the historians' attention on human action; it also brought a great deal of realism to historical explanation. At the same time the treatment of history as narrative of unrelated events limited the explanation to the occurrence of each event individually, largely devoid of a broad historical perspective which could have suggested inter-relationship among the events as a whole. Once human will became the basis of the explanation of events, the ruler's will, in view of his position, understandably assumed pivotal significance in the entire approach. From this, it was just a short step to treating the events of a reign as the manifestation of the ruler's will or nature.

It may be noted here parenthetically that the medieval Indian historical approach differs very substantially from the medieval European approach. In the works of medieval European historians, most of whom were ecclesiasts, historical events are treated as a manifestation of divine will. This treatment necessarily implied the conception of history as an organic whole, for in God's will the past, the present and the future constitute a well integrated plan, each event falling in place within that plan. Thus, as Collingwood remarks, ". . . .in their anxiety to detect the general plan of history, and their belief that this plan was God's and not man's, they tended to look for the essence of history outside history itself by looking away from man's actions in order to detect the plan of God, and consequently, the actual detail of human actions became for them relatively unimportant, and they neglected that prime duty of the historian: a willingness to bestow infinite pains on discovering what actually happened."[1]

These features of medieval Indian history writing have vitally influenced modern works on medieval India. Many of our most important works have been set within the dynastic or regnal form. Within the dynastic whole the chapters coincide with the regnal unit. The focal point of these works is the imperial court, and the contents are almost entirely related to political history—the accession of rulers, wars, rebellions, etc. (Almost as an afterthought,

[1]*The Idea of History*, Oxford, 1946, p. 55. Interestingly, in a recent analysis of medieval Indian historiography, an attempt has been made to establish that the medieval Indian historians treated history as a branch of theology and that historical causation, for them, lay in divine will. See Peter Hardy, *Historians of Medieval India*, London, 1960. It appears that the author has sought to apply the medieval European historical approach to medieval Indian historiography, the very basic difference in the social, political and intellectual contexts as well as the difference in the respective social positions of the historians notwithstanding.

chapters are sometimes added dealing with social and economic conditions and cultural achievements of a particular ruler or a dynasty, perhaps due to the influence of the growing Western interest in social, economic and cultural history during the late 19th and early 20th centuries.) All this directly corresponds to the chief features of our sources. It is significant, for instance, that until recently even in the field of political history, few attempts had been made to analyze even the composition of the ruling class in terms of various groups—racial, religious, regional, etc.—and their interests which at times converged at a point and at others diverged and which, corresponding to their strength, were able to influence the course of the evolution of various imperial policies. That such studies can at one stroke blast many of our long-cherished notions has been effectively demonstrated by the studies of Athar Ali (*The Mughal Nobility Under Aurangzeb*) and Iqtidar Alam Khan ("The Nobility Under Akbar and the Development of His Religious Policy").

With regard to the attitude towards the sources of information, the modern historians have for long treated the works of medieval historians as "authorities." Their method of investigation was limited to elementary and technical matters in general—collation of evidence and tentative acceptance of evidence where neither its corroboration nor its negation was available, etc. Very little attempt was made to question and understand the basic framework —the assumptions, attitudes and viewpoint—of the medieval historian before making use of the information from his work. The collation of evidence minus the investigation of the general framework of an informant—whether a book or a person—was also the highest point of development that medieval Indian history writing had reached in the hands of Abul Fazl.

In most of the modern works, there is an absence of a conscious theoretical framework or a general historical explanation. This absence is not the result of a conscious revolt against generalization in history as is the case with some of the present-day European and American historians and thinkers, but a carry over from the medieval Indian historical tradition. On the other hand, while explanation of each event and each policy is offered, the interconnections among the events and between events and social and state structures are seldom established or analyzed. That is, the independent entities of individual events and policies, apart from reigns and dynasties, are rather jealously maintained. However, whenever there has been a break in this pattern, like K. M. Ashraf's *Life and Conditions of the People of Hindustan*, or Irfan Habib's *Agrarian System of Mughal India*, it is because the author has rejected the framework of his sources.

Secondly, most modern historians have tended to explain historical causation more or less entirely in personal terms, that is, in terms of the personal will, or at best, disposition, of the ruler. Thus Balban's despotism is explained in terms of his iron will; and Ala-ud-din Khalji's conquests in terms of his ambitious nature; and Akbar's liberal religious policy in terms of his liberal disposition. The influence of medieval Indian historians' approach is clearly discernible in this explanation.

Finally, the medieval historians have succeeded in subtly imposing even their own viewpoint on the modern historians. Until recently the subject of study by modern historians has generally centred round the imperial court and within it the rebellions, wars, etc., have claimed the largest share of attention. All this corresponds to the parallel features of medieval Indian history writing. Secondly, while the medieval historians' anxiety to preserve the empire's unity and stability is understandable for reasons explained earlier, the same standard has generally been accepted by the modern historians as well. The establishment of a mighty empire and its expansion under a strong ruler are looked upon with great favour by the medieval as well as modern historians, and its disintegration touches the same melancholy emotional and intellectual chords in both.

Thus, in the absence of a *general* study of the framework of our sources, even the particular pieces of information could not at times be examined in their proper perspective. Barani, for example, repeatedly emphasizes the point that Sultan Muhammad Tughlaq's nature comprised an imbalanced mixture of contradictory qualities[1] and in the relevant chapter of his *Tarikh* he describes the events of Muhammad Tughlaq's reign in a manner so as to illustrate this point. This emphasis is understandable only in the context of

[1] Barani, *Tarikh*, pp. 459, 496-497, 505-507.

his theory that every Sultan's nature comprises contradictory qualities and it is a balanced mixture of these that results in success.[1] Secondly, Barani treats the events occurring during the reign of a Sultan as the manifestation of his nature. Therefore, when we accept his statement on the contradictory qualities of Muhammad Tughlaq's nature and advance it as *the* cause, or even as *a* cause, of the Sultan's failure, we are also accepting his theory of contradictory qualities and his treatment of history and historical causation, perhaps without our knowing it. Similarly, when we portray Akbar as "a seeker after the Truth" and his religious policy as uniformly "secular" throughout his reign, we do so within the framework set by Abul Fazl in his *Akbar Nama*; or, when we sometimes treat the history of medieval India as a story of a continual conflict, or even as the story of an undisturbed peace, between Hindus and Muslims, and for our evidence quote passages from Minhaj and Barani and Afif and Badauni or Abul Fazl and Nizam-ud-din Ahmad, we do so ignoring the fact that we are using evidence picked up from court histories where only the various conflicts and compromises, including communal, *within the ruling class* have been described or implied and thus the evidence concerned is applicable only to the ruling class and not to the whole society. Or, when we feel more concerned with the rise and fall of dynasties and empires than with changes in the social and economic organization, we have probably not yet decided to depart from the pattern set by medieval historians.

These comments are not meant to be a criticism, much less a denigration, of modern works on our medieval history. These are all the works of some of our best historians and one needs the labours of a lifetime to be able to stand up and criticize them. These comments have been made only to establish the relevance of the study of medieval historiography to history writing in our own day. That is, it is only when we consciously adopt a framework of our own—a framework different from that of the medieval historians—that we would be able to alter our attitude to our sources of information and use them as "sources" rather than

[1]*FJ*, pp. 85-89.

as "authorities." And we can adopt a different framework only if we alter our whole attitude towards history itself, for which, in turn, it is necessary to be in constant touch with the latest developments in the methodology of other sciences; and to possess an active and deep progressive commitment to the society of our day.

Bibliography

A. Historiography

Louis Althusser, *For Marx*, *tr.* Ben Brewster, London, 1969.

H. E. Barnes, *A History of Historical Writing*, 2nd revised edn., New York, 1963.

Isiah Berlin, *Historical Inevitability*, Oxford, 1954.

Marc Bloch, *The Historian's Craft*, Manchester, 1954.

J. Burckhardt, *Judgement on History and Historians*, London, 1959.

H. Butterfield, *Man on His Past: A Study of the History of Historical Scholarship*, Cambridge, 1955.

———, *The Whig Interpretation of History*, London, 1968 (first published 1931).

Grace Cairns, *Philosophies of History*, London, 1963.

E. H. Carr, *What is History?*, London, 1962.

R. G. Collingwood, *The Idea of History*, Oxford, 1946.

Committee on Historiography (ed.), *Theory and Practice in Historical Study*, New York, n.d

Benedetto Croce, *History as the Story of Liberty*, *tr.* Sylvia Sprigge, London, 1941.

———, *History: Its Theory and Practice*, *tr.* Douglas Ainslie, New York, 1960.

Arthur C. Danto, *Analytical Philosophy of History*, Cambridge, 1965.

H. P. R. Finberg (ed), *Approaches to History*, London, 1962.

Patrick Gardiner, *The Nature of Historical Explanation*, London, 1952.

——— (ed.), *Theories of History*, The Free Press of Glencoe, 1962.

W. B. GATHE, *Philosophy and the Historical Understanding*, London, 1964.

PETER GEYL, *Debates with Historians*, London, 1955.

L. GOTTSCHALK (ed.), *Generalization in the Writing of History*, Chicago, 1963.

PETER HARDY, *Historians of Medieval India*, London, 1960.

MUHIBBUL HASAN (ed.), *Historians of Medieval India*, Meerut, 1968.

SIDNEY HOOK, *Hero in History: A Study in Limitation and Possibility*, New York, 1943.

V. JOSHI, *Problems of History and Historiography*, Allahabad, 1946.

ERICH KAHLER, *The Meaning of History*, London, 1941.

ANTONIO LABRIOLA, *Essays on the Materialistic Conception of History*, New York, 1966 (first published 1903).

BERNARD LEWIS and P. M. HOLT (eds.), *Historians of the Middle East*, London, 1964.

JOHN LEWIS, *Marxism and the Open Mind*, London, 1957.

GEORGE LUKACS, *History and Class Consciousness*, *tr.* Rodney Livingstone, London, 1971.

MUHSIN MAHDI, *Ibn Khaldun's Philosophy of History*, London, 1957.

D. S. MARGOLIOUTH, *Lectures on Arabic Historians*, Calcutta, 1930.

FRIEDRICH MEINECKE, *Historicism*, London, 1972.

R. L. P. MELBURN, *Early Christian Interpretations of History*, London, 1954.

HANS MEYERHOFF (ed.), *The Philosophy of History in Our Time*, New York, 1959.

ARNALDO MOMIGLIANO, *Studies in Historiography*, London, 1966.

L. B. NAMIER, *Avenues of History*, London, 1952.

C. H. Philips (ed.), *Historians of India, Pakistan and Ceylon*, London, 1961.

G. V. PLEKHANOV, *The Development of the Monist View of History*, Moscow, 1965.

———, *Fundamental Problems of Marxism*, London, 1969.

KARL R. POPPER, *The Poverty of Historicism*, reprint, London, 1966.

Problems of Historical Writing in India, proceedings of seminar held at New Delhi, January 1963.

G. J. Renier, *History: Its Purpose and Method*, London, 1961.
H. P. Rickmam (ed.), *Meaning in History: W. Dilthey's Thoughts on History and Society*, London, 1961.
F. Rosenthal, *A History of Muslim Historiography*, Lieden, 1952.
Ferdinand Schevill, *Six Historians*, Chicago, 1956.
Denis Sinor, *Orientalism and History*, Cambridge, 1954.
J. W. Thompson, *A History of Historical Writing*, 2 vols., New York, 1958.
W. H. Walsh, *An Introduction to Philosophy of History*, 5th edn., London, 1958.
A. G. Widgery, *The Meanings in History*, London, 1967.

B. Primary Sources (MSS, Texts and Translations)

Abul Fazl, *Akbar Nama*, 3 vols., Bib. Ind., Calcutta, 1873-87. English *tr.*, H. Beveridge, 3 vols., Bib. Ind., Calcutta, 1897-1921.
The first draft of the *Akbar Nama* is lying in the British Museum (Rieu, I, p. 2476). I have consulted the transcript of the variation between the first and the final drafts at the Research Library, Department of History, Aligarh Muslim University.
———, *Ain-i-Akbari*, H. Blochmann (ed.), 2 vols., Bib. Ind., Calcutta, 1872-77. English *tr.* of Vol. I, H. Blochmann revised by D. C. Phillott, 2nd edn., Bib. Ind. Calcutta 1939 and of Vols. II and III by H. S. Jarrett revised and further annotated by J. N. Sarkar, Bib. Ind., 1949 and 1948 respectively. While I have also consulted the 3 vols. Munshi Nawal Kishore edn. of the *Ain* (Lucknow, 1869), I have referred only to the Bib. Ind. edn., of the text.
———, *Insha-i-Abul Fazl*, 3 vols., Delhi University Library MS, No. 0164, 4 MS 51x, dated 1237 H./1821-22 A.D.
———, *Munajat-i-Abul Fazl*, S.A.A. Rizvi (ed.), *Medieval India Quarterly*, Vol. I, Aligarh, 1950.
———, *Ayar-i-Danish*, published by Munshi Nawal Kishore under the title *Nigar-i-Danish*, Lucknow, 1902.
Shams Siraj Afif, *Tarikh-i-Firuz Shahi*, M. Wilayat Husain (ed.), Bib. Ind., Calcutta, 1888-91.
Al-Beruni, *Kitab-ul-Hind*, *tr.* Edward C. Sachau as *Al-Beruni's*

India, 2 vols., popular edn., London, 1910.

AMIR KHUSRAU, *Qiran-us-Sadain*, Muhammad Ismail (ed.), Aligarh, 1918.

———, *Miftah-ul-Futuh*, Shaikh Abdur Rashid (ed.), Aligarh, 1954.

———, *Khazain-ul-Futuh*. I have used only the English *tr.*, M. Habib under the title *Campaigns of Ala-ud-din Khalji being the Khazain-ul-Futuh (Treasures of Victory) of Hazrat Amir Khusrau of Delhi*, Madras, 1931.

———, *Dewal Rani-Khizr Khan* also known as *Ashiqa*, M. Rashid Ahmad (ed.), Aligarh, 1917.

———, *Nuh Sipihr*, M. Wahid Mirza (ed.), Bib. Ind., Calcutta, 1948-50.

———, *Tughlaq Nama*, Syed Hashmi Faridabadi (ed.), Aurangabad, 1933.

BABUR PADSHAH, *Babur Nama*, *tr.* A.S. Beveridge, 2 vols., London, 1922.

ABDUL QADIR BADAUNI, *Muntakhab-ut-Tawarikh*, 3 vols., Bib. Ind., Calcutta, 1865-69. English *tr.* of Vol. I, G. S. Ranking; of Vol. II, W.H. Lowe; of Vol. III, W. Haig; all three published in Bib. Ind. series, Calcutta, 1898, 1924 and 1925 respectively.

———, *Najat-ur-Rashid*, MS Habibganj collection, No. Farsi 21/115, Maulana Azad Library, Aligarh Muslim University.

BAIRAM KHAN, *The Persian and Turki Diwans of Bayram Khan Khan-i-Khanan*, ed. Denison Ross, Bib. Ind., Calcutta, 1910.

BAKHTAWAR KHAN, *Mirat-ul-Alam*, MS, No. Farsi Tarikh 51, Maulana Azad Library, Aligarh Muslim University. The author's name is so listed in the Library's catalogue, though the work belongs to Shaikh Muhammed Baqa, Baqa.

ZIA-UD-DIN BARANI, *Tarikh-i-Firuz Shahi*. Saiyad Ahmad Khan (ed.), Bib. Ind., Calcutta, 1862.

———, *Fatawa-i-Jahandari*, *tr.* M. Habib and Mrs Afsar Khan under the title *Political Theory of the Delhi Sultanate*, Allahabad, n.d. The translation carries an introduction and a very penetrating study of the life and thought of Barani by M. Habib.

SHAIKH FARID BHAKKARI, *Zakhirat-ul-Khawanin*, Vol. I, Syed Moinul Haq (ed.), Karachi, 1961.

MUHAMMAD BIHAMAD KHANI, *Tarikh-i-Muhammadi*, portion dealing with the account of Firuz Tughlaq and minor kingdoms from 1351 to 1438 *tr.* Mohammad Zaki, Bombay, 1972.

BAYAZID BIYAT, *Tazkira-i-Humayun-wa-Akbar*, M. Hidayat Husain (ed.), Bib. Ind.. Calcutta, 1941.

SUJAN RAI BHANDARI, *Khulasat-ut-Tawarikh*, Zafar Hasan, (ed.), Delhi, 1918.

SHAIKH NUR-UL-HAQ DEHLAVI, *Zubdat-ut-Tawarikh*, MS, Br. Mus Add. 10580.

HENRY ELLIOT and JOHN DOWSON, *History of India as Told by Its Own Historians*, 8 vols , London, 1867-77.

ILAHADAD FAIZI SIRHINDI, *Akbar Nama*, MS, Br. Mus. Or. 169.

MIRZA MUNSHI KASHMIRI FANI, *Dabistan-i-Mazahib*, Nawal Kishore edn., Lucknow, 1904.

ABUL QASIM FARISHTA, *Tarikh-i-Farishta*, also known as *Gulshan-i-Ibrahimi*, 2 vols., Bombay, 1832.

FIRUZ SHAH TUGHLAQ, *Futuhat-i-Firuzshahi*, Shaikh Abdur Rashid (ed.), Aligarh, 1954.

GULBADAN BEGAM, *Humayun Nama*, text ed. and *tr.*, Mrs A. S. Beveridge, Royal Asiatic Society, London, 1902.

HASAN ALI KHAN, *Tawarikh-i-Daulat-i-Sher Shahi*, a part of the text and R.P. Tripathi's *tr.* of another part published in *Medieval India Quarterly*, Vol. I, No. 1, Aligarh, 1950. S. A. A. Rizvi has convincingly challenged the authenticity of the fly-leaf of the published portion of the text, but the genuineness of the text has remained unquestioned so far.

IBN BATTUTAH, *Rehla*, ed. and *tr.* from Arabic by A. Mahdi Husain under the title *The Rehla of Ibn Battutah*, Baroda, 1953.

ISAMI, *Futuh-us-Salatin*, A. Mahdi Husain (ed.), Agra, 1938.

MUHAMMAD KABIR BIN SHAH ISMAIL, *Afsana-i Shahan*, MS Br. Mus. Add. 24409.

JAHANGIR PADSHAH, *Tuzuk-i-Jahangiri*, Saiyid Ahmad Khan (ed.), Ghazipur and Aligarh, 1863-64. English *tr.*, Rogers in 2 vols., H. Beveridge (ed.), and published under the title *The Memoirs of Jahangir*, London, 1909-14.

JAUHAR AFTABCHI, *Tazkirat-ul-Waqiat*, MS, Br. Mus. Add. 16711.

MUNSHI MUHAMMAD KAZIM, *Alamgir Nama*, M. Khadim Husain and M. Abdul Hai (eds.), Bib. Ind., Calcutta, 1865-73.

KHAFI KHAN, *Muntakhab-ul-Lubab*, Kabiruddin Ahmad and W. Haig (eds.), Bib. Ind., Calcutta, 1869-1925.

KHWAND MIR, *Qanun-i-Humayuni*, M. Hidayat Husain (ed.), Bib. Ind., Calcutta, 1940,

ABDUL HAMID LAHORI, *Padshah Nama*, M. Kabiruddin and M.A. Rahman (eds.), Bib. Ind., Calcutta, 1867-68.

MANU, *Manusmriti*, *tr.*, Buhler, Oxford, 1886.

MINHAJ-US-SIRAJ, *Tabaqat-i-Nasiri*, William Lees and M. Abdul Hai (eds.), Bib. Ind., Calcutta, 1863-64. English *tr.* in 2 vols. by H. G. Raverty, Bib. Ind., Calcutta, 1881. A new edn. in 2 vols. prepared by Abdul Hai Habibi and published by Anjuman-i-Tarikh-i-Afghanistan, Kabul, 1963 and 1964 is no great improvement on the Bib. Ind., text.

MUATAMAD KHAN, *Iqbal Nama-i-Jahangiri*, Munshi Nawal Kishore edn., Lucknow, 1870.

MALIK ZADAH MUNSHI, *Nigar Nama-i-Munshi*, Nawal Kishore edn., Lucknow, 1882.

SHAIKH RIZQULLAH MUSHTAQI, *Waqiat-i-Mushtaqi*, MS, Br. Mus. Or. 1929.

ABUL BAQI NIHAVANDI, *Masir-i-Rahimi*, Hidayat Husain (ed.), 3 vols., Bib. Ind., Calcutta, 1910-31.

NIZAM-UD-DIN AHMAD, *Tabaqat-i-Akbari*, B. De (ed.), 3 vols, Bib. Ind. (Vol. III revised and partly edited by M. Hidayat Husain), Calcutta 1913, 1927, 1931 and 1935. English *tr.*, B. De, the third volume of the *tr.* consisting of two parts, revised, edited and completed, with a Preface, by Beni Prashad, Bib. Ind., Calcutta, 1927-39.

NIZAM-UL-MULK, *Siyasat Nama*, *tr.* under the title *The Book of Government*, H. Darke, New Haven, 1960.

ARIF QANDHARI, *Tarikh-i-Akbari*, Haji Syed Muinuddin Nadwi, Syed Azhar Ali Dehlavi and Imtiaz Ali Arshi (eds.), Rampur, 1962.

ALA-UD-DAULA QAZWINI, *Nafais-ul-Maasir*, MS, Subhanullah collection, Farsi 920/45, Maulana Azad Library, Aligarh Muslim University.

ASAD BEG QAZWINI, *Tarikh-i-Risala-i-Asad-Beg Qazwini*, MS, Br. Mus. Or. 1996.

RASHID-UD-DIN FAZLULLAH, *Jami-ut-Tawarikh*, portions relating to India in Karl Jahn (ed.), *Rashid al-Din's History of India* (including text), The Hague, 1965.

ABBAS SARWANI, *Tuhfa-i-Akbarshahi*, also known as *Tarikh-i-Shershahi*, MS, India Office Library Persian MSS I. O. 218

SHAH NAWAZ KHAN, *Maasir-ul-Umra*, M. Abdur Rahim and

Ashraf Ali (eds.), 3 vols., Bib. Ind., Calcutta, 1888-91.
AHMAD THATTAVI *et al.*, *Tarikh-i-Alfi*, MS, Br. Mus., Or. 465.
AHMAD YADGAR, *Tarikh-i-Shahi*, M. Hidayat Husain (ed.), Bib. Ind., Calcutta, 1939.
YAHYA BIN AHMAD SIRHINDI, *Tarikh-i-Mubarakshahi*, M. Hidayat Husain (ed.), Bib. Ind., Calcutta, 1931.

C. EUROPEAN SOURCES

FRANCOIS BERNIER, *Travels in the Mogul Empire, 1965-68. tr.* A. Constable, 2nd edn. revised by V. A. Smith, London, 1916.
W. FOSTER (ed.), *The Embassy of Sir Thomas Roe, 1615-19*, London, 1926.
——— (ed.), *Early Travels in India 1583-1619*, London, 1927. The editor has included in it the accounts of travels in India by Fitch, Mildenhall, Hawkins, Finch, Willington, Coryat and Terry.
PIERRE DU JARRIC, *Akbar and the Jesuits*, *tr.* C. H. Payne, London, 1926.
JOANNES DE LAET, *The Empire of the Great Mogol*, *tr.* J. S. Hoyland and annotated by S. N. Banerjee, Bombay, 1928.
MONSERRATE, *Commentary*, *tr.* J. S. Hoyland and annotated by S. N. Banerjee, Oxford, 1922.
FRANCISCO PALSAERT, *Romonstrie*, *tr.* W.H. Moreland and P. Geyl under the title *Jahangir's India*, Cambridge, 1925.
J.B. TAVRRNIER, *Travels in India*, *1640-67*, *tr.* V. Ball, 2nd edn. revised by W. Crooke, London, 1925.
JEAN DE THEVENOT and GIOVANNI CARERI, S.N. Sen (ed.), *Indian Travels of Thevenot and Careri*, New Delhi, 1949.

D. MODERN WORKS

ABDUL AZIZ, *The Mansabdari System and the Mughal Army*, Lahore, 1945.
AZIZ AHMAD, *Political History and Institutions of the Early Turkish Empire in India*, Lahore, 1949.
———, *Studies in Islamic Culture in the Indian Environment*,

Oxford, 1964.

M. B. AHMAD, *The Administration of Justice in Medieval India*, Aligarh, 1941.

SAIYAD AHMAD, *Umra-i Hunud* (Urdu), Aurangabad, 1932.

K. M. ASHRAF, *Life and Conditions of the People of Hindustan*, Delhi, 1959.

M. ATHAR ALI, *The Mughal Nobility Under Aurangzeb*, Bombay, 1966.

FREDERICK AUGUSTUS, *Kaiser Akbar*, *tr.* Mrs A. S. Beveridge as *The Emperor Akbar*, 2 vols., Calcutta, 1890.

MUHAMMAD HUSAIN AZAD, *Darbar-i-Akbari* (Urdu), Lahore, 1898.

THEODORE DE BARY (ed.), *Sources of Indian Tradition*, New York, 1958.

MARC BLOCH, *Feudal Society*, *tr.* L. A. Manyon, 2 vols. (the pagination is continuous), Chicago, 1964.

CARL BROCKELMANN, *History of the Islamic Peoples*, London, 1959.

P. N. CHOPRA, *Some Aspects of Society and Culture During the Mughal Age* (1526-1707), 2nd edn., Agra, 1963.

YOHANAN FRIEDMANN, *Shaykh Ahmad Sirhindi*, Montreal, 1971.

R. E. FRYKENBERG, *Land Control and Social Structure in Indian History*, Wisconsin, 1969.

M. A. GAHNI, *Pre-Mughal Persian in Hindustan*, Allahabad, 1941.

———, *A History of Persian Language and Literature at the Mughal Court*, Allahabad, 1929.

U. N. GHOSHAL, *A History of Indian Political Ideas*, Bombay, 1959.

B. N. GOSWAMI and J.S. GREWAL, *The Mughals and the Jogis of Jakhbar*, Simla, 1967.

———, *The Mughal and Sikh Rulers and the Vaishnavas of Pindari*, Simla, 1969.

G. E. VON GRUNEBAUM, *Medieval Islam: A Study in Cultural Orientation*, 2nd edn., Chicago, 1953.

IRFAN HABIB, *The Agrarian System of Mughal India* (1556-1707), Bombay, 1963.

MOHAMMAD HABIB, *Hazrat Amir Khusrau of Delhi*, Delhi, 1927.

———, *Sultan Mahmud of Ghaznin*, 2nd edn., Delhi, 1951.

———, *Politics and Society during the Early Medieval Period*, K. A. Nizami (ed.), Delhi, 1974.

A. B. M. HABIBULLAH, *The Foundation of Muslim Rule in India*,

2nd edn., Allahabad, 1961.

IBN HASAN, *The Central Structure of the Mughal Empire*, reprint, New Delhi, 1970.

HADI HASAN, *Mughal Poetry: Its Cultural and Historical Value*, Madras, 1951.

S. H. HODIVALA, *Studies in Indo-Muslim History*, Bombay, 1939; *Supplement*, Bombay, 1957.

A. MAHDI HUSAIN, *The Tughlaq Dynasty*, Calcutta, 1963.

S. M. IKRAM, *Muslim Civilization in India*, A. T. Embree (ed.), New York, 1964.

IQTIDAR ALAM KHAN, *The Political Biography of a Mughal Noble: Munim Khan Khan-i-Khanan, 1497-1575*, New Delhi, 1973.

W. IRVINE, *The Army of the Indian Moghuls*, reprint, New Delhi, 1971.

R. P. KHOSLA, *The Mughal Kingship and the Nobility*, Allahabad, 1934.

D. D. KOSAMBI, *An Introduction to the Study of Indian History*, Bombay, 1956.

H. KRUGER (ed.), *Kunwar Mohammad Ashraf: An Indian Scholar and Revolutionary, 1903-1962*, Indian edn., Delhi, 1969.

K. S. LAL, *History of the Khaljis*, 2nd edn., Bombay, 1967.

———, *Twilight of the Sultanate*, Bombay, 1963.

R. LEVY, *Social Structure of Islam*, Cambridge, reprint, 1962.

BERNARD LEWIS, *The Arabs in History*, London, 1954.

E. MACLAGAN, *The Jesuists and the Great Mogul*, London, 1932.

R. C. MAJUMDAR (ed.), *History and Culture of the Indian People*, Vols. V and VI, Bombay, 1957 and 1960 respectively.

M. WAHID MIRZA, *Life and Works of Amir Khusrau*, Calcutta, 1935.

W. H. MORELAND, *The Agrarian System of Moslem India*, Allahabad, 1929.

———, *India at the Death of Akbar*, London, 1920.

———, *From Akbar to Aurangzeb*, reprint, New Delhi, 1972.

M. MUJEEB, *The Indian Muslims*, London, 1967.

S. H. NASR, *An Introduction to Islamic Cosmological Doctrines*, Massachusettes, 1964

———, *Science and Civilization in Islam*, Massachusettes, 1966.

S. B. P. NIGAM, *Nobility Under the Sultans of Delhi*, A.D. *1206-1398*, Delhi, 1968.

K. A. NIZAMI, *Some Aspects of Religion and Politics in India during the Thirteenth Century*, Aligarh, 1961.

———, *Salatin-i-Delhi ke Mazhabi Rujhanat* (Urdu), Delhi, 1958.

W. G. ORR, *A Sixteenth Century Indian Mystic*, London, 1947.

R. N. PRASAD, *Raja Man Singh of Amber*, Calcutta, 1966.

MICHAEL PRAWDIN, *The Mongol Empire : Its Rise and Legacy*, London, 1967 (first published 1940).

K. R. QANUNGO, *Sher Shah and His Times*, 2nd edn., Bombay, 1965.

I. H. QURESHI, *The Administration of the Sultanate of Delhi*, 5th revised edn., Delhi, 1971.

———, *The Administration of the Mughal Empire*, Karachi, 1966,

———, *The Muslim Community of the Indo-Pakistan Sub-continent (610-1947)*, 'S-Gravenhage, 1962.

M. L. RAYCHAUDHURY, *Din-i-Ilahi*, Calcutta, 1941.

S. A. A. RIZVI, *Muslim Revivalist Movements in Northern India in the Sixteenth and Seventeenth Centuries*, Agra, 1965.

E. I. J. ROSENTHAL, *Political Thought in Medieval Islam*, Cambridge, 1962.

P. SARAN, *The Provincial Government of the Mughals, 1556-1658*, Allahabad, 1941.

———, *Studies in Medieval Indian History*, Delhi, 1952.

JADU NATH SARKAR, *Mughal Administration*, Calcutta, 1920.

SATISH CHANDRA, *Parties and Politics at the Mughal Court (1707-1740)*, Aligarh, 1959.

SRI RAM SHARMA, *The Religious Policy of the Mughal Emperors*, 2nd edn., Bombay, 1962.

I. H. Siddiqi, *Some Aspects of Afghan Despotism in India*, Aligarh, 1969.

N. A. SIDDIQI, *Land Revenue Administration Under the Mughals*, Bombay, 1970.

V. A. SMITH, *Akbar the Great Mogul*, Oxford, 1917.

W. C. SMITH, *Modern Islam in India*, Lahore, 1943.

MADHU TANDON, *Historical Analysis of Kabir's Poetry*, M. Phil. Dissertation, Jawaharlal Nehru University, New Delhi, 1974 (unpublished).

TARA CHAND, *Influence of Islam on Indian Culture*, 2nd edn., Allahabad, 1963.

R. P. TRIPATHI, *Some Aspects of Muslim Administration in India*, Allahabad, 1936.

———, *Rise and Fall of Mughal Empire*, 3rd edn., Allahabad, 1963.

E. WELLESZ, *Akbar's Religious Thought Reflected in Mogul Painting*, London, 1952.

E. JOURNALS AND PERIODICALS

S. S. ABDUR RAHMAN, "Futuh-us-Salatin," *Ma'arif* (Urdu), Vol. 44, No. 2, 1939.

BASHIR AHMAD, "Abul Fazl and Shaikh Mubarak," *Oriental College Magazine*, Lahore, May 1952.

S. H. Barani, "Zia-ud-din Barani," *Islamic Culture*, 1938.

H. BEVERIDGE, "The Sources of the *Akbar Namah*," *Journal of the Asiatic Society of Bengal*, Vol. XIV (New Series), 1918.

———, "The Memoirs of Bayazid (Bajazet) Biyat," *J. A. S. B.*, Vol. LXVII, Part I, No. 4, 1898.

H. BLOCHMANN, "Badaoni and His Works," *J.A.S.B.*, Vol. 38, Part I, 1869.

E. B. COWELL, "The Kiran-us-Sadain of Mir Khusrau," *J.A.S.B.*, Vol. 29, 1860.

IRFAN HABIB, "Problems of Marxist Historical Analysis," *Enquiry*, Monsoon 1969.

———, Presidential Address, Section II, *Proceedings of Indian History Congress*, Varanasi Session 1969, Patna, 1970.

———, The Technology and Economy of Mughal India," Dev Raj Chanana Memorial Lecture, 1970 (mimeo).

———, "Potentialities of Capitalistic Development in the Economy of Mughal India," *Enquiry*, Winter 1971.

MOHAMMAD HABIB, "Chishti Mystic Records of the Sultanate Period," *Medieval India Quarterly*, Vol. I, No. 2, 1950.

A.B.M. HABIBULLAH, "A Re-evaluation of the Literary Sources of the pre-Mughal History," *Islamic Culture*, 1941.

S. NURUL HASAN, "Sahifa-i-Nat-i-Muhammadi of Zia-ud-din Barani," *Medieval India Quarterly*, Vol. I, Nos. 3 & 4, 1950.

A. MAHDI HUSAIN, "Mahmud of Ghazna Idolized by Isami," *Proceedings of Indian History Congress*, 1944.

———, "A Critical Study of the Sources of Medieval India (1320-1526)," *Islamic Culture*, 1957.

HIDAYAT HUSAIN, "Contemporary Historians of the Reign of Shah Jahan," *Islamic Culture*, 1941.

IQTIDAR ALAM KHAN, "The Nobility Under Akbar and the Development of His Religious Policy," *Journal of Royal Asiatic Society*, London, 1968, Parts 1 & 2.

———,"The Turko-Mongol Theory of Kingship," *Medieval India: A Miscellany*, Vol. II, Aligarh, 1972.

SAVITRI CHANDRA, "Tulsidas' Concept of Rulership," *Proceedings of Indian History Congress*, Muzaffarpur Session 1972, New Delhi, 1973.

SHAIKH ABDUR RASHID, "Zia-ud-din Barani; A Study," *Aligarh Muslim University Journal*, 1942.

V. A. SMITH, "The Date of Akbar's Birth," *The Indian Antiquary*, Vol. XLIV, 1915.

W. C. SMITH, "The Mughal Empire and the Middle Class, A Hypothesis," *Islamic Culture*, 1944.

———, "Lower Class Uprisings in the Mughal Empire," *Islamic Culture*, 1946.

F. CATALOGUES AND BIBLIOGRAPHIES

H. ETHE, *Catalogue of Persian Manuscripts in the Library of the India Office*, 2 vols., Oxford, Vol. I, 1903, Vol. II, 1937.

CHARLES RIEU, *Catalogue of the Persian Manuscripts in the British Museum*, 3 vols., London, Vol. I, 1879; Vol. II, 1881; Vol. III, 1883; Supplement, 1895.

C. A. STOREY, *Persian Literature: A Bio-bibliographical Survey*, 2 parts, London, 1927-39 and 1953 respectively.

V. D. B. TARAPOREVALA and D. N. MARSHALL, *Mughal Bibliography*, Bombay, 1962.

Index

Other books by the Same Author

Feudalism and Non-European Societies, Frank Cass, London, 1985 (co-edited with T.J. Byres) comprising debate centred on Harbans Mukhia's "Was There Feudalism in Indian History?". Originally a special double issue of *The Journal of Peasant Studies*, 1985. Hindi tr. *Feudalism aur Ghair-Europiya Samāj*, Granth Shilpi, New Delhi, 1998.

The Feudalism Debate, Manohar Publishers, New Delhi, 2000, a revised edition of *Feudalism and Non-European Societies*.

French Studies in History, Vol. 1: *The Inheritance*; Vol. 2: *The Departures*, (co-edited with Maurice Aymard), Orient Longman, New Delhi, 1988 and 1990, comprising some 35 articles of the front-rank French historians on medieval/early modern European history.

Perspectives on Medieval History, Vikas Publishing House, New Delhi, 1993. An anthology. Hindi tr. *Madhyakālīn Bhārat: Nayé Āyām*, Rajkamal Prakashan, New Delhi, 1998. Urdu tr. *'Ahd-i wusta kā Hindustān*, Fiction House, Lahore, 2003.

Religion, Religiosity and Communalism, co-edited with Praful Bidwai and AchinVanaik, Manohar Publishers, New Delhi, 1996.

The Mughals of India, Blackwell Publishers, Oxford, 2004. Indian reprint Wiley 2005 and later. Hindi tr. *Bharatiya Mughal*, Aakar Books, Delhi, 2008.

Issues in Indian History, Politics and Society, Aakar Books, Delhi, 2009. A collection of Mukhia's newspaper articles and select book reviews.

Exploring India's Medieval Centuries: Essays in History, Society, Culture and Technology, Aakar Books, Delhi, 2010, an enlarged version of *Perspectives.*

History of Technology, vol. II, Medieval India, Indian National Science Academy, New Delhi 2012 (edited).

Understanding India: Indology and Beyond, co-edited with Jaroslav Vacek, Charles University, Prague, 2012.

Founding Editor, *The Medieval History Journal*, published by SAGE Publications from New Delhi, London, Los Angeles, Singapore and Washington DC.